Decision Support for Global Enterprises

Annals of Information Systems

Volume 1:
Managing in the Information Economy: *Current Research Issues*
Uday Apte, Uday Karmarkar

Decision Support for Global Enterprises

edited by

Uday Kulkarni
Arizona State University

Daniel J. Power
University of Northern Iowa

Ramesh Sharda
Oklahoma State University

 Springer

Uday Kulkarni
Arizona State University
Tempe, AZ, USA

Daniel J. Power
University of Northern Iowa
Cedar Falls, Iowa, USA

Ramesh Sharda
Oklahoma State University
Stillwater, OK, USA

Library of Congress Control Number: 2006936086

ISSN: 1934-3221 / 1934-3213 (e-book)
ISBN-10: 0-387-48136-2 (HB)   ISBN-10: 0-387-48137-0 (e-book)
ISBN-13: 978-0-387-48136-4 (HB) ISBN-13: 978-0-387-48137-1 (e-book)

Printed on acid-free paper.

9 8 7 6 5 4 3 2 1

springer.com

Table of Contents

III. SUCCESSES AND FAILURES: *Learning from Experience*

IV. EVOLVING TECHNOLOGIES: *Next Generation Systems*

Preface

What are the obstacles and challenges faced in building Decision Support Systems (DSS) for global enterprises? In multinational firms, computerized decision support systems must support managers with diverse national and cultural backgrounds who are working in many nations. This staffing reality creates a major overarching challenge. To bring the global DSS community together, SIGDSS of the Association of Information Systems organizes an International Conference on Decision Support Systems every other year. The purpose of ICDSS 2007 is to promote discussion and interaction among members of the information systems community with research interests in cutting edge decision support systems. The emphasis is on emerging enterprise decision making processes, increasing needs of decision-making and reasoning under uncertainty, new infrastructure for decision making in organizations and society, the role of web technologies, and emerging theories and practices for knowledge management.

This book of refereed papers is based upon selected papers submitted and reviewed for presentation at the 9th International Conference on Decision Support Systems. The papers are clustered into four categories that represent areas of significant research and applications in the DSS domain: Decision Support for Global Enterprises.

The conference was hosted at the Indian Institute of Management, Calcutta, India. A strong local hosting team worked hard to organize this meeting. This team deserves our grateful thanks: Professor Amitava Bagchi who served as the conference General Co-Chair; Professors Ambuj Mahanti and Rahul Roy, Local Arrangements Co-Chairs; the Local Arrangements Team consisting of Debashis Saha, Balram Avittathur, and Partha Sarathi Dasgupta; Dinesh Varma, Conference Manager, and Victor Mukherjee, Manager, Mgt Dev Centre. We also acknowledge financial support provided by Teradata Corporation as a sponsor of ICDSS 2007.

Papers for this volume were selected competitively after a rigorous review by an outstanding program committee. We acknowledge the efforts of the following referees:

Amitava Dutta, George Mason University
Bartel Van de Walle, Tilburg University
Benjamin Shao, Arizona State University
Carmine Sellitto, Victoria University - Melbourne
Choong Kwon Lee, Georgia Southern University
Daewon Sun, Notre Dame University
Deepak Khazanchi, University of Nebraska at Omaha
Derek Nazareth, University of Wisconsin - Milwaukee
Eugene Kim, University of Hartford
Faiz Currim, University of Iowa
Goutam Dutta, Indian Institute of Management - Ahmedabad
Haluk Demirkan, Arizona State University

J.P. Shim, Mississippi State University
Jacques Ajenstat, University of Quebec at Montreal
Karen Corral, Arizona State University
Michael Goul, Arizona State University
Mike Hart, University of Cape Town
Murray E. Jennex, San Diego State University
Narasimha Bolloju, City University of Hong Kong
Nazrul Islam, Asian Institute of Technology - Bangkok
Peter Keenan, University College - Dublin
Sean B. Eom, Southeast Missouri State University
Stanislaw Stanek, University of Economics in Katowice
Varghese Jacob, University of Texas at Dallas
Vijayan Sugumaran, Oakland University

We believe that this book presents a good compendium of recent DSS research in the global context.

Ramesh Sharda, Conference General co-chair
Daniel J. Power and Uday Kulkarni, Program co-chairs

I. OVERVIEW:
Concepts, Theories, and Frameworks

Understanding Decision Support Systems for Global Enterprises

Daniel J. Power[1], Ramesh Sharda[2], Uday Kulkarni[3]

[1] University of Northern Iowa, Cedar Falls, IA 50614, U.S.A
[2] Oklahoma State University, Stillwater, OK, 70478, U.S.A
[3] Arizona State University, Tempe, AZ, U.S.A

daniel.power@uni.edu[1], ramesh.sharda@okstate.edu[2], uday.kulkarni@asu.edu[3]

Abstract. Globalization of markets is changing the structure of business enterprises and hence the need for and design of computerized decision support systems. Trying to understand how decision support systems can and should evolve in a global business environment is difficult, but this article draws on current best practices, examples of deployments of available technology and trends to make some sense of the problem. Six deployment issues are examined for the five broad categories of decision support systems. The need for further research is apparent given the inadequacy of our current knowledge.

Keywords: Decision support, globalization, decision support systems, DSS.

1 Introduction

According to a number of sources, the English and Dutch East India trading companies of the early 17th Century were the first global enterprises. Modern global enterprises have a similar broad reach, but conduct business in a much more complex trading environment. Four hundred years ago a ship would depart Europe to trade in India or Asia and would return with goods that were quickly absorbed into local markets. The captain of the ship was an autonomous decision maker about what to buy and sell. Today global products and services are produced and delivered in a technologically sophisticated environment of trade and commerce. Consumer demand is more difficult to predict and managerial decisions are more time sensitive. Managers make decisions in an electronic trading environment where markets change rapidly and consumer demands are increasingly difficult to forecast. Performance monitoring is complex, production is globally distributed, documents are written in many language and communications are primarily electronic.

This article explores the characteristics of global enterprises and examines how they may and do impact computerized decision support needs. Research on DSS in global enterprises is rather limited. Iyer [7] and Iyer and Schkade [8] describe a specific DSS built for global enterprises and the lesson learned. McDonald [12] extends this in the context of global marketing DSS. There is general Information Systems research related to global enterprises, for example Tractinsky and Jarvenpaa [9], Peppard [16], Myers and Tan [14], processes. When documents are a key part of a decision making process, paperless is "best" and the only practical alternative in a global enterprise. With document-driven DSS, language becomes a crucial issue. One also has to consider the differences in organizational patterns across countries.

3.4 Knowledge-Driven DSS

Knowledge refers to what one knows and understands. In a global enterprise, knowledge can be especially hard to share and maintain. Knowledge-driven DSS can expand the base of explicit knowledge in global enterprises and facilitate distribution, access and retrieval of such knowledge. Conversion of local knowledge to a global scope is however a huge challenge.

3.5 Model-Driven DSS

One might assume that model-driven DSS are the same in localized or global enterprises, but in many cases such systems will differ in the complexity of the quantitative model and in the demands placed upon the user interface. For example, it may be necessary to rapidly convert solutions into various currencies or to deal with widely differing tax rates and tariffs.

3.6 Enterprise Architecture

Integrating decision support systems in an enterprise architecture for a global enterprise remains challenging. A computing architecture reflects the translation of the overall vision of an enterprise into specific technology solutions. More work is needed to incorporate decision support into an evolving distributed architecture. In the next section we discuss some of the issues that are especially relevant for global DSS developers and users.

4   Obstacles to Building DSS for Global Enterprises

So what are the obstacles and challenges faced in building DSS for global enterprises? In multinational firms, computerized decision support systems must support managers with diverse national and cultural backgrounds who are working in many differing countries. This staffing reality creates a major overarching challenge. Some of the more focused obstacles to using technology to support decision-making in global enterprises include: accounting and currency issues, cultural differences, differing legal regulations, electronic communications limitations, telecommunications and computing infrastructures, and time zone differences (cf., Power [17]). Let's look at these issues in more detail.

4.1. Accounting and Currency Issues

In data-driven DSS, one seeks a consistent, meaningful version of the truth about an enterprise's activities over a multi-year time span. Creating and maintaining a version of the truth for decision making is much harder in a global enterprise because of accounting and currency issues. Accounting and other business practices differ from country to country and this makes getting accurate financial reports and consolidating them difficult. Also, currency conversion and fluctuations is another ongoing source of challenge in designing data-driven and some model-driven DSS. According to an analysis in Accounting Software News, "Only a handful of accounting packages process multiple currencies in compliance with FASB Statement no. 52" and other internal standards (check accountingsoftwarenews.com/charts/currency.htm) Also, one needs to keep in mind that accounting refers to a "formal system of collecting, organizing and reporting financial data" primarily intended to inform people interested in the financial status and progress of a firm. Accounting systems are not sophisticated decision support systems. Even when a global company follows generally accepted accounting principles (GAAP), they need to add, disaggregate and interpret data to provide data-driven decision support. Accounting data in a DSS data store should reconcile with accounting systems, but that is not enough to insure usefulness of the system. For example, data on units sold may be much more important than sales revenue when comparing sales operations in various countries. A good data-driven DSS should help managers make meaningful comparisons despite accounting and currency differences in local operations.

4.2 Cultural Differences

The purpose of a Decision Support System is to inform decision-makers and ignoring cultural issues may create misinformation or misinterpretation [2]. Culture consists of "assumptions about 1. human nature, 2. causality, 3. the possible, 4. the desirable, 5. the appropriate, 6. the nature of the physical environment, and 7. the relationship of human beings to their fellows" ([6], p. 78, from [13]). For example, not all cultures have the same assumptions about group decision-making and hence the use of a Group DSS may be resisted by some potential participants. In some cultures, the norm is that all should have an equal voice in decision-making. Some cultures encourage an open and collaborative problem-solving atmosphere. Some cultural norms support detailed meeting notes and a very structured decision-making process. Other cultures have conflicting norms. People have multiple overlapping group memberships and varied personal and cultural histories that can impact their decision behavior. For example, "native" English speakers benefit because English is the unofficial language of business and technology. This cultural reality may create a language arrogance and communication barrier between managers. Culture impacts evaluations of DSS layout and design and the use of a specific DSS. Word choice can cause confusion in screen displays. Also, colors and icons may have different emotional and political meanings based upon cultural history. In building DSS, designers need to be sensitive to cultural issues associated with decision makers and with stakeholders like customers and suppliers. Also, because of cultural differences promoting the use of DSS and evidence-based decision-making is a challenge in many countries (cf., [24]).

4.3 Differing Legal Regulations

Complex government regulations create a barrier to global expansion and increase the challenge of building DSS. For example, in some countries regulations specify data collection and security rules. Also, some countries have data import/export restrictions. According to Pratt [22], "European laws require much higher levels of data security and privacy, even as they apply to accessing employees' information." Pratt identifies seven key areas to watch out for: 1. Labor Relations, 2. Privacy, 3. Procurement, 4. Documentation, 5. Taxes, 6. Legal Systems, and 7. Variability of laws and regulations from country to country. This legal complexity makes it harder to aggregate data assembled from global operations. Also, knowledge-driven DSS become harder to construct. The many small-scale, high-frequency risks that result from the current global regulatory jungle make building all types of DSS much more costly.

4.4 Electronic Communication Limitations

In a global corporation, much of the communication is electronic. "Electronic communication" means that communication is by means of data messages and a digital medium. There are a smaller proportion of "real" face-to-face meetings and until recently few meeting used Interactive Video. Instead, bulletin boards and email have proliferated. This environment tends to isolate managers in different parts of a company. Also, this behavioral change means that there will be less spontaneous and informal communication in a company. To keep from getting "out of touch", managers need to work harder to communicate feelings and develop trust relationships. Communications-driven DSS should probably include pictures of participants and background materials. The changes in communications medium and associated limitations may improve some group outcomes. For example, there may be more anonymous brainstorming and better documentation of decision rationales. Lisa Kimball [10] argues "too many teams fail to consider key qualities of different media in their choices about when and how to use the full range of communications channels available to them." The benefits of various media for decision-making meetings needs to be better understood and must be considered by team leaders.

4.5 Telecommunications and Computing Infrastructures

Telecommunications access, reliability, and standards differ from country to country. In many countries, the government owns or controls the communication industry and it may be difficult to install communication lines. Also, costs are a major factor. Costs for telecommunications vary around the world. Throughout the Middle East, telecommunications infrastructures are expanding, but Africa still has a weak infrastructure. Many observers have noted that traditional telecommunications, computing and media "haphazardly" intersect. Some possible solutions to these infrastructure problems are Virtual Private Networks and satellite systems. Technological infrastructure constrains DSS choices and creates implementation problems.

4.6 Time Zone Differences

There is a complex array of time zones throughout the world. Having global operations makes it harder for companies to have "real-time meetings" and to have overlapping working hours for collaborating employees. But operating in many time zones can create decision support opportunities to reduce decision cycle times and reduce decision "handling costs". In some situations, the time zone of origin for a transaction matters and in others it is not relevant in decision making. Operating in multiple time zones creates both an opportunity and a challenge for collaborative work and communications.

Table 1 summarizes the above global DSS issues and our assessment of the relevance of the issues to specific types of DSS. The perceived importance of an issue is rated as low, moderate, or high. We recognize that such ratings are at best a conjecture at this stage, but they are proposed as a starting point to generate discussion of these issues for various types of DSS.

Table 1: Importance of Global DSS Issues for Different DSS Categories

Issues → DSS Types ↓	Accounting and Currency Issues	Cultural differences	Differing legal regulations	Electronic communication limitations	Telecom and infrastructure	Time zone differences
Communications-driven	Low	High	Medium	High	High	High
Data-driven	High	Medium	Medium	Medium	Medium	Low
Document-driven	Medium	Medium	High	Low	Medium	Low
Knowledge-driven	Medium	High	High	Medium	Medium	Low
Model-driven	Medium-High	Medium	Low	Medium	Low	Low

For communication-driven DSS, not recognizing the cultural sensitivities can be a major obstacle, in addition to the differences in electronic communication facilities and the telecom infrastructure of various countries. On the other hand, in the case of data-driven DSS, being able to properly transform decision-support data across currency and other measurement units should be the highest priority. For document and knowledge-driven DSS, familiarity with the cultural contexts and also the legal landscapes while interpreting the explicit documents and/or tacit knowledge is an important consideration.

Can these obstacles be overcome? YES. Building web-based DSS is a way to reduce telecommunications and computing infrastructure obstacles. One solution to cultural obstacles is planning and implementing DSS so that they can more easily be adapted to specific local languages. Localizing a Decision Support System can include: allowing space in user interfaces for translation of text into languages that require more characters; developing DSS with products like Web editors or authoring tools that can support international character sets (Unicode); creating graphic images that are universal in meaning; and using examples in help systems and software documentation that have global meaning. At a minimum the six major issues discussed above must be addressed in the evaluation of a proposed DSS that will have a global reach.

5 Examples of DSS in Global Enterprises

Let's examine some examples in the context of the expanded DSS framework: Communications-driven DSS, Data-driven DSS, Document-driven DSS, Knowledge-driven DSS and Model-driven DSS. Also, it should be noted that managers in global enterprises like Procter & Gamble use software for decision support special studies (cf., [15])

5.1 Communications-Driven DSS

Groupware, chat, Videoconferencing, and web-based bulletin boards are increasingly common in global enterprises. In a 2002 case study, eRoom Staff documented how more than 100 Naval Medicine CIOs and their staffs access eRoom through industry-standard Web browsers [3]. The U. S. Navy Bureau of Medicine manages 77 hospitals and regional service providers in locations inside the U.S. as well as overseas-based military installations, combat field hospitals and Navy ships at sea.

Recently, WebEx launched WebEx WebOffice in India to support distributed project management and outsourced development coordination for overseas partners and clients (03/07/2006). In 2001, Procter & Gamble chose Polycom for worldWide video communications support. Hewlett Packard (HP) has 13 Halo Collaboration Studios installed at its facilities worldwide. Halo Collaboration Studio is a high-end video conferencing facility built by HP in partnership with DreamWorks Animation SKG (12/12/2005).

To use Halo, organizations purchase at least two Halo rooms set up for six people each. "There are three plasma displays in each room that enable participants to see those they are collaborating with in life-size images. The rooms come equipped with studio-quality audio and lighting and participants use a simple on-screen user interface to begin collaborating". "Participants can easily share documents and data directly from their notebook PCs with individuals in other rooms using a collaboration screen mounted above the plasma displays."

5.2 Data-Driven DSS

In a recent case study at DSSResources.com, SAS staff explain how Briggs & Stratton uses SAS BI to consolidate information and deliver it globally to manufacturing offices, particularly in North America, China and Europe [23]. The case describes a global data-driven, executive management system with scorecards. More than 50 people in the company are hands-on information producers. For the past few years in the oil business within Shell International, a Category Management Business Solution (CMBS) has been used in seven countries, including Germany, UK and Netherlands. Data is gathered from more than 2,500 sites with 100 head office users [1].

At Maytag International, in a somewhat dated example, DI-Diver was used to track sales and analyze profitability for refrigeration, laundry, floor care, cooking and dishwasher product categories [11]. DI-Diver reports included sales dollars, unit totals, revenue, cost, warranty, and gross margin information for 1,700 SKU's and 1,000 customers. The data was updated monthly and distributed to users over a LAN. For remote users the updated information was distributed on a CD.

Two July 2005 press releases described decision support applications at Airbus and Hellmann Worldwide Logistics. Airbus expanded its use of an Applix TM1 solution to approximately 100 controllers at 16 Engineering Competency Centers located in France, Germany, the UK, and Spain. Hellmann is an air and sea freight shipping company that serves customers from 341 cities in 134 countries. Hellmann selected BusinessObjects XI to provide real-time access to customer related information such as tracking and tracing statuses, invoicing, inventory, and KPI management.

Buckman Labs standardized on Information Builders' software for global information integration (01/30/2006). It uses WebFOCUS to generate sales analysis reports. The company has annual sales of $429 million, produces 700 different products, and employs over 1,500 people working in more than 90 countries. ABN AMRO selected Teradata Data Warehouse to build a platform for business decision support in Asia (02/15/2006). ABN AMRO is an international bank with more than 3,000 branches in more than 60 countries and territories. The data warehouse will support business development of ABN AMRO consumer businesses in Asia. Regional headquarters in Hong Kong will be able to view the region's total business as well as the performance of each individual country's business, and each country will have a view of its own data. The focus is on DSS for customer relationship management, customer revenue analysis, and monitoring credit risk metrics. On March 21, 2006 Cognos announced Fresh Del Monte purchased the Cognos Performance Management solution. Fresh Del Monte is a leading global producer and distributor of fruit and vegetable products in Europe, Africa, and the Middle East.

5.3 Document-Driven DSS

In a press release dated March 10, 2006, "Dr. Scheller Cosmetics speeds time-to-market with Captaris Workflow", Captaris Workflow software was used to automate the approvals process for Dr. Scheller research and marketing materials. Dow Corning automated workflow capabilities and created templates using the Documentum ECM platform to ensure the consistency of all Web content while enabling business units to manage the content. DuPont Engineering has a document-driven system with more than 2,100 users worldwide. The system contains more than one million CAD drawings and other project documentation.

5.4 Knowledge-Driven DSS

Moody's Risk Management Services uses a knowledge-driven system to support the needs of commercial lending institutions. Over one third of the top 100 commercial banks in the US and Canada along with some of the largest industrial and financial companies in the world use FAST (Financial Analysis Support Techniques) software for credit analysis. Also, Hewlett Packard deployed a Web-based system to provide "quick, accurate hardware sizing, network configuration, and usage recommendations for SAP Business Information Warehouse implementations" (cf., exsys.com/case.html).

5.5 Model-Driven DSS

Standard Bank, one of the largest banks in South Africa, has operations in 17 countries. It was one of the early adopters of credit scoring and customer-level decisioning from Experian-Scorex (08/30/2005). ILOG announced on February 14, 2006 that Taiping Life, a leading Chinese insurer, chose ILOG JRules for its underwriting system so that it could expand its underwriting in Asia. There are many other model-driven scheduling, simulation and optimization DSS examples in global enterprises similar to those found in more local or country-centered enterprises.

6 Conclusions

This article has identified the unique factors that need to be considered in developing DSS by examining the five DSS categories. Further research is necessary to validate the conceptual conjectures made in Table 1. Research is also needed to identify a more comprehensive collection of DSS applications that may have been built for one location and then adapted/extended to other locations. For example, what are the unique systems analysis and design issues in changing from rapid prototyping at one location to installing a similar DSS at another location? How do situational factors impact DSS implementations across geographic boundaries? As a research field, DSS has grown and proliferated around the globe. However, our studies have tended to be focusing on localized DSS implementations rather than on global DSS implementations. It is now time to extend DSS studies to incorporate the issues raised by deploying DSS that can truly support global enterprises.

Acknowledgment. Some of the material in this chapter originally appeared in DSS News Ask Dan! Columns [18, 19, 20, 21].

References

1. Business Objects Staff, "Shell Delivers the New Face of Fuel Retailing with Business Objects", Business Objects, Inc., 2000, posted at DSSResources.COM September 2, 2001.
2. Davis, A., D. Fu, "Culture Matters: Better Decision Making through Increased Awareness," Interservice/Industry Training, Simulation, and Education Conference (I/ITSEC) 2004, http://www.stottlerhenke.com/papers/IITSEC-04-culture.pdf.
3. eRoom Staff, "Naval Medicine CIOs use collaboration and knowledge-sharing decision support application", eRoom, Inc., 2002, posted at DSSResources.COM August 2, 2002.
4. Ford, D.P., Connelly, C.E., and Meister, D. B., "Information systems research and Hofstede's culture's consequences: an uneasy and incomplete partnership", IEEE Transactions on Engineering Management, Vol. 50, Issue 1, 2003, pp. 8-25.
5. Friedman, T. L., "The World Is Flat: A Brief History of the Twenty-First Century," Farrar, Straus and Giroux, April 2005, ISBN: 0374292884.
6. Gaenslen, F., "Culture and Decision Making in China, Japan, Russia, and the United States", World Politics, 39, 1986, pp. 78-103.
7. Iyer, R. K., "Information and Modeling Resources for Decision Support in Global Environments," Information & Management, Vol. 14, Issue 2, 1988, pp. 67-73.
8. Iyer, R. K. and Schkade, L., "Management Support Systems for Multinational Business," Information & Management, Volume 12, Issue 2, 1987, Pages 59-64.
9. Tractinsky, N. and Jarvenpaa, S. L., "Information Systems Design Decisions in a Global Versus Domestic Context", Management Information Systems Quarterly, Vol. 19, No. 4, 1995, pp. 507-534.
10. Kimball, L., "Choosing Media Strategically for Team Communications," (Group Jazz) http://consortium.caucus.com/pw-choosemedia.html .

11. Lyons, T., "Maytag International Refines Data Distribution with DI-Diver", Dimensional Insight, Inc., February 2001, posted at DSSResources.COM February 28, 2001.
12. McDonald, W., "Influences on the Adoption of Global Marketing Decision Support Systems: A Management Perspective", International Marketing Review, Vol. 13, Issue 1, 1996, pp. 33-45.
13. Melberg, H. O., "Culture and Decision Making: A Review of an Article by F. Gaenslen, 1996, http://www.geocities.com/hmelberg/papers/960904.htm
14. Myers, M. D. and Tan, F. B., "Beyond Models of National Culture in Information Systems Research", Journal of Global Information Management, Vol. 10, Part 1, 2002, pp. 24-32.
15. Palisade Staff, "Procter & Gamble Uses @RISK and PrecisionTree World-Wide", Palisade Corp., Spring 2001, posted at DSSResources.COM May 22, 2001.
16. Peppard, J., "Information Management in the Global Enterprise: An Organising Framework", European Journal of Information Systems, Vol. 8, Num. 2, 1999, pp. 77-94.
17. Power, D.J. Decision Support Systems: Concepts and Resources for Managers, Greenwood/Quorum, 2002.
18. Power, D. J., "How is BPM related to DSS?", DSS News, Vol. 6, No. 19, August 28, 2005.
19. Power, D.J., "What is involved in providing decision support for global enterprises?", DSS News, Vol. 7, No. 3, January 29, 2006.
20. Power, D.J., "What are the obstacles associated with building DSS for global enterprises?", DSS News, Vol. 7, No. 6, March 12, 2006.
21. Power, D.J., "What are examples of decision support systems in global enterprises?", DSS News, Vol. 7, No. 7, March 26, 2006.
22. Pratt, M., "Global Legal Gotchas: How to avoid hidden traps in international laws," Computerworld, February 20, 2006.
23. SAS Staff, "Briggs & Stratton harnesses operational data", posted at DSSResources.COM December 2, 2005.
24. Yoder, R., A. Arabaji, M. A. and Siam C., "Building and Sustaining an Evidence-Based Decision-Making Culture: Can it be done?," APHA Meeting Oct 21-25, 2001, apha.confex.com/apha/129am/techprogram/paper_27202.htm .

Cited Press Releases

07/12/2005   Airbus expands use of Applix TM1 solution.
07/12/2005   Hellmann Worldwide Logistics optimizes performance with BusinessObjects XI.
08/30/2005   Experian-Scorex enables enterprise-wide decisioning for Standard Bank of South Africa.
12/12/2005   HP unveils Halo Collaboration Studios: Life-like communication leaps across geographic boundaries.
01/30/2006   Buckman Labs standardizes on Information Builders' software for global information integration.
02/14/2006   Leading Chinese insurer Taiping Life chooses ILOG JRules for its underwriting system.
02/15/2006   ABN AMRO selects Teradata Data Warehouse to build a robust foundation for business development in Asia.
03/07/2006   WebEx launches WebEx WebOffice in India: An on-demand collaboration solution for distributed project management and outsourced development.
03/10/2006   Dr. Scheller Cosmetics speeds time-to-market with Captaris Workflow.
03/21/2006   Fresh Del Monte moves to Cognos Performance Management solution.

Sources of Unstructuredness in Decision Situations: Towards a framework for DSS Development

Sanjiv D. Vaidya[1], Priya Seetharaman[1]

[1] MIS Group, Indian Institute of Management Calcutta,
Diamond Harbour Road, Joka, Kolkata – 700104, India

sdvaidya@iimcal.ac.in, priyas@iimcal.ac.in

Abstract. Decision support systems (DSS) are computer-based information systems which support unstructured or semi-structured managerial decisions in organizations. While it is yet to be recognized on a wide scale, DSS have become extremely important in today's world. Many reengineering exercises are actually built around DSS. A knowledge management infrastructure often fails as organizations cannot derive support for specific decisions from it. DSS are generally aimed at reducing the unstructuredness in a decision situation. A decision situation consists of the decision itself, the decision maker and the organizational environment. An attempt at developing a DSS essentially involves an attempt at reducing unstructuredness in the decision situation. This paper presents a framework which would allow decision analysts to identify such specific sources of unstructuredness at a much more refined level than the analysis available in the literature today.

Keywords: Decision Support Systems, Unstructuredness, Decision process, Decision-making style

1 Introduction

In an organizational environment, one of the three main roles of a manager involves making decisions and implementing them. Such decision making processes involve identifying and choosing among alternative solutions to organizational problems. Researchers from various disciplines have attempted to study and analyze the decision making process in organizations. While the dominant focus has been to define models of decision making, there has also been considerable work on analyzing the various factors which affect decision making within organizations.

Democratization of Information Technology (IT) has given rise to greater use of IT support for organizational decision making. One of the most important IT-based systems in organizations is a class of systems called Decision Support Systems. Decision Support Systems (DSS) can be defined as computer-based information systems which support unstructured or semi-structured managerial decisions in organizations. While it is yet to be recognized on a wide scale, DSS have become extremely important in today's world. There are two important reasons for this. First, increasing complexities in an organization's environments imposes greater challenges in organizational decision making. Second, DSS form fundamental building blocks of many IT-based strategic initiatives such as business process reengineering, knowledge management, customer relationship management etc.

Many reengineering exercises are actually built around DSS. A knowledge management infrastructure often fails as organizations cannot derive support for specific decisions from it. It is therefore important for us as IS researchers to understand the process of DSS design and development in greater depth than we do right now. This paper is an attempt in that direction.

Prior literature has argued that the aims of DSS, in general, are two fold namely, supporting the semi-structured decisions and, in the long run, reducing the unstructuredness in a decision situation. "Decisions are *programmed*[1] to the extent that they are repetitive and routine, to the extent that a definite procedure has been worked out for handling them so that they don't have to be treated de novo each time they occur" [18]. Unstructuredness therefore refers to the extent to which decisions are not programmed.

An attempt at developing a DSS essentially involves an attempt at reducing unstructuredness in the decision situation. In order to be able to do this, the DSS development team, particularly the decision analyst, should be able to identify the specific sources of unstructuredness in the situation. This paper presents a framework which would allow decision analysts to identify such specific sources of unstructuredness at a much more refined and comprehensive manner than the analysis available in the literature today. In discussing such a framework, the paper also presents a set of propositions relating to the specific sources and the degree of unstructuredness.

2   The Decision Situation – A Definition

Every decision has a certain inherent degree of structure about it. Keen and Morton [8] differentiate structured and unstructured decisions in the following manner. In unstructured decisions, the human decision maker must provide judgment and evaluation as well as insights into the problem definition. They also distinguish perceived structure from deep structure and contend that it is important for IS researchers to consider perceived structure especially in the context of DSS design and development. This is important mainly because in organizational decision making, the context plays a significant role in determining both the decision process and the contents. Kasanen, Wallenius, Wallenius and Zionts [7] highlighted the importance of structured decision making through four caselets each of which presented a different organizational decision situation.

The procedure and the substance of the decision are extensively influenced by the context [19]. Keen and Morton [8] argue that the term "system" in the name DSS itself implies both the manager and the machine and that the system considerations include the wider context in which the manager is operating. A model or a program (DSS) cannot be built in isolation from that wider context.

---

[1] Simon uses the word 'programmed' but subsequent authors have preferred the word 'structured'.

Using this line of thought, we describe the decision situation as *the context or boundary comprising of the decision, including the procedure and the substance, the decision maker(s) and the organizational environment in which the decision is made.*

These three factors taken together form, in total the decision situation to be supported by a "DSS". A DSS should support not just "a decision" but a decision situation i.e. it should support "a decision maker making a decision in a certain organizational environment". It can be seen from the above discussion that, development of an effective DSS would require the DSS team to have a very good understanding of the decision itself, the different types of decision makers and the environment in which the decision is made. This means that the DSS team has a formidable task on hand, particularly while analyzing and modeling the decision.

This paper aims to provide a framework for analyzing this decision situation through identification of the sources of unstructuredness. Using this framework, the DSS team should be able to identify the extent of unstructuredness in the respective decision situation. Following such identification, the team should be able to segregate the structured portion of the decision situation and ascertain the extent of support that can be provided by a DSS.

3   The Framework

The aim of this framework, as already mentioned is to aid the DSS team in identifying the sources of unstructuredness in the given decision situation. There are three potential sources of unstructuredness:

1.   The decision itself
2.   The decision maker and
3.   The organizational environment

We will examine these three constructs in detail and identify micro level dimensions for each of them. In doing so, the purpose is to provide a list of dimensions which when examined will provide the DSS team a comprehensive and complete understanding of the decision situation. Each section first delineates the dimensions that form the main construct and provides a set of propositions suggesting the nature of influence of the dimension on degree of unstructuredness of the respective construct. This is followed by an analysis of relationships between established typologies of the constructs and the degree of unstructuredness of the decision situation construct.

3.1   The Decision

A decision can be described as a conscious choice of solution to an organizational problem, among different alternative solutions. A decision is made using data or substance and through a process or procedure. "Substantive aspects relate to what of decision making, while the procedural aspects relate to how decisions are made" [19]. Both these aspects – data and process can be unstructured and the degree of unstructuredness of both is likely to impact the degree of unstructuredness of the decision and therefore the decision situation. Stabell argues that one of the reasons why it is difficult to describe and diagnose decision behaviour is because the procedure and substance of the decision are highly interdependent. Let us examine these two aspects of the decision in greater depth.

3.1.1 Data

Data refers to informational inputs to the decision. Data can vary in the degree of structure. Three main sources of unstructuredness of data arise from complexity, uncertainty and the ambiguity in the data.

Complexity: Complexity refers to the amount of information or quantum of information that has to be processed. This may arise from the wide variety and range of information. For instance, consider a decision to choose a candidate from thousands of potential applicants. The quantum of information to be processed is thus vast. Also consider a decision to diversify into a new product. The potential range of products could be enormous thus leading to a massive set of data to be processed. Such high levels of information inputs leads to greater levels of unstructuredness in the decision as there is a need to integrate such volumes of data inputs. Moreover, variations in data also necessitate dissimilarity in the manner in which such data are processed. Therefore,
Proposition: Higher degree of complexity in data is likely to lead to higher degree of unstructuredness in the decision.

Uncertainty: Uncertainty refers to the difference between the amount of information required for the decision and the amount of information already possessed by the decision maker [20]. In other words, uncertainty arises from lack of information. Sources of uncertainty include
a.   Deficiency of anticipation, wherein the information cues required for a decision to be made cannot be anticipated.
b.   Deficiency of acquisition, which denotes the inability to acquire the information required to make the decision.
These two deficiencies are likely to impact the unstructuredness of the decision, as they reduce the availability of the needed information. Thus,
Proposition: Higher degree of uncertainty of data is likely to lead to higher degree of unstructuredness in the decision.

Ambiguity: Ambiguity or equivocality refers to the multiplicity of meaning conveyed by the information cues [21]. Ambiguity arises from the inability to present a unique interpretation of the available data. Such decisions thus cannot be easily made as it is difficult to completely and precisely analyze the decision-related data. Therefore,

Proposition: Higher degree of ambiguity in data is likely to lead to higher degree of unstructuredness in the decision.

3.1.2 Process

Process refers to the various methods or procedures of making the decision using various data inputs gathered. Kasanen, et. al [7] presented a set of questions which can be used to understand organizational decision making process. Simon [18] defined the three phases of decision making, intelligence, design and choice. In the intelligence phase, the decision maker scouts for possible conditions in the environment calling for a decision. In the design phase, possible alternative solutions are delineated and analyzed, while in the choice phase, the alternative course of action is chosen from amongst these alternatives. Simon later extended the framework to include implementation and review or control. For the purpose of this paper, let us focus on the first three phases of the decision making process as these are directly related to design and development of the DSS.

Unstructuredness in the decision process is likely to arise when at least one of these three phases are unstructured [8]. Unstructuredness in one of the phases is likely to give rise to variability in the decision making process across decision situations, thus calling for a non-programmed or undefined procedure to conduct the process. Therefore

Proposition: Higher degree of unstructuredness in intelligence, design or choice phases of the decision making process are likely to lead to greater unstructuredness in the decision.

Unstructuredness in any of the three phases is likely to occur when the phase is complex, uncertain or ambiguous. Let us examine these three sources of unstructuredness in the context of the decision process:

Complexity: Multitude of steps or variety in activities of the decision process is likely to make the decision process more complex for the decision maker to handle. While whether a certain level of complexity is manageable or not depends on the individual's cognitive capacity, it is still possible to define an "absolute complexity" on the basis of extent of information processing involved. Therefore,

Proposition: Higher level of complexity in decision process is likely to lead to higher degree of unstructuredness in the decision.

Uncertainty: Uncertainty in decision process refers to the unavailability of information regarding how the decision is made. This could be due to the inherent inability of the decision maker to describe the decision process. Keen and Morton [8] argue that unstructuredness in a decision problem could occur because it may not be possible to define the conditions that allow us to recognize the problem or because the decision maker may be unable to specify the methodologies to solve the problem. These two deficiencies are likely to impact the unstructuredness of the decision process, as they reduce the awareness of the decision maker as regards the decision process. Thus,

Proposition: Higher degree of uncertainty of decision process is likely to lead to higher degree of unstructuredness in the decision.

Ambiguity: Ambiguity of the decision process refers to unclear procedure. Among other reasons, this could be due to multiplicity of decision models or absence of prior occurrence of the decision situation. Ambiguity arises from the inability to present a unique representation of the decision process. In such cases it is difficult to completely and precisely model the decision process. Therefore,

Proposition: Higher degree of ambiguity in decision process is likely to lead to higher degree of unstructuredness in the decision.

3.2 The Decision Maker

Different individuals have different styles of decision making. Some are naturally inclined to make decisions in a systematic manner by collecting the necessary data, processing and analyzing it in a detailed manner etc. On the other hand, there are decision makers who are comfortable with using mainly their intuition. The importance of decision making style of the decision maker can hardly be exaggerated. Some authors have studied the impact of decision making style of aspects such as firm performance (see for instance, [4]). We will examine some inherent characteristics of decision makers which influence the degree of unstructuredness in the decision situation [16].

Tolerance for Ambiguity: This refers to the degree to which the decision maker is comfortable with low levels of clarity in decision process or data.

Risk Tolerance: Decision makers vary in their aversion to risk. Some decision makers are innately more risk taking than others.

Leadership Style: Managers usually adopt authoritative, democratic, consultative or bureaucratic leadership styles. When the decision makers are authoritative it is likely to cause greater levels of unstructuredness than when the style is consultative or democratic.

Information gathering style: When managers are perceptive individuals in their information gathering styles, they are likely to focus on relationships between data items look for deviations from their expectations. Receptive thinkers, on the other hand, focus on the details than the overall patterns [11].

Information evaluation style: Managers adopting intuitive information evaluation styles keep the overall problem in mind, rely on unverbalized cues, jump alternatives while systematic thinkers approach the problem in a methodical manner moving through an increasing refinement of analysis [11].

Creativity: Creative decision makers are likely to adopt innovative, novel ways of making the decision. They are hence likely to be erratic and unpredictable.

Task versus People orientation: High task-orientation decision makers focus on getting things done and achievements unlike people oriented managers who are more focused on the relationship with people and how to make them comfortable.

Table 1. Decision-related Characteristics of Decision Maker

Characteristic of Decision maker	Relationship to Degree of Unstructuredness
Tolerance for Ambiguity	Positive
Risk Tolerance	Positive
Leadership Style: Authoritative	Negative
Leadership Style: Democratic/Consultative	Positive
Leadership Style: Bureaucratic	Negative
Information Gathering Style: Perceptive	Positive
Information Gathering Style: Receptive	Negative
Information Evaluation Style: Intuitive	Positive
Information Evaluation Style: Systematic	Negative
Creativity	Positive
Task orientation	Negative
People orientation	Positive

3.2.1 Typology of Decision Makers and Degree of Unstructuredness

Rowe and Boulgarides [17] discuss a four-class typology of decision makers based on their value orientation (relational or logical) and tolerance for ambiguity (low and high). Their classes include Analytical, Directive, Conceptual and Behavioral. It is possible, using their description of the four types to conclude that directive decision makers are likely to face lowest degree of unstructuredness followed by analytical, behavioral and conceptual.

Due to restrictions on space, we will not examine other more comprehensive personality typologies such as the Myers-Briggs Type Indicator which can also be related to the degree of unstructuredness due to the decision maker. It must be remembered though, that managers have a dominant style with back-up styles; some almost always rely on their dominant style while others are more flexible. Hence while these typologies give us a good idea of the impact of style on unstructuredness, they should not be taken as fixed or rigid classes.

Let us now examine the third source of unstructuredness – the organizational decision environment.

3.3 Organizational Environment

The degree of unstructuredness or structuredness in a decision situation also depends on the organizational environment in which the decision is taken. The organizational decision environment includes characteristics of the domain in which the organization functions and the immediate domain in which the decision is being made. The directly impacting environment is the immediate decision environment. While this may include environment external to the organization depending on the type of decision (say Operational Control/Management Control/Strategic Planning discussed in [6]), it will be shaped by the legacy environment present in the organization. In the long term, the legacy environment of the organization is also affected by the external factors. By legacy environment we refer to organization structure, organization culture, etc. which authors have argued are influenced by the external environment in which the organization operates. For instance, Galbraith [5] argued that task uncertainty influences the ability of decision makers to pre-plan or to make decisions about activities in advance of their execution.

Lawrence and Lorsch [9] postulated that greater turbulence in the external environment necessitates greater differentiation among the subparts of the organization and therefore such organisations required elaborate integration mechanisms to avoid loss of coordination among differentiated subparts. Miles and Snow [12] and Mintzberg [14] have also discussed how the external environment of an organization affects the various dimensions of the organization's internal environment.

The following section examines in greater detail the internal environment characteristics that influence the decision environment. The broad factors include organization structure, organization culture and power distribution in the organization.

3.2.1 Organization Structure

Organization structure is defined as "the sum total of the ways in which (an organization) divides its labor into distinct tasks and then achieves coordination between them" [13]. This structure therefore also determines the decision making structure of the organization which not only tells us who makes what decisions but also tells us the way in which the decisions should be made and the boundaries within which the decision makers are allowed to operate. Such decision boundaries, decision hierarchies and control mechanisms define the unstructuredness of the decision situation.

While numerous theorists have argued about what constitutes organization structure, Robbins [16] puts forth that the following three dimensions are the core dimensions and encompass all other factors: complexity, formalization and centralization. In the following subsections, we will examine each of these in detail in an attempt to theorize the relationship between organization structure and the degree of unstructuredness in the organization decision situation.

Complexity: This refers to the degree of differentiation that exists within the organization. Three parameters contribute to complexity of the organization. They are horizontal differentiation, vertical differentiation and spatial differentiation.

Horizontal differentiation refers to "degree of differentiation between units based on orientation of members nature of tasks they perform, and their education and training" [16]. The greater the horizontal differentiation, the more complex the organization will be as it makes it increasingly difficult for the organization to coordinate and integrate organization activities. Thus when organization encounter higher degrees of horizontal differentiation they are likely to face greater unstructuredness in their decision situations. Horizontal differentiation arises from specialization – functional or social. Higher levels of specialization of tasks are likely to give rise to greater need for task coordination. This may also result in greater vertical differentiation.

Vertical differentiation refers to the depth in the structure. In other words, vertical differentiation captures the number of hierarchical levels in the organization. It also reflects the span of control which defines the number of subordinates a manager can effectively manage. Therefore, higher levels of vertical differentiation lead to higher degree of unstructuredness in decision situations in organizations.

The third dimension of complexity is spatial differentiation. This refers to the extent of geographical spread of the organization and its various units. When organizations are more geographically and spatially differentiated, the complexity of the organization is also high. Greater spatial differentiation necessitates integration. Communication, control, coordination needs increase, thus giving rise to higher degree of unstructuredness.

Thus all three differentiation factors increase degree of unstructuredness as they increase complexity thus making integration necessary yet difficult. Thus we can say

Proposition: Organisations having higher degree of complexity are likely to have higher degree of unstructuredness in their decision environment

Formalization: The degree to which jobs in an organization are standardized is referred to as formalization. Robbins [16] argues that when formalization is low, employees are likely to behave in relatively a more non-programmed manner. Low formalization allows greater degree of freedom and flexibility but also causes greater unstructuredness in the decision environment in organizations. On the other hand, highly formalized organizations or departments are likely to have well-defined procedures, explicit organization rules and job description. While this restricts the freedom, the employee will have lower inputs in terms of how and what is to be done. Therefore, a structured decision environment will be prevalent in such formalized organizational environments.

Proposition: Organizations having higher degree of formalization are likely to have lower degree of unstructuredness in their decision environment.

Centralization: When decision making authority is concentrated at one point, an organization is said to be centralized. While it is impossible to strictly hypothesize the relationship between centralization and degree of unstructuredness in the organization decision environment, it is highly likely that higher degree of centralization will lead to lower degree of unstructuredness in the organization decision environment. Quite often decentralization provides greater information inputs to the decision maker and also allows for lower intermediary channels of information transmission to the decision maker. In other words,

Proposition: Organizations having higher degree of centralization are likely to have lower degree of unstructuredness in their decision environment.

Structural Typologies: Organizational theorists have put forth typologies based on various structural parameters. In this section we analyse two of the popular and simple typology frameworks to understand the relationship between organization structure and decision environment.

Burns and Stalker [3] analyzed the various kinds of organization environments and their influence on the structure of the organization. Using rate of change of external environment they argued that organization can be broadly classified as having mechanistic or organic structures. Using their classification it is possible to delineate the degree of unstructuredness in organizational decision environment. For instance, mechanistic organization structures perform routine tasks and therefore rely more heavily on programmed tasks. On the other hand, organic structures are more adaptive, flexible and have loose job definitions. Thus,

Proposition: Organizations having greater orientation towards a mechanistic structural form are likely to have lower degree of unstructuredness in their decision environment than organizations with orientation towards an organic structural form.

A similar analysis can be conducted using Mintzberg's five classes of organization based on their structure. Mintzberg [13] presented five configurations of organization design options including simple structure, machine bureaucracy, professional bureaucracy, divisional structure, adhocracy. For our examination here, let us look at machine bureaucracy and adhocracy. Machine bureaucracy refers to the organization design which emphasizes standardization. Because such organization face simple and stable external environments, they are likely to have highly routine operating tasks, high degree of formalization and high degree of centralization. In comparison, adhocratic organizations face extremely complex and dynamic environments and thus have few rules, are highly flexible, decentralized and have a high degree of social specialization. Therefore,

Proposition: Machine bureaucracies are likely to have lower degree of unstructuredness in their organizational decision environment than adhocracies.

It must be remembered that since these typologies are not strict watertight compartments, the influence of the characteristics of a particular type on the degree of unstructuredness of organizational decision environment is also likely to be affected by such overlaps.

In the same way, using the Miles and Snow [12] typologies of Defenders, Prospectors and Analyzers, we can understand the relationship between the external organization environment, the organization structure and the degree of unstructuredness in the organizational decision environment. Prospectors for instance, are those organizations that face a dynamic external environment and react by having a loose structure, low degree of formalization and a high degree of centralization. Defenders, in contrast, are organizations that operate in relatively more stable environments and respond through high horizontal differentiation, centralized control, high degree of formalization. We can therefore conclude:

Proposition: Organizations adopting the prospector strategy are likely to face higher degree of unstructuredness in their organizational decision environment than organizations that adopt a defender strategy.

Proposition: Organizations adopting the analyzer strategy are likely to face lower degree of unstructuredness in their organizational decision environment than organizations that adopt a prospector strategy but higher degree of unstructuredness in their organizational decision environment than organizations that adopt a defender strategy.

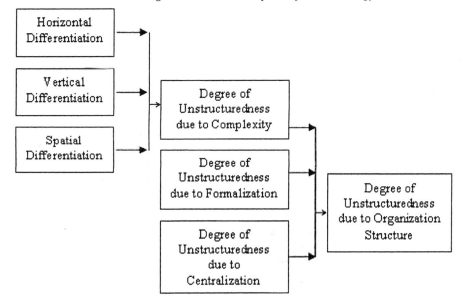

Figure 1: Degree of Unstructuredness due to Organization Structure

   Having examined the influence of organization structure on the degree of unstructuredness in the decision environment, let us now examine the impact of organization culture on the organization decision environment.

3.2.2 Organization Culture

Culture defines "the way things are done around here". In other words, "a pattern of shared basic assumptions.....that has worked well enough to be considered valid and therefore ..... as the correct way to perceive, think and feel in relation to those problems" [16].

A common way of understanding culture is through the organizational artefacts or visible signs; the espoused values or values projected to employees; and basic assumptions incorporated in the way employees view things in the organization and thus act. Robbins [16] describes ten dimensions of organization culture include individual initiative, risk tolerance, clarity in direction, integration, management support, control, identity, reward system, conflict tolerance and communication patterns. While some of these relate to the structural dimensions, some others focus on behavioral dimensions. The structural dimensions such as integration, control, reward systems, etc. were dealt with in the previous section on organization structure. We will focus here on the influence of the behavioral aspects of organization culture on the degree of unstructuredness of decision environment.

Individual Initiative: This refers to the degree of responsibility, freedom and independence that individuals have [16]. In other words, in an organization where individual initiative is high, employees are encouraged to independently make decision and have a certain degree of freedom to act. This of course, would be within the boundaries fixed by their roles and responsibilities. Such organizations, other things remaining the same are likely to encounter greater level of unstructuredness in their decision situation. This is mainly because allowances for individual initiatives permits employees to adopt their own mental model of decision making instead of a pre-determined decision making process or structure. Thus variations in the decision situation increase thus leading to greater unstructuredness in the decision environment as faced by the employees.
Proposition: Organizations encouraging individual initiatives are likely to face higher degree of unstructuredness in their decision environment.

Risk Tolerance: Risk tolerance refers to the "degree of which employees are encouraged to be aggressive, innovative and risk-seeking". In an organization where there is a high level of risk tolerance, it is also likely that individuals make decision in a more unstructured fashion. Innovativeness encourages unstructuredness mainly because innovativeness brings in instability or uncertainties. Further, organizations that encourage aggressiveness and competitiveness are also likely to have greater unstructuredness in decision situations.
Proposition: Organizations having higher levels of tolerance to risk are likely to face higher degree of unstructuredness in their decision environment.

Direction: Clarity in objectives and direction provides a degree of structuredness in organizational decision making situations. For instance, in an organization where the objectives are very clearly defined and the direction or path towards those objectives is very clearly defined and explicit, employees are clear about performance expectations. This leads to a high degree of structuredness in decisions they make. In contrast, consider an organization where the objectives are loosely defined or the means to meet those objectives are not very clearly defined, such organizations are likely to have very unstructured decision environments.

Proposition: Organizations having greater clarity in their directions are likely to face lower degree of unstructuredness in their decision environment.

Management Support: A closely related aspect is that of management support and guidance. When top management or superiors of the decision maker do not provide very clear communication, guidance, direction or support to the subordinate, then the organizational decision environment is likely to be highly unstructured. Employees can be expected to feel vague and unclear about decision making process and achieving the organizational objectives.

Proposition: Organizations encouraging greater superior support and guidance are likely to face lower degree of unstructuredness in their decision environment.

Communication Patterns: The degree to which organizational communications are restricted to formal hierarchy or authority determines the extent of structuredness in the organizational decision environment. If communications in the organization are restricted to organizational hierarchical authority, the decision maker can be expected to handle far fewer opinions and suggestions, thus reducing the degree of unstructuredness. Employees are also likely to feel more constrained to express their opinions. On the other hand, when organization communication is not restricted to formal authority, informal groups may exist and individual specific variations are allowed. Therefore,

Proposition: Organizations where communication patterns are restricted to formal channels are likely to face lower degree of unstructuredness in decision environments.

Conflict Tolerance: An associated dimension is that of conflict tolerance. When organizations encourage employees to air their criticisms, grievances, etc. openly, they are said to be conflict tolerant. Higher levels of such tolerance allow greater participation of employees in the organizational decision making processes. Such participation gives rise to greater unstructuredness in the organizational decision environment.

Proposition: Organizations where communication patterns are restricted to formal channels are likely to face lower degree of unstructuredness in decision environments.

Typologies of Culture and Degree of Unstructuredness: Robbins [16] describes the concept of fit between an organization's culture and its external environment through two common strategies adopted by organizations – market-driven and product-driven approaches. He argues that organizations opting for market-driven organization culture fit strategies tend to have higher degree of unstructuredness in their decision environments as they will emphasize greater individual initiatives, risk taking and conflict tolerances. In contrast to that, organizations adopting product-driven strategies tend to fit cultures that emphasize high control, low risk and conflict tolerance and do not encourage individual initiatives as they prefer operating in stable environments. Marakas [10] extends this argument to the decision environment by contending that market-driven organization tend to have higher degree of unstructuredness in their organizational decision environments, while product-driven organizations tend to have lower degree of unstructuredness. This would affect the technologies that they adopt. For instance, product-driven orientation supports routine technologies like assembly line etc.

The structure of decision may also depend on how informal the organization culture is. There are many such environmental factors which affect the degree of structure in a decision.

It must also be remembered that cultures which are strong tend to have stable or constant degree of structuredness, while organizations that have weak cultures where the core values are not intensely held are more likely to have flexibility and therefore a less stable degree of structuredness.

3.2.2 Power and Political Environment

Power refers to an individual's capacity to influence decision making. The role of power of individuals in organizations therefore assumes importance especially when there are differences in either the preferences towards solutions to decision problems or in the very definition of the situations. Political decision makers are thus, people who can appear to represent the organizational interests while at the same time look after their own interests. Astley and Sachdeva [1] argue that there are three sources of power. These include (1) hierarchical authority, (2) resource control and (3) network centrality. Let us consider each of these sources in greater detail and understand how they influence the structuredness of the overall decision situation in the organization.

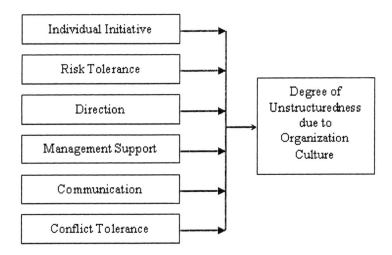

Figure 2: Degree of Unstructuredness due to Organization Culture

Hierarchical Authority: Formal authority in the organization is a source of power. Power can be "viewed as the product of formal decree". This hierarchical authority provides the decision maker the power to make the decision within the formal authority provided to him/her. It thus allows him/her to use his preferences and predispositions in making the decision. If the hierarchical authority is greater in the context of the decision the decision environment is likely to be more unstructured. For instance, if the decision maker is not authorized by virtue of his organizational hierarchy with respect to this decision, he is more likely to make a decision which will be more acceptable in the organization, hence will be inclined to do so in a structured and pre-determined manner.
Proposition: Greater the power due to hierarchical authority, higher is the degree of unstructuredness in the organization decision environment.

Resource Control: If the source of power of a decision maker is the control over resources either physical or information, it is likely to affect the degree of structuredness in the decision environment. Lower control over physical or information resources related to the decision force decision makers to adopt greater structured decision process in order to circumvent or make do with lower access to the resource.
Proposition: Greater the power due to resource control, higher is the degree of unstructuredness in the organization decision environment.

Network Centrality: Network centrality refers to the power gained from positions that allow the decision maker to integrate other functions or to reduce organization dependencies. In a well-differentiated organization the network is dependent on this integration mechanism which allows a stable network of interactions. When the power due to such network centrality is greater, it is very likely that the decision environment in the organization becomes more unstructured. Higher levels of power due to network centrality is mainly because there are more nodes to interconnect in the network, or there is greater dependency on the network centrality due to higher levels of spatial, vertical or horizontal differentiation.

Proposition: Greater the power due to network centrality, higher is the degree of unstructuredness in the organization decision environment.

Power possessed and exercised by the decision maker can therefore be an important source of unstructuredness. The importance of its role is also dependent on the importance of the decision itself.

Under pressure of time, an otherwise structurable decision may have to be taken in a highly unstructured manner. Short term pressures like time pressures also affect the organizational decision environment. These may be caused by spikes in some aspects of the external environment caused due to unanticipated factors or unforeseen exigencies. Such sudden spikes cause sudden time pressures for one-time decisions. Such decisions are likely to be taken in a situation where the external environment assumes a high level of importance and hence there is an increased unstructuredness in the decision situation.

Proposition: Lesser the availability of time to make decision, higher is the degree of unstructuredness in the organization decision environment.

A summary of the framework is presented in Figure 3.

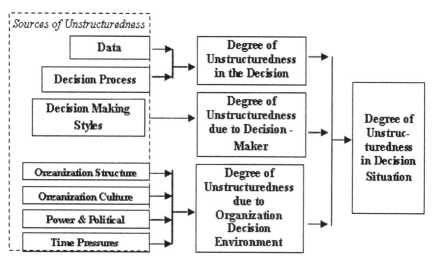

Figure 3: Summary of Framework for DSS Development - Sources of Unstructuredness in Decision Situations

4 Conclusion

This paper presented a framework for DSS development using the various sources of unstructuredness as the basis identifying the potential support of DSS. This framework, it is believed, would allow decision analysts to identify specific sources of unstructuredness in a more refined and comprehensive manner. The paper also presented a set of propositions relating to the specific sources and the degree of unstructuredness.

While this paper restricts itself to presenting a theoretical framework for DSS development, it is also necessary to test it and validate it. Hypothetical examples have been used during the theory development process by the authors to strengthen the framework, but empirical validation is on the future agenda. Situations similar to the decision situations documented in Austin, Sole and Cotteleer [2] or Covina, et. al [4] can be used to highlight the importance of the framework.

Decision analysts can identify the specific sources of unstructuredness, the extent of such unstructuredness and thus prioritize development of DSS to tackle them. Such a process used for a specific decision, especially those that are strategically important may aid managers in using IT support for organizational decision making, more efficiently and effectively.

5 References

1. Astley, G., and Sachdeva, P. Structural Source of Intraorganizational Power: A Theoretical Synthesis. Academy of Management Review (9) 1984.
2. Austin, R.D., Sole, D. and Cotteleer, M.J. Harley Davidson Motor Company: Enterprise Software Selection. Harvard Business School Case Study. 2003, Number: 9-600-006.
3. Burns, T., and Stalker, G.M. The Management of Innovation Tavistock, London, 1961.
4. Covina, J.G., Slevin, D.P., Heeley, M.B. Strategic decision making in an intuitive vs. technocratic mode: structural and environmental considerations. Journal of Business Research (52) 2001, pp 51-67.
5. Galbraith, J. Designing Complex Organizations Addison-Wesley, Reading, MA, 1973.
6. Gorry, G.A., and Scott Morton, M.S. A Framework for Management Information Systems. Sloan Management Review (13:1) 1971, pp 55-70.
7. Kasanen, E., Wallenius, H., Wallenius, J. and Zionts, S. A Study of High-Level Managerial Decision Process, with Implications for MCDM Research. European Journal of Operational Research (120) 2000, pp 496-510.
8. Keen, P.G.W., and Morton, M.S. Decision Support Systems: an Organizational Perspective Addison-Wesley, Reading, MA, 1978.
9. Lawrence, P., and Lorsch, J. Differentiation and Integration in Complex Organizations. Administrative Science Quarterly 1967, pp 1-30.
10. Marakas, G.M. Decision Support Systems in the 21st Century Prentice Hall, 2002.
11. McKenney, J., and Keen, P. How Managers' Minds Work. Harvard Business Review (52:3) 1974, pp 79-90.
12. Miles, R.E., and Snow, C.C. Organizational Strategy, Structure and Process McGraw-Hill Book Co, New Delhi, 1978.

13. Mintzberg, H. The Manager's Job: Folklore and Fact. Harvard Business Review (53:4) 1975, pp 49-61.
14. Mintzberg, H. The Structuring of Organisations Prentice Hall, Englewood Cliffs, N.J, 1979.
15. Porter, M.E., and Millar, V.E. How Information gives you Competitive Advantage. Harvard Business Review (63:4) 1985, pp 149-160.
16. Robbins, S.P. Organizational Behavior Prentice Hall of India, New Delhi, 2002.
17. Rowe, A.J., and Boulgarides, J.D. Managerial Decision Making Prentice-Hall, Upper Saddle River, NJ, 1992.
18. Simon, H.A. The New Science of Management Decision, (3rd ed.) Prentice Hall International, Englewood Cliffs, NJ, USA, 1960.
19. Stabell, C.B. A Decision Oriented Approach to Building Decision Support Systems in: Building Decision Support Systems, J.L. Bennett (ed.), Addison-Wesley, Reading, MA, 1983, pp. 221-260.
20. Tarafdar, M. Determinants of Certain Characteristics of Information Technology Deployment in Organisations: A Theoretical Explanation in: Department of Management Information Systems, Indian Institute of Management Calcutta, Calcutta, 2001.
21. Weick, K.E. The Social Psychology of Organizing Addison-Wesley, Reading, MA, 1969.
22. Wood, R.E. Task Complexity: Definition of the Construct. Organizational Behavior and Human Decision Processes (37) 1986, pp 60-82.

Critical Success Factors for Implementation of Business Intelligence Systems: A Study of Engineering Asset Management Organizations

William Yeoh[1], Andy Koronios[1], Jing Gao[1]

[1] Strategic Information Management Lab,
School of Computer and Information Science,
University of South Australia, Mawson Lakes, 5095 Australia

{William.Yeoh, Andy.Koronios, Jing.Gao}@unisa.edu.au

Abstract. Much of IS literature suggests that various factors play pivotal roles in the implementation of an information system; however, there has been little empirical research about the factors impacting the implementation of business intelligence (BI) systems, particularly in engineering asset management organizations. There is an imperative need for a critical success factors (CSFs) approach to enable BI stakeholders to focus on the key issues of implementing BI systems. The authors conducted in-depth interviews with 15 BI practitioners of engineering asset management domain to identify factors critical for successful implementation of BI systems. Based on the findings, this study identifies ten CSFs that are crucial for implementing BI systems. This paper presents and discusses the findings, as well as puts forward recommendations for further research. This paper will be of particular interest to those researchers and practitioners who are studying, providing consultancies, planning or implementing BI systems.

Keywords: Critical Success Factors, Business Intelligence Systems

1 Introduction

Due to competition resulting from deregulation and from increasingly complex business environments, engineering asset management organizations (EAMOs) such as electricity, gas, water and waste utilities and railway companies are particularly concerned with accessing timely and actionable information which will enhance decision support and improve the bottom line. Although computerized operational and transactional systems do provide information to run the daily operations, what business managers often need are different kinds of information that can be readily used for integrated engineering asset management. They need to understand their respective businesses from multiple perspectives, to carry out 'what-if' predictive analysis and to make strategic and tactical decisions based on that actionable information.

According to British Standards Institute [1], engineering asset management is the "systematic and coordinated activities and practices through which an organization optimally manages its assets and their associated performance, risks and expenditures over their lifecycle for the purpose of achieving its organizational strategic plan". In other words, effective engineering asset management optimizes asset utilization, increases output, maximizes availability, and lengthens the asset lifespan, while simultaneously maintaining the lowest long-term cost rather than short-term savings in order to reap the maximum value. Furthermore, it is impossible to optimize asset lifecycle profits if the various business functions are not synchronized or aligned with each other [2]. This requires integration and synchronization of management plans and practices at all levels, from asset needs definition to the asset retiring stage. In order to achieve that, there should be a focused approach on engineering asset management and its interrelationships with other processes and systems [3]. As a result, the asset operation, maintenance, human resource, procurement, inventory control, financial and other business functions are considered inter-dependent and mutually supportive, from the perspective of the achievement of overall enterprise goals. This would enable knowledge workers to use this multidimensional information to plan and schedule business functions such as asset availability, asset maintenance, rehabilitation, and replacement activities in the most effective and efficient manner.

The information environment in these organizations, however, is typically fragmented and characterized by disparate operational, transactional, and legacy systems, spread across multiple platforms and diverse structures [4]. EAMOs store vast amounts of asset-oriented information, and business users often have difficulty locating the best information for their decision support, resulting in suboptimal management performance. Yet, with the many millions of dollars of investment in ERP-style systems, engineering enterprises have been storing large volumes of transactional data, leading to increased difficulties in analysing, summarizing and extracting reliable information. In response to these growing pressures, engineering asset management organizations are compelled to improve their business execution and management decision support through the implementation of a BI system.

A BI system is, as Negash [5] explains, "a strategic information system capable of providing actionable information through a centralized data repository, sourced from numerous sources, transformed into meaningful information via BI analytical tools, to facilitate business insights leading to informed decisions". A successful BI system implementation presents EAMOs with a unified, new and thorough insight across the entire range of its engineering asset management functions. Consequently, critical information from many different sources of an asset management enterprise can be integrated into a coherent body for strategic planning and effective allocation of assets and resources. Hence, the various business functions and activities are analyzed collectively to generate more comprehensive information in support of management's decision making process. BI systems come as standardized software packages from such vendors as Business Objects, Cognos, Hyperion Solutions, Microstrategy, Information Builders, Oracle and Actuate, and they allow customers to adapt them to their specific requirements. IDC Research expects that the BI market will enjoy a compound annual growth rate of 23 percent, and report US$3.3 billion dollars turnover in the Asia Pacific region alone [6]. Forrester's 2005 study further indicates that BI had the top spot in enterprises' list of planned application purchases [7]. The 2005 annual survey of CIOs conducted by Gartner similarly found that

BI was runner-up on their list of the top ten technology priorities [8]. These findings are echoed by Merrill Lynch's CIOs spending surveys in February and September of 2005 which revealed that BI retained a consistent place in the top three spending priorities [9].

1.1   Research Problem and Objectives

The implementation of a BI system is not a simple activity to purchase a combination of software and hardware, but rather a complex undertaking and requires requisite infrastructure, resources, and includes a variety of stakeholders, such as project teams, steering committees, key BI users, external consultants, and BI vendors. A typical expenditure in these systems, including all BI infrastructure, packaged software, licenses, training and entire implementation costs, is always measured in millions of dollars. The IS literature contains many studies that investigate the factors that impact the implementation of an information system. While these studies are helpful, a BI system is substantially different from a traditional operational or transactional system. Specifically, the key infrastructural component – a data warehouse - is a subject-oriented, integrated, time-variant, and non-volatile collection of data than conventional online transactional processing (OLTP) systems [10]. A complex data structure must be maintained in order to provide an integrated view of the organization's data so users can query across departmental boundaries for dynamic retrieval of rich decision-support information. Moreover, the implementation of a BI system has to deal with a variety of stakeholders, functional needs, data management, technical issues, and broader enterprise integration and consistency challenges. Furthermore, there is a high degree of complexity in the system's architecture, owing to the unstable back-end systems originating from multiple data sources, and the vast volume of data to be processed [11]. This data is used to generate standard reports, and to support the decision making process of knowledge workers as well as ad hoc power users. Therefore, the complexities of implementing a BI system and its far reaching business implications justify a more focused look at the system implementation issues separately from those of traditional OLTP systems.

Much IS literature suggests that various factors play pivotal roles in the implementation of an information system. However, despite the increasing interest in, and importance of, BI systems, there has been little empirical research about the critical success factors (CSFs) impacting the implementation of BI systems, particularly in EAMOs. The gap in the literature is reflected in the low level of contributions to international conferences and journals. Moreover, as a BI system is primarily driven by the IT industry, most of the existing BI system literature consists of anecdotal reports or quotations based on hearsay. According to Ang and Teo [12], the implementation of an enterprise-wide information system is a major event and is likely to cause organizational perturbations. This is even more so in the case of BI system implementation. BI project planning and implementation always involves a vast amount of resources and a variety of stakeholders over a period of months, requiring simultaneous attention to a wide variety of organizational, human, budget, technical and project variables. Therefore, rigorous academic research to identify the CSFs for successful implementation of BI systems is of great importance and urgency.

The goal of this study is to identify the CSFs for implementation of BI systems, particularly within engineering asset management organizations. With a systematic investigation about the existing scenarios, the findings presented in this article can certainly help those EAMOs which are studying or planning to implement BI systems by focusing on those critical issues, and hence harnessing the success of such a resource-intensive and large-scale undertaking. Furthermore, academia can use the results from this study as a basis to initiate other related studies in the area of BI system implementation. The remainder of this paper has been structured as follows. The next section briefly describes concepts of critical success factors before elaborating on the research methodology for identifying CSFs crucial for implementation of BI systems. The fourth section then outlines the data analysis approach. In the fifth section the authors discuss the findings of the study, followed by the conclusion, and finally proposals for further research initiatives.

2   Critical Success Factors: Definition and Concepts

The concept of Critical Success Factors (CSFs) was first introduced by Daniel [13] and later popularized by Rockart [14] as a mechanism to identify the information needs of CEOs. Since then it has become a popular approach in a number of studies linking business and IT [15]. According to Rockart [14], CSFs are those few critical areas where things must go right for the business to flourish. These limited areas are those in which results, if they are satisfactory, will ensure successful competitive performance for the organization. If results in these areas are not adequate, the organization's effort for the period will be less than desired [16]. The emphasis here is on 'few' and must go 'right'. As the number of CSF is limited, senior management is able to constantly focus on the CSFs until they are successfully achieved [17].

Greene and Loughridge [18] further add that the identification of CSFs can help to clarify the nature and amount of resources that must be gathered to permit the development team to concentrate their efforts on meeting priority issues, rather than what the available technologies will allow. Evidently, these key areas of activity would need consistent and careful attention from top management if BI system implementation and thus organizational goals were to be attained. In other words, CSFs are high-level management considerations as distinct from a detailed set of project deliverable specifications. Hence, a set of CSFs identified for the development of any major information system, such as a BI system, is fundamentally different from the set of interlinked detailed tasks which must be accomplished satisfactorily to ensure a project's successful completion [19]. Consequently, the success of BI system implementation may not be fully ensured by meeting the required CSFs, but failure to consider the CSFs will be a major constraint for the organization.

Although CSFs were initially introduced to determine the information needs of executives, the approach has been extended to cover other areas of information system research. Despite the limited literature on entire BI system implementation issues, there exists a significant body of CSFs literature about the implementation of information systems, data warehouses, ERP systems and software projects. As a BI system is an enterprise-wide implementation effort similar to ERP and data warehouse, the adoption of a CSF approach is therefore considered appropriate in this study of BI systems.

3 Research Methodology

The majority of previous studies have used well-established research methods, such as questionnaire surveys and case studies, to examine the key factors for their respective information system research. However, the purpose of the present research was not to test hypotheses but rather to identify a set of CSFs for implementation of BI systems, particularly within engineering asset management enterprises. The authors wanted to explore and identify CSFs perceived to be important by the interviewees, and so they chose a research method which would allow for the emergence of whatever factors and issues that BI system managers and consultants considered significant. Grounded theory approach was thus deemed to be most appropriate for this study because it ensures deep context categories and facilitates the "discovery of a theory from data systematically obtained from social research" [20, 21].

Although there is a plethora of anecdotal literature on success factors for systems implementation, the suggested factors seem to focus primarily on general information systems, ERP, MRP, and data warehouses. There is still no clear and comprehensive examination on the CSFs for implementation of entire BI systems. Therefore there is an urgent need for a fresh approach to the present research topic and grounded theory methodology can provide a new perspective in this study. In other words, rather than begin this research with a preconceived hypothesis that needs to be proven, the researchers started with a general area of study and allowed the CSFs to emerge from the gathered data. According to Glaser and Strauss [20], the grounded theory approach is about building theory, not testing it. Hence the CSFs resulting from this study is considered as an integrated set of propositions; however, the verification of this result is left to other better suited research methods such as questionnaire survey [21]. This methodology thus allows the researchers to be open to the issues that will emerge from the data and to avoid derailments in the form of assumptions about what ought to be found in the data.

For data collection, fifteen BI systems experts (as shown in Table 1) who had been involved substantially in the implementation of BI systems within engineering asset management domain were selected and included in the study. They consisted of senior consultants from BI consultancy firms, BI project managers, and system managers within implementation companies. The BI systems products included Cognos, Business Objects, Oracle, Hyperion, Microstrategy, Information Builder, SPF Plus, Actuate and Informatica. In addition, these experts represented a diverse range of engineering asset management organizations. They include public utilities, such as electricity, gas, water, and waste management, and infrastructure-intensive enterprises such as oil, gas and railway companies. It should be noted that some of the large organizations have had several implementation projects and that they chose to implement the BI systems in a series of phases. Most of the EAMOs are very large companies with engineering assets worth hundreds millions of dollars and have committed immense expenditure to BI projects, so the expertise of the participants represented the most up-to-date knowledge of BI systems implementation in a broad range of engineering asset-intensive industries.

Table 1. Interviewees and their BI Systems Experience in EAMOs

Current Position	Company Type	BI System	EAMOs' Industry Sector
Principal Consultant	BI Consultancy	Business Objects, Information Builder, Cognos, Oracle	Electricity, Gas, Water & Waste utilities, Oil & gas production, Public transportation authority
Principal Consultant	BI Consultancy	Cognos, Business Objects, Actuate	Telecommunications, Airlines, Municipal utility
Senior Consultant	BI Consultancy	Oracle	Energy utilities
Business Information System Manager	Implementation company	Informatica, Oracle	Water utility, Waste Water utilities
Senior Principal consultant	BI Consultancy	Cognos, Hyperion, Microstrategy, Business Objects	Electricity, Gas, Water utilities, Telecommunications
Senior Advisor	Implementation company	Hyperion, Informatica, Oracle	Rail infrastructure and fleets
Consultant	BI Consultancy	IBM, Oracle, Cognos	Municipal utilities, Public transportation authority
System Manager	Implementation company	SPF Plus, IBM	Electricity utility
Project Manager	Implementation company	Hyperion, Informatica, Oracle	Rail infrastructure and fleets
System Support Engineer	BI Vendor	Cognos	Energy utilities, logistic transportation company
Business Decision Support Manager	Implementation company	Informatica, Oracle, Hyperion	Rail infrastructure and fleets
Principal Consultant	BI Consultancy	Oracle, Business Objects	Energy utilities, Rail infrastructure
Manager Risk Management	Implementation company	Business Objects, Oracle	Electricity utility
Project manager	Implementation company	Business objects, Oracle	Water and waste utilities
Principal Consultant	BI Consultancy	Microsoft	Energy utilities, Oil & Gas production

Semi-structured in-depth interviews were chosen as the primary source of data for this study because this particular technique would provide the researchers with a deeper understanding of the relevant issues than would have been possible by a closed-ended survey or structured interviews. It allows for dynamic exploration and clarification of comments made by the respondents in pursuing issues of particular significance that relate to the research question [22] – which asked 'what are the CSFs for implementation of BI systems in EAMOs?'. In other words, this technique allows flexibility in the sequencing of questions and in the depth of exploration. The authors conducted face-to-face interviews (and phone interviews in some cases due to geographical constraints), and these varied in duration from one to one and half hours. At commencement of the interviews it was explained that the study focused on CSFs that facilitated the implementation success in terms of infrastructure performance and process performance. The infrastructure performance consists of three major IS success dimensions proposed by Delone and McLean [23, 24], namely system quality, information quality and system use, whereas process performance is composed of meeting time-schedule and budgetary constraints. After the interviews, further clarifications (if any) were made by follow-up phone calls and email communications. However, the authors were cautious about over relying on key informants, and whenever possible they sought to corroborate emerging findings by seeking contrary evidence from other interviewees and from documentation and presentation materials provided by the interviewees.

4 Data Analysis

All the qualitative data collected were analyzed according to the grounded theory approach. This approach encourages the emergence of a theory from the data set by constantly comparing incidents of codes with each other and then abstracting related codes to a higher conceptual level [21, 25, 26]. The objective of the present research was to identify the CSFs that influence the implementation of BI systems in engineering asset management enterprises. Hence, it is considered to be very important to determine what emerges from the data regarding interpretations of the CSFs for implementing BI systems.

The data analysis began simultaneously and progressively during the data collection stage of the research. When the researchers began conducting interviews it was noted that more refined questions evolved from the emerging qualitative data. According to Strauss and Corbin [27], refining the collection of data in conjunction with the data analysis could further validate the patterns and themes that emerge. Based on the analysis of previous interviews, the researchers revised the interview questions, and most of the time some new questions were added for subsequent interviews.

The transcribed interviews resulted in 38 pages of single-spaced text. After several reviews of the interview transcripts, open coding occurred. Open coding is "the analytic process through which concepts are identified and their properties are discovered in the data" [28]. This line-by-line analysis commenced by identifying and coding key terms and significant sentences which contain particular feelings, thoughts or experiences that answering present research question – the CSFs for implementation of BI systems. As each incident was coded, the researchers then compared it with other coded incidents within the data set in order to uncover similarities and differences. Strauss and Corbin [28] further explain that the goal of labelling is to give a common heading to similar phenomena or concepts, and more importantly to note the reoccurring concepts or patterns within the data.

Following the open coding, the subsequent stage took all the coded data in open coding and subjected them to a process of constant comparison analysis [20, 28]. Through an iterative clustering process the researchers grouped identical codes and labeled them as a unique cluster. While the clusters were being formed the process of developing and integrating the clusters into a set of more general themes was occurring concurrently. Finally, all the themes were integrated. The authors identified the central insights emerged from the aggregated themes. The analysis was stopped when the researchers believed that the point of theoretical saturation has been reached. This means that no new concepts, properties or dimensions will emerge during analysis. Saturation is "the state in which the researcher makes the subjective determination that new data will not provide any new information or insights for the developing categories" [29].

To illustrate the entire analysis process, within the interview transcripts, data specific to the "users must be included in the effort" was identified and coded during open coding; then the researchers constantly compared this code with other similar concepts and this has led to the development of a unique cluster, known as "formal and interactive user involvement", and at the same time this particular cluster or CSF was further categorized into organizational dimension. Eventually, the combination of all dimensions formed the conceptual framework of CSFs for implementation of BI systems. In short, the whole analysis process evolved from coding concepts to grouping concepts into dimensions and then to integrating dimensions into a conceptual framework of CSFs.

5 Findings and Discussion

Based on findings of the research, Figure 1 depicts a conceptual framework of CSFs that lead to the successful implementation of BI systems, particularly in engineering asset management enterprises. The CSFs are categorized into three main dimensions, namely organizational dimension, project dimension and infrastructure dimension. Within each dimension there are a number of independent CSFs which would impact the success of BI systems implementation. The implementation success of this research takes into account two key dimensions: infrastructure performance and process performance. The infrastructure performance draws parallels to the three major IS success variables described by Delone and McLean [23, 24], namely system quality, information quality and system use, whereas process performance can be assessed in terms of time-schedule and budgetary considerations for the overall project. The discussion of each of the CSFs findings is as follows.

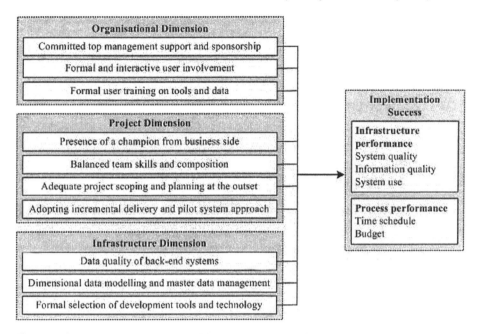

Figure 1. Conceptual Framework of Critical Success Factors for Implementation of BI Systems

5.1 Organizational Dimension

Committed Top Management Support and Sponsorship: In the organizational dimension, evidences from the qualitative findings revealed that top management support was held to be indispensable for successful BI system implementation in engineering asset management enterprises. The interviewees asserted that consistent support and sponsorship from top management make it easier to secure the necessary operating resources such as funding, human skills, organizational support, and other requirements throughout the implementation process. One interviewee pointed out that "if you don't have top level sponsorship – it is doomed!" Another one stated firmly, "no money, no system." This observation is reasonable and expected because the whole BI system implementation effort is a costly, time-consuming, resource-intensive process. Hence, adequate funding is vital if the development team is to overcome implementation obstacles and deliver on the project milestones. In particular, adequate funding would enable the development team to access the appropriate BI tools and technology. The respondents indicated that the selection of BI system components such as ETL tools, data-cleansing software, database management systems, data warehouses, query tools, analytical tools and hardware that are needed for optimized BI application must not be jeopardized because of a lack of funding. Otherwise, the project scope will have to be realigned accordingly and this may present a threat to user expectations. Moreover, without dedicated support from top management, the BI project may not receive the proper recognition and hence the support it needs to be successful. This is simply because users tend to conform to the expectations of top management and so are more likely to accept a system backed by their superiors. As pointed out by one participating manager, "BI applications take internal time and resources and without an executive communicating the importance and aligning resources the project will not be successful." Many interviewees further indicated that such support was best when it was accompanied by close monitoring of, and interaction with, the BI projects. In this regard, a steering committee was established to provide a balanced check between management needs and project effort. Specifically, senior management set up a structured mechanism for regular monitoring of implementation progress. Apart from these, top management support was deemed critical to solve the organizational resistance and conflicts that may arise during the course of a complex project.

Formal and Interactive User Involvement: The importance of formal and interactive user involvement was recognized by the interviewees. Evidence from the interviewed respondents indicates that better user participation included in the implementation effort can lead to better communication of their needs, which in turn can help ensure successful implementation of the system, for as a BI consultant stated, "they are the ones going to use the system." This CSF is particularly important when the initial requirements for a system are unclear, as is the case with many of the decision-support applications that a BI system is designed to sustain. As indicated by a BI consultant, "Users should be an important partner in building and delivering the right system. Without their consistent input, we technicians cannot deliver the right system." Supporting this view was the observation of another consultant who commented that, "Users must be included in the effort. There must be a sense of ownership by the users." Apparently, interactive user participation throughout the implementation cycle can help meet their information needs and format requirements, and this finding is congruent with an observation by one project manager who noted, "How can the development team design and implement a BI system to meet the users' needs without their involvement?" Meanwhile, another interviewee mentioned that, "...if the BI project does not involve adequate user participation, then the project is not likely to be successful because the BI application will not satisfy the end users." Consequently, the data dimensions, business rules, metadata and data context that are needed by business users must be identified and incorporated into the system. Moreover, many consultants advocated that users should be consulted on the selection of user interface and query tools as they are the prime users. In short, when users are actively involved in the project, they have a better understanding of the potential benefits and this makes them more likely to accept the system on completion.

Formal and Adequate User Training on BI Tools and Data Environment: The research findings also show that the formal and systematic training for end users must not be ignored when aiming for successful BI system implementation in EAMOs. Many interviewees indicated that adequate training can help users to speed up the system adoption and to explore the required information in a more effective manner. One project manager posed the following question; "Will the users of a BI system know how to use it? If not, how are they going to make use of the BI application?" Furthermore, interviewees emphasized that training should not only focus on the technology itself, but also on the associated data and maintenance issues. This training is important to equip users to understand and experience the features and functions, and to learn about the configured environment, the available data and business rules of the BI applications. In this regard, a manager added that "Providing user training…gives them comfort, or the users just go back to the source systems as much as they can." In order to facilitate more conducive training sessions, it is also critical to separate power users from casual ones because individuals may have different needs and expectations. Since users are accountable for making the BI system produce returns on investment, it is critical for companies to view user training as an investment rather than a cost in order to reap greater benefits from the project implementation.

5.2 Project Dimension

Presence of a Champion from Business Side: Turning now to the project dimension, the majority of respondents believed that having the right business manager to lead the project is critical for implementation success. One project manager explicitly emphasized that "You must have a champion from business side." This CSF was unanimously supported by all respondents who maintained that the project leader, or so-called 'champion', must have business expertise, be technically-knowledgeable, and be committed to the success of the project. According to them, a business-centric champion would view the BI system primarily in strategic and organizational perspectives, as opposed to over focusing on technical aspects. As noted by a BI consultant, "The team needs a champion. By a champion, I do not mean someone who knows the tools. I mean someone who understands the business and the technology and is able to translate the business requirements into a BI architecture for the system." Furthermore, he or she must possess excellent communication and interpersonal skills. This is because many organizational issues, such as conflict of data ownership, can be more difficult to resolve than technical challenges which can be overcome through technical solutions [12]. In fact, a BI project coordinator commented that "technological issues can sort out later; it is getting users' understanding and showing value to them that are more difficult." Hence, a champion must be unswerving in promoting the benefits of the new BI system and must help resolve any internal disputes that are impacting the project. Also, the interviewees indicated that the champion must be able to motivate his or her team to channel their energies into overcoming both technical and organizational obstacles to better meet project objectives. Consequently, the selection of a champion may determine the cohesion and success of BI system implementation.

Balanced Team Skill and Composition: All interviewees stressed that the composition, skills, and aptitude of a development team have a major influence on the success of the BI systems implementation. The development team should be composed of those personnel who possess technical expertise and those with a strong business background because the interviewees stressed that BI system is a business-driven project to provide enhanced managerial decision support. Hence, IT expertise is needed to implement the technical aspects, whereas the definition of data architecture especially during the planning phase must be under the realm of business personnel. A project manager spoke to this point simply stating, "Best of both worlds." The interviewees further maintained that these project members must desire to work as a collective team and be able to work and interact well with users, demonstrating excellent interpersonal skills and communication capabilities. A principal consultant put it this way, "They must like each other and be smart and dedicated." This particular point can be well understood since a BI system is a relatively new and complex technology, yet the entire implementation effort in such EAMOs always involves intense intra-organizational communications and immense resources. In addition, many respondents indicated that it is better to empower the project leader to choose his or her best team. An effective model has been the small team comprising up to ten people who are knowledgeable, skilled, and dedicated, and who like and respect each other in order to strive for project success. Therefore, EAMOs management must pay greater attention to this CSF for successful implementation of a BI system.

Adequate Project Scoping and Planning at the Outset: The grounded study found that for successful BI system implementation in EAMOs it is necessary to carefully take into account the important factor of project planning and scope definition. According to them, proper scoping and planning allows the development team to concentrate on the best opportunity for improvement. To be specific, scoping that clearly focuses on high impact process helps to set clear parameters and develops a common understanding as to what is in scope or excluded from. Moreover, it is the foundation on which the operating resources, including budget and time frame, are built. A system manager contended, "The success of 90 percent of our BI projects is determined prior to the first day. This success is based on having a very clear and well-communicated scope, having realistic expectations and timelines, having the appropriate budget set aside, and having the right resources committed to the effort." Another BI consultant further stressed that "This can be the undoing of all projects!" The same consultant further explained, "The information environment (of EAMOs) is typically fragmented… it is often characterized by silos of systems." Hence, adequate scoping and planning enables the team members to focus on crucial milestones and pertinent issues while shielding them from becoming trapped in unnecessary events. Moreover, the interviewees were well aware that adequate project planning also facilitates flexibility and adaptability to changing requirements within the given timeframe and resources, especially in implementing a complex EAMO-specific BI system. One consultant pointed out that the "Just do it" philosophy and the excuse of "What a waste of time developing a detailed project plan, yet no one exactly follows the plan" are warning signs of project failure. Therefore, the critical scoping and planning session allows a documented consensus on the BI project, provides a liberal platform to which all relevant BI stakeholders can speak and thus avoids misunderstanding and denial of responsibilities.

Adopting Incremental Delivery and Pilot System Approach: The interviewees also indicated that it is advisable to start small and adopt an incremental delivery approach because large-scale change efforts are always fraught with greater risks given the substantial variables to be managed simultaneously. This finding was stressed by many of the interviewees. For instance, a system manager asserted that "(Incremental delivery)...reduces the risks of the big bang approach." Another senior consultant explained in detail, "You cannot role out the whole BI system at once, but people want to see some key areas. You need to do data marts for a couple of key areas and then maybe a small number of other key reports in an attempt to keep all stakeholders happy. Then, when the first release is done and you get some feedback, you can work on other data mart areas and enhance existing subject areas over time." Obviously, an incremental delivery approach that starts off with a pilot system is always valuable as proof of a concept; that is, constructing a fairly small BI application for a key area in order to provide tangible evidence for both executive sponsors and key users. A majority of the interviewees recommended a pilot system that offers clear forms of communication and a better understanding in an important business area would convince organizational stakeholders of the usefulness of BI system implementation. As a result of a successful pilot project, senior management are keen and motivated to support larger scale BI efforts. A project manager stated that "People need to see how the reports will look before committing large amounts of money." Another manager added, "Business organizations are always looking to see immediate impact, and such an incremental delivery approach could provide some results in a short time. In addition, business changes very fast and as such an incremental delivery approach provides the tools for delivery of needed requirement. Moreover, a scalable approach allows for building a long-term solution as opposed to a short term one." Consequently, this pilot-tested system could be further expanded and enhanced into an enterprise-wide BI system. The pilot system could include additional data sources, attributes, and dimensional areas for fact-based analysis, and it could incorporate external data from suppliers, regulatory bodies and industrial benchmarks. Undoubtedly, an incremental delivery approach allows an EAMO to concentrate on crucial issues, so enabling teams to prove that the system implementation is feasible and productive for the enterprise.

5.3 Infrastructure Dimension

Data Quality of Back-end Systems: In terms of infrastructure dimension, the research findings indicate that the quality of data, particularly at the back-end systems, is crucial if a BI system is to be implemented successfully. Data quality will affect the quality of management reports, which in turn impact the decision outcomes. Speaking to this point, a BI consultant asked, "If the data is corrupt then what is the point?' While another consultant further contended that "If the source systems are unreliable, maybe you shouldn't do a BI project." According to the interviewees, a primary purpose of the BI system is to integrate 'silos' of data sources within EAMOs for further analysis so as to improve the decision making process. However, most EAMOs face great difficulties because it is found that the data in their source systems are not reliable and of poor quality [4]. These problems may be due to the lack of concern on the part of field maintenance workers and a lack of enforcement by managers. A senior consultant commented in detail,

"This is the most underrated and underestimated part of nearly every BI development effort. Much effort is put into getting the data right the first time, but not near enough time is spent putting in place the data governance processes to ensure the data quality is maintained." Thus, the combined efforts of the development team and business units are required to assess the quality of the data sources and to put appropriate data-cleansing processes in place, especially during the data capture process. Frontline and field workers should be made responsible for their data source and hence data quality assurance. Furthermore, the EAMO should initiate corresponding efforts to improve the quality of the data in such back-end systems as operational, maintenance, procurement, contract management, work management and inventory control, because unreliable data sources will have a ripple effect on the BI applications and subsequently the decision outcomes.

Dimensional Data Modeling and Master Data Management: A BI system provides EAMOs users with a dimensional view of data such as demographics of engineering assets, and each of the dimensions has measures in terms of throughput or productivity. In order to have consistent dimensions and measures across subject areas, the interviewees asserted that it is important for development team to identify and establish consensus on the dimensions and measures that will be used in the system's data model. A senior consultant described the situation this way; "Not understanding dimensional modelling will cause lots of grief later on and make it difficult to answer some questions." Therefore, it is crucial to get it right the first time with a star schema and well-designed dimensions. Prior to that, many interviewees stressed that the information needs of organizational key users must be identified to enable the decision regarding the data requirements which will satisfy their expectations and information needs. As stated by a BI consultant, "Otherwise the model will not be reflective of the organization." Consequently, the development team would use those requirements to develop an enterprise-wide dimensional model that is business orientated. Furthermore, it is typical for an EAMO to have hundreds of varying terms with slightly different meanings, because different business units tend to define terms in ways that best serve their purposes. For instance, a maintenance unit might define assets as physical engineering equipment or machines, whereas a financial department might include capital and buildings. Often an accurate data may have been captured at the source level; however, the record cannot be used to link with other data sources due to inconsistent data identifier. This is simply because data values that should uniquely describe entities are varied in different business units. Once an organization collects a large number of reports it becomes harder to rearchitect these areas. As a result, a cross-system analysis is important to help profiling a uniform 'master data set' which is in compliance with business rules. Hence, the development of a master data set on which to base the logical data warehouse construction for BI system will ease terminology problems.

Formal Selection of Development Tools and Technology: Apart from the CSFs discussed above, the interviewees indicated that the selection of development tools and technology impacts the efficiency and effectiveness of BI development efforts as much as other CSFs, particularly if the tools are not well understood by the development team. In fact, the tools and technologies involved in BI systems, especially for EAMOs, are different from those used with operational systems because the BI effort requires advanced data extraction, transformation and loading software, data-cleansing programs, database software, and multidimensional analysis tools. Many of those tools and software are expensive, not just for their initial costs but in maintenance and user training expenses. Therefore, the selection of these important development technologies and tools must meet the needs of business and be compatible to EAMO's disparate back-end systems. The interviewees indicated that using a business-driven approach to select against defined goals can significantly increase the success rate of getting most optimized tools and technology. This business-based approach builds upon consensus across departmental boundaries and therefore is more likely to meet user requirements. A project manager stated firmly that, "a BI system that is not business driven, is a failed system." Meanwhile, another system manager expressed the view that, "These tools must match the requirements of organization, users and the project." Otherwise, the whole implementation effort will suffer from inappropriate development technologies that do not meet the EAMOs' requirements of strategic asset management. Furthermore, one interviewee advised that the development team should not let an external consultant make important decisions on matters such as software selection. This is because the skills and experience of the consultant may hinder the individual's judgment from offering an independent recommendation. Thus the critical factor of tools selection cannot be taken lightly to ensure implementation success.

6 Conclusion and Future Research

This paper has reported the exploratory results that aimed to critically identify the CSFs for the implementation of BI systems in engineering asset management organizations. This research drew upon semi-structured and in-depth interviews with 15 BI systems practitioners who have been involved extensively in implementing BI system for integrated engineering asset management. An analysis of the findings demonstrated that there is a combination of CSFs peculiar to successful BI system implementation. Senior management, project sponsors, project leaders, project members, and end-users all play critical roles in respective CSF.

Moreover, this study reveals a clear trend towards multi-dimensional challenges in implementing BI systems. The research indicates that the CSFs exist in three main dimensions, namely an organizational dimension, a project dimension, and an infrastructure dimension. Amongst the findings, CSFs such as committed top management support, interactive user involvement, team skills and composition, quality of data sources, adequate project scoping, incremental delivery approach and scalable system design are decisive for the success of such an undertaking. While the specific CSFs vary somewhat among BI systems and general IS studies, it appears that there is a new understanding of factors associated with infrastructure projects like BI systems which can be used in future research. Many CSFs of BI system implementation are probably the same as the IS development. However, there is a great difference with the technical CSFs like dimensional data modeling and master data management issues because the technical issues vary with the nature of the infrastructure system.

From a practical standpoint, the findings of this study help BI stakeholders of EAMOs both to identify and to concentrate on the CSFs, especially in the planning of a BI system. Such outcomes will help them to improve the effectiveness and efficiency of their implementation activities and thus achieve a greater degree of success in eventual user adoption. Furthermore, this paper has important implications for research and practice. To be specific, the findings and conceptual model suggest that in investigating the CSFs for BI systems implementation, researchers should not only focus on the technical context but also take into account the factors of organizational and project perspectives to provide a more comprehensive research approach. For practitioners, the findings would enable them to better manage their implementation of BI systems if they understand that such implementations involve multiple success factors occurring simultaneously and not merely the technical aspect of the system.

For further research, it is planned that a survey with multiple EAMOs will be conducted using a structured questionnaire based on the findings. As it stands, this research was exploratory in nature and further empirical research in other industries may shed light on where and how the research findings can influence the success of a BI system implementation.

Acknowledgments. This research is conducted through the Cooperative Research Centre for Integrated Engineering Asset Management (CIEAM). The support of CIEAM partners is gratefully acknowledged.

References

1. British Standards Institute: Publicly Available Specification for the 'Optimal Management of Physical Infrastructure Assets' (PAS-55) (2004)
2. Eerens, E.: Business Driven Asset Management for Industrial and Infrastructure Assets. Victoria, Australia: Le Clochard (2003)
3. Bever, K.: Understanding Plant Asset Management Systems. Maintenance Technology, July/August (2000) 20-25.
4. Haider, A., & Koronios, A.: Managing Engineering Assets: A Knowledge Based Approach through Information Quality, Proceedings of 2003 International Business Information Management Conference, Cairo:IBIMA (2003)
5. Negash, S.: Business intelligence. Communications of the Association for Information Systems, vol 13, (2004) 177-195
6. Giang, R.: Asia/Pacific Business Intelligence Solutions Market Spending Dynamics. IDC Research Group (2002)
7. Wirth, J. Top 10 Trends in Business Intelligence, viewed 11 May 2006
8. http://www.b-eye-network.com/view/2717?jsessionid=8417aae931842

9. Gartner Press Release: Gartner Survey of 1,300 CIOs Shows IT Budgets to Increase by 2.5 Percent in 2005, viewed 11 August 2006, http://www.gartner.com/press_releases/asset_117739_11.html
10. CIO, Business Intelligence, viewed 11 April 2006, http://www.cio.com/specialreports/business_intelligence.html
11. Inmon, W.: Building the Data warehouse. Wellesley, MA: QED Technical Publishing Group (1992)
12. Sen, A. & Jacob, V.: Industrial-Strength Data Warehousing. Communications of the ACM vol 41(9) (1998) 28-31
13. Ang, J., & Teo, T.: Management issues in data warehousing: Insights from the Housing and Development Board. Decision Support System, vol 29(1), (2005) 11-20
14. Daniel, R.H.: Management data crisis. Harvard Business Review. Sept-Oct (1961) 111-112
15. Rockart, J.: Chief Executives Define Their Own Data Needs. Harvard Business Review, vol 57(2) (1979) 81-93
16. Rockart, J. & Hoffman, J.: System delivery: Evolving new strategies, Sloan Management Review, vol 33(4) (1992) 21-31
17. Ives, B., Jarvenpaa, S. & Mason, R.: Global business drivers: Aligning information technology to global business strategy, IBM System Journal, vol 32(1) (1993) 4-16
18. Khandelwal, V.: What the Australian CEOs want from IT, Journal of Research and Practice in Information Technology, vol 32(3) (2000)151-167
19. Greene, F. & Loughridge, F.: The Management Information Needs of Academic Heads of Department in Universities: A Critical Success Factors Approach'. A Report for the British Library Research and Development Department. Sheffield: Department of Information Studies, University of Sheffield (1996)
20. Dobbins, J.: On a Generalized CSF Process Model for Critical Success Factors Identification and Analysis, PhD Thesis, George Washington University (2000)
21. Glaser, B. & Strauss, A.: Discovery of grounded theory: Strategies for qualitative research. Chicago: Aldine (1967)
22. Glaser, B.: Basics of grounded theory analysis. Mill Valley, CA: Sociological Press (1992)
23. Minichiello, V., Aroni, R., Timewell, E. & Alexander, L.: In-depth interviewing: researching people. Melbourne, Vic: Longman Cheshire (1990)
24. DeLone, W. & McLean, E.: The Quest for the Dependent Variable. Information System Research, (1992) 60-95
25. DeLone, W. & McLean, E.: The DeLone and McLean Model of Information Systems Success: A Ten-Year Update. Journal of Management Information Systems, vol 19 (2003), 9-30
26. Glaser, B.: Theoretical sensitivity: Advances in methodology of grounded theory. Mill Valley, CA: Sociological Press (1978)
27. Glaser, B.: Doing grounded theory: issues and discussions. Mill Valley, CA: Sociology Press (1998)
28. Strauss, A. & Corbin, J.: Basics of qualitative research: grounded theory procedures and techniques. Newbury Park, CA: Sage (1990)
29. Strauss, A. & Corbin, J.: Basics of qualitative research: Techniques and procedures for developing grounded theory (2nd ed.). Thousand Oaks, CA: Sage (1998)
30. Creswell, J.: Educational research: Planning, conducting, and evaluating quantitative and qualitative research. New Jersey: Merrill Prentice Hall (2002) 450-452.

Support for Collaborative and Distributed Decision Making

Schalk Pienaar[1], Ananth Srinivasan[1], David Sundaram[1]

[1]Department of Information Systems and Operations Management,
University of Auckland, Auckland, New Zealand

Schalk.PIENAAR@rbos.com, {a.srinivasan, d.sundaram} @auckland.ac.nz

Abstract. Our research addresses issues of design and implementation of a framework and architecture for distributed decision making. While decision support technologies have been studied for a number of years the emergence of new standards and internet technologies provides us with an opportunity to address current problems in distributed and collaborative decision making. This class of problems has become increasingly relevant with collaborative business models such as supply and demand chains and e-business. In particular, the increasing global nature of organizational work involves collaboration across national boundaries. This has become a common business model and technology support for such activity is the focus of our work. In this paper we discuss the design of a generator that supports distributed decision making. We do this by leveraging emerging standards and technologies like Web Services, SOAP, and WSDL. Features such as ad-hoc integration, location independence and platform independence are supported in a manner that addresses independence, flexibility, interoperability, and workflow management. We present a discussion about a design prototype and associated examples using the stock market as an application domain.

Keywords: distributed decision making, organizational collaboration, decision support design, system generators.

1 Introduction

A reality of modern organizations and the manner in which they function is one of collaborative work. Increasing levels of the global reach of many organizations today has made it essential for us to pay attention to collaborative business models. Business processes that span multiple business units in multiple countries have assumed a level of importance that demands formal attention from researchers. Perhaps the two most important business models that exemplify collaborative work that is largely enabled by a technological infrastructure are supply chains and e-business. In both cases, it is imperative that business processes that span organizational boundaries be defined and supported for the efficient functioning of the participants. These processes may span national boundaries in order to completely define a particular unit of work in a focal organization. The infrastructure that supports such processes (transaction as well as decision oriented) must take into account the fact that multiple organizations must work in a synchronized manner to accomplish organizational goals. The requirements under such a scenario transcend a single enterprise to one of multiple enterprises working in a coordinated fashion. High level modeling has become a core aspect defining the requirements in a way that ensures that the systems that are designed to support such activity align properly with multi-enterprise level objectives. Requirements that are determined in this fashion can ensure that systems work efficiently and in unison to accomplish the goals [5, 14].

Integration of systems that exist in multiple organizations is the key to success in a multi- organizational environment. The issue of IT relatedness across multiple business units has been highlighted as a significant antecedent to organizational performance [17]. However, achieving proper integration is often fraught with risks due to poorly defined business processes (and associated decision processes) and technological heterogeneity.

In this paper, we focus on support for collaborative and distributed decision making in the context of business and technological environments outlined above. Specifically our emphasis is on design aspects that enable distributed decision making with effective systems support. We outline a framework that explicitly supports the modeling and execution of distributed business processes. We consider variations in both business process complexity and organizational boundary definitions and the implications for design. Finally, we show examples of our implementation to demonstrate and highlight the important requirements of such a system.

Distributed decision making needs a level of technology support that places particular demands on the designer. These include issues such as independence, flexibility, interoperability, ad-hoc integration and workflow management. As the predominant business model continues to shift towards integration of diverse and distributed organizational systems, the requirements of distributed decision making need special attention.

By leveraging the opportunities provided by technologies and protocols like Web Services [8, 12] and SOAP [2], we develop a Distributed Decision Support System Generator (DDSSG) that helps distributed decision makers make better decisions more easily. This is accomplished in three phases described in the following sections. The first is to provide a Distributed Decision Making Model to summarise the needs of the distributed decision making environment. The second is to provide a Distributed Decision Making Lifecycle that describes the phases of building a Distributed Decision Support System. The third is to develop a framework and architecture that support this lifecycle, and a prototype that implements the framework and architecture as a proof of concept.

2 Distributed Decision Making: Conceptual Underpinnings

Langley, Mintzberg, Pitcher, and Posada [13] view decision making as a complex network of issues (Figure 1) bound by a multitude of linkages. From this network, decisions or actions emerge periodically. These decisions and actions are driven by insights, various "affective factors", or the rationale of the decision makers. Langley *et al* [13] liken the model to a moving stream, in which issues float along, *"sometimes getting washed up on shore as actions, sometimes sinking and disappearing, and often bumping into each other with the effect of changing another's direction, slowing one down, speeding one up, joining two together, or having a single burst into several new ones"*.

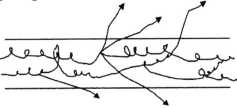

Figure 1. Organizational Decision Making as Interwoven, Driven by Linkages [13]

When we translate this rather abstract model of interwoven linkages into an organizational framework context, the enterprise framework presented by Curran and Kcllcr [3] is what we can expect to see. Here, points of decision making functionality are linked to each other via abstracted interfaces in a network that supports organizational information processing (Figure 2). The process flows in the network, represented by lines between objects, are analogous to the "issue streams" described by Langley *et al* [13].

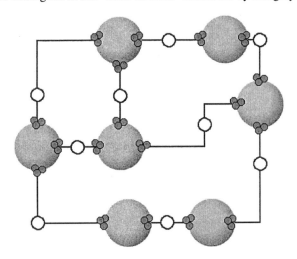

Figure 2. The New Age Enterprise Framework [3]

Drawing from the Langley *et al* [13] model, and from Curran and Keller's [3] framework, we are able to distil a conceptual model for distributed decision making. We do this simply by focussing on the interactions of decision makers as the "issue stream" moves, because these interactions are what any distributed system needs to address to succeed.

Decision makers in an organization are capable of several interactions as the stream moves. They may interact with their own system, a system of a fellow decision maker within the same organization, a system of a decision maker in another organization, or an external system provided by a "service provider". These interactions are summarised in Figure 3, which shows our proposed Distributed Decision Making Model.

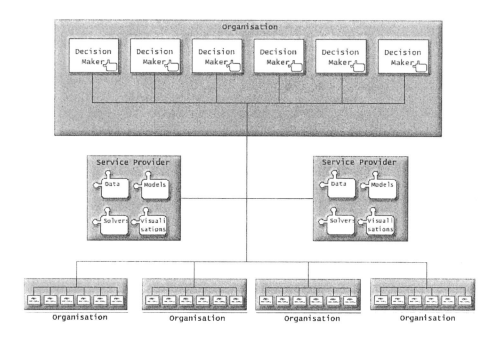

Figure 3. The Distributed Decision Making Model

The model contains a set of decision making entities, including decision makers, organizations, service providers, and decision making components. By addressing the interactions of the decision making entities, we can form a picture of the processes that occur when a distributed decision is being made. Each of the entities is bound by a network, which enables the bi-directional flow of information between them.

3 Modeling the Distributed Decision Making Lifecycle

In this section we look at important issues associated with a generic modelling lifecycle and adapt it to the needs of a distributed decision making environment. In the following sections we develop a design framework to guide the implementation of the lifecycle ideas.

The modelling life cycle involves a number of phases that provide cradle-to-grave modelling (scenario-building) support [6, 10, 11].

- Formulation of the model - support the modeller to create the model
- Integration of the model with data/instantiation of the model - support the modeller in the instantiation of the model
- Integration of the model with appropriate solvers - allow the modeller to link to a variety of solver technologies
- Use/execution of the model - allow the modeller to solve the model/problem using a particular instance of the model
- Analyzing, reporting, and explaining the results of the model
- Perform what-if analysis on the model by changing the solvers and/or data and/or model versions
- Reformulation of the model if necessary - reformulation of the model by changing either its structure or behaviour or both
- Storage of the model - storage of the instance of the model as well as the structure and behaviour of the model
- Retrieval of the model - retrieval of model instance information as well as information relating to the structure and behaviour of the model
- Termination or removal of the model - removal of the model instance as well as removal of a particular behaviour of the model or part of the model structure or the whole model itself

When adapted to address the concerns of distributed decision making [13] we can extract a Distributed Decision Making Lifecycle, which specifies phases of importance to our design. This lifecycle consists of the following phases, which outline the main needs of distributed decision makers based on the ideas thus far discussed. The phases of the lifecycle are iterative; while they are generally linear, non-linear movement between them should also be supported:

1) Generate & manipulate (proxy) components - support the decision maker to create and use distributed and heterogeneous decision making components
2) Access heterogeneous and distributed decision making components – allow the decision maker to have access to components on different platforms and at different locations
3) Analyze heterogeneous and distributed decision making components – allow the decision maker to analyze the distributed and heterogeneous components to determine their nature and functionality
4) Select desired functionality – allow the decision maker to choose which functions of the components they desire to use based on their analysis

5)   Map heterogeneous and distributed decision making components – support the decision maker in connecting distributed and heterogeneous data, model, solver and visualization components together to form a scenario

6)   Map parameters of heterogeneous and distributed decision making components – support the decision maker to specify which parameter of the components should exchange data when a scenario is run

7)   Run a distributed solver to execute distributed scenario – allow the decision maker to run a scenario by 'pulling' data from and 'pushing' data to distributed components

8)   Analyze results – allow the decision maker to analyze the results that are generated through the execution of the solver

9)   Store the distributed scenario – support the decision maker to store the distributed scenario including its structure, details of distributed components, etc.

10)   Retrieve a distributed scenario – support the decision maker to retrieve stored scenarios for further use

4 Distributed Decision Support System Generator Framework

The Distributed Decision Support System Generator *framework* that we propose pays particular attention to the needs of the distributed decision making/modeling lifecycle process proposed earlier. We explicitly link the components of the framework to the phases of the lifecycle process.

Many of the building blocks that we use in the modelling lifecycle described above have been well established in traditional DSS literature [16]. It is important that these be recognized as the key components that enable instance generation. The volume, complexity, and distribution of data are defining characteristics of the data component of our framework. Further, models allow us to specify rules by which data can be manipulated. Such manipulation may be simple (e.g. re-arranging the data with a customer focus) or quite complex (e.g. generating growth forecasts for a family of products). Solvers are implementation specific components that can integrate data and model components to produce a manipulated result. Visualizations allow a user to depict problem instances in a form that is most appropriate for the task at hand. A problem instance is defined as a scenario which is a particular combination of the above components that best describes a task at hand. The concept of scenarios allow problem instances to be formally created and managed as persistent objects in an application, much like any other component that needs to be available to a user.

The core of the framework is the Distributed Decision Support System Generator (DDSSG) Kernel, which is the engine that makes the system run. Any combination of components (model, data, solver, and visualization) can be plugged into the kernel to create a scenario, or specific DSS. In line with the Distributed Decision Making Model proposed earlier, components may "belong" to users within an organization, users within another organization, or service providers, who are either component development specialists, or other developers exposing useful parts of the functionality of a larger system.

This framework is valuable because it is a representation of the key tangible elements needed to support the phases of the proposed Distributed Decision Making Lifecycle. Issues such as access to distributed and heterogeneous components, integration of distributed and heterogeneous components, and scenarios are collected and organized. With the broad perspective it offers, we can begin to refine our concepts, and define a more detailed system framework.

Keeping in mind the distributed decision making and support requirements, and examining the advantages and limitations of the various architectures we synthesized a more detailed system framework (Figure 4) for distributed decision support.

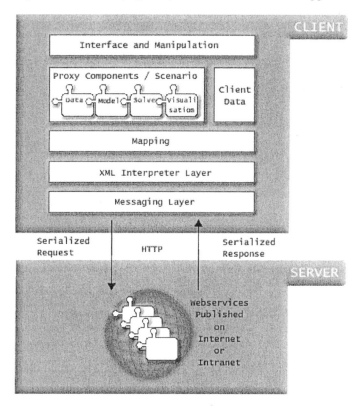

Figure 4. The DDSSG Framework

The DDSSG framework is based on a client server model. More specifically, the DDSSG client is actually an 'intelligent client' (a thin client with sophisticated user interface and data access capabilities) and the Web Services it consumes are the servers.

This framework allows us to portray in even more detail the tangible ingredients required to support the phases of the Distributed Decision Making Lifecycle, and its interactions. These ingredients will now be addressed in some more detail.

4.1 The Client

The client is made up of six key elements: the User Interface and Manipulation Layer, the Proxy Components Layer the Client Data Layer, the Mapping Layer, an XML Interpreter Layer, and a Messaging Layer. The Interface Layer sits above all of the elements as it is used to manipulate them. The Proxy Components Layer is the layer that is the center of most interaction, so it sits directly under the User Interface Layer. The Client Data Layer assists in generating certain proxy components so it is adjacent to the Proxy Components Layer. The Mapping Layer sits between the Proxy Components Layer and the rest of the system as it is the integrating tool. The XML Interpreter Layer allows the proxy components to be generated and to talk to the servers, so it is in the middle of the client. Finally, the Messaging Layer is where messages are sent and from and passed back into the system.

4.2 The User Interface and Manipulation Layer

The User Interface and Manipulation Layer consist of a graphical user interface that uses a presentation language and an action language [16] in order to allow the user to visualize and manipulate parts of the system. This layer is the key tool to the decision maker when performing operations on distributed components. It supports most of the phases of the Distributed Decision Making Lifecycle by making them easy for an inexperienced programmer or decision maker to perform.

4.3 The Proxy Components Layer

According to the Merriam-Webster dictionary, a proxy is "a person (or object) authorized to act for another". The Proxy Components Layer is in a sense (from the user's point of view at least) the central focus point of the detailed DDSSG framework. The Proxy Components Layer contains localized 'proxy' components, objects that provide a client-side representation of the actual component at the server with which they are trying to communicate. Providing a proxy component allows the user to view and manipulate the component without having to refer to the server where the real component resides, and therefore reduces network traffic and associated time lags involved in basic component operations. The Proxy Components Layer is a critical enabler of the entire Distributed Decision Making Lifecycle. Almost all of the phases of the lifecycle involve proxy components, which allow the decision maker to easily manipulate distributed and heterogeneous Web Services. This makes their details, such as platform and implementation, transparent to the user.

4.4 The Client Data Layer

The Client Data Layer allows the decision maker to access databases. The purpose of this is to retrieve data to populate a component, or update the data in the database with data values that have been derived through executing a scenario. The Client Data Layer is essential in the running of distributed scenarios as it is often the starting point of the data flow of the scenario. It supports the 'execution of solvers' phase in the Distributed Decision Making Lifecycle by allowing the decision maker to send data to distributed decision making components.

4.5 The Mapping Layer

The Mapping Layer allows the user to link decision making components (data, model, solver, visualization) of the DDSSG together. For example, if a user wishes to plug a specific data component into a model component, a means to enable and record this operation is required. That is the role of the Mapping Layer. It could allow the user to connect a parameter representing a certain date in the data component, to the corresponding date parameter in the model component. Once this connection has been made, the Mapping Layer will store it so that it can be further manipulated. Therefore, the Mapping Layer support phases five, six and seven (mapping and execution) of the Distributed Decision Making Lifecycle.

4.6 The XML Interpreter Layer

Since the Client/Server model is a distributed model, a standardized means of communicating between the client and server is required. The communication must be able to cope not only with servers that are situated remotely, but also employ different platforms, operating systems, and communication software. Since XML is an accepted standard for interoperability between heterogeneous systems, a layer that reads and encodes messages to and from XML for sending and receiving is required to implement this communication. This layer acts as the communications hub of the framework, preparing messages for sending and receiving between the client and server. The processes of encoding and decoding messages in XML are called serialization and de-serialization respectively. The XML Interpreter Layer is a crucial element of the framework. It strongly enables almost all of the integration related phases of the Distributed Decision Making Lifecycle, including access and analysis, mapping of components and parameters, and running the distributed solver. Enablement in these areas is through the use of various forms of XML (like SOAP and WSDL), which enable previously difficult-to-attain levels of integration between heterogeneous and distributed components to be realized.

4.7 The Messaging Layer

Once a message has been prepared for sending by the XML Interpreter Layer, a layer is needed to handle the asynchronous sending and receiving of the message and its reply. This is the role of the Messaging Layer. The Messaging Layer will send a serialized message via a certain protocol, and then listen for the response. When the response arrives, the Messaging Layer will return it to the XML Interpreter Layer for further processing. Therefore, the Messaging Layer is essential in supporting the phases of the Distributed Decision Making Lifecycle, as distributed communication is a requirement for their success.

4.8 The Server

The server is where the components that are 'plugged' into the client physically reside. A single client may use components from multiple servers. Hence, the server part of the framework diagram does not refer to a single server, but rather to the fact that components are served to the client from multiple distributed sources. Thus the DDSSG Framework adopts a multiple service provider model. A server could be any web server that publishes Web Services for the client to use. In addition, the server could just as easily reside on the same machine as the client itself as on the other side of the world.

5 Design Guidelines and Implementation

Now that we have provided an overview of the DDSSG framework, this section will explore its implementation with reference to the phases of the proposed Distributed Decision Making Lifecycle and the design guidelines inherent therein. We will examine each of the phases in turn, using examples from a typical process of building a distributed scenario with the DDSSG to illustrate how the phases are addressed.

5.1 Phase One: Generating and Manipulating (Proxy) Components

---
Design Guideline 1
The system should support the decision maker to create and use distributed and heterogeneous decision making components.

The workflow interface of the DDSSG enables users to easily add and manipulate proxy components to the Canvas as icons from a Toolbox. It masks the complexity of using distributed Web Services as components. Figure 5 depicts a *Canvas* where three components (a data component, a model component, and a solver component) have just been added. The design of the Canvas easily enables the user to construct a scenario by dropping icons from the toolbox onto the Canvas.

Once the components have been added to the Canvas, they represent the proxy components. They are (at this point) blank representations of real-world components that will be 'filled in', or instantiated, later. They may be positioned about the Canvas as required, and operated on using the Editor Panel. The creation of proxy components is a powerful tool for distributed interoperability because it allows the decision maker to ignore the complexity, location and implementation of the real Web Service that the proxy object represents. It also allows the decision maker to operate on the parameters of the Web Service without having to communicate directly with the Web Service.

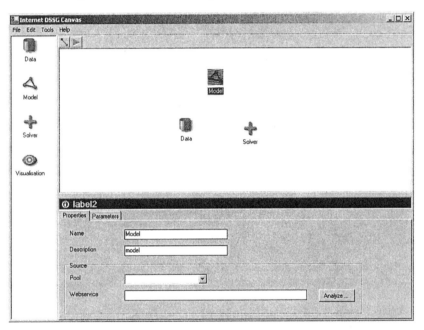

Figure 5. Adding Components to the Canvas

5.2 Phase Two: Accessing Heterogeneous and Distributed Components

> ***Design Guideline 2***
> The system should allow the decision maker to have access to components on different platforms and at different locations.

Accessing a distributed Web Service is achieved by querying its WSDL interface through the use of HTTP, which is supported in the .NET Framework by the *XMLTextReader* base class. The user provides a URL for the WSDL file and the DDSSG uses that URL to initialise an *XMLTextReader* object. Once the Web Service has been accessed, the WSDL that describes the Web Service is loaded into an XML Document object, which is another .NET base class that allows the developer to manipulate the DOM (Document Object Model) of an XML document.

5.3   Phase Three: Analyzing Heterogeneous and Distributed Components

> *Design Guideline 3*
> The system should allow the decision maker to analyze distributed and heterogeneous components to determine their nature and functionality.

The XML Document object created by the DDSSG is then analyzed to determine what implementation of SOAP the Web Service uses. For example, a Web Service may be implemented in SOAPLite, ApacheSOAP, MS.NET SOAP, Delphi, and so forth. There are several patterns of elements within each WSDL file that reveal this information. Once the implementation type has been discovered, the DDSSG reads the WSDL to extract the information about the methods of the Web Service, and what their parameters are.

5.4   Phase Four: Selecting Desired Functionality

> *Design Guideline 4*
> The system should allow the decision makers to choose which functions of components they desire to use based on their analysis.

Once the WSDL file has been processed, the DDSSG generates a form that shows the decision maker what methods are implemented by the Web Service and what the parameters of those methods are. The user may then select one of those methods as an input, and one of them as the output for that input. Generally, for each Web Service, an input procedure and its equivalent output procedure will need to be selected. Selecting the desired procedures of the Web Service populates the proxy component with the parameters of those procedures. Up to this point in the sample session, we have three blank components: a data component, a model component, and a solver component. However, our data component contains no actual data, our model component contains no model parameters, and our solver component does not have any active functionality available to it as of yet. To move forward we will begin by populating the data component, then the model, and then the solver component.

Populating the Data Component To populate the data component, we need to link it to a database. The connection string to the database can be constructed manually or through the process of stepping through a well defined procedure. Figure 6 shows the interaction that prompts the user to select an OLEDB Provider.

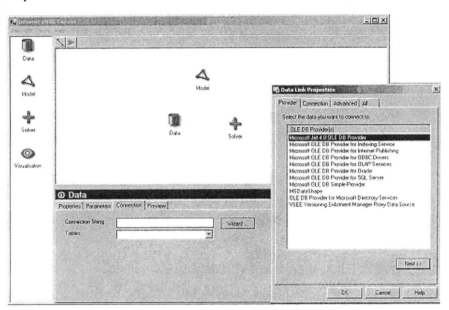

Figure 6. Using the Data Connection Wizard

Once the provider is chosen, the user selects the database file. The *Tables listbox* gets populated with a list of all of the tables in the chosen database. The user sets up the data component by selecting a table from this list. In this sample session, we will select the *StockSymbols* table, as we are going to try and build a stock value scenario. Figure 7 shows the user selecting the *StockSymbols* table from the *Tables listbox*.

Once the table has been selected, the DDSSG sets up the proxy component for the database. At this point, the data component is fully populated. The next step is to populate the model component.

Populating the Model Component Populating the model component requires that the decision maker query a Web Service to view its description and decide which parts of its functionality they wish to use in their model. The DDSSG lets a user query a Web Service description by typing the URL of the Web Service's WSDL description file into the Web Service textbox, and using an "Analyze" functionality. This action returns the Web Service window, as shown in Figure 8.

At this point, the DDSSG sends a request to the URL entered by the user. The request returns a description of the Web Service in a WSDL file format. The DDSSG uses the XML Interpreter to parse the file, determine which implementation of SOAP the Web

Service uses (e.g., Microsoft.NET, VelocigenX, etc.), and present the usable procedures of the Web Service in a *treeview* for the user to select from.

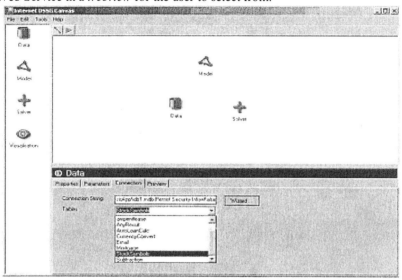

Figure 7. Selecting the Table from the Database

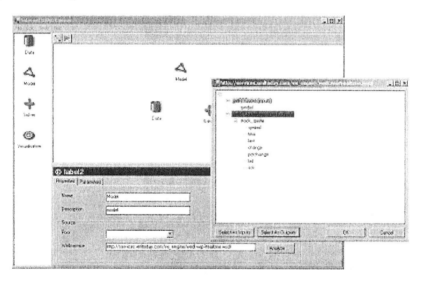

Figure 8. Analyzing a Web Service

Figure 9 shows the model now populated with the parameters generated once the inputs and outputs for the component have been selected. Inputs are shown in green and outputs in red. Once the user has selected the inputs and outputs, the DDSSG uses the proxy component factory to transform the description of the Web Service into a proxy component that the user can manipulate on the client.

In the *Parameters* tab in the Editor Panel, the input parameters are shown in black type, and the output parameters are shown in red type. In Figure 9, we can now see that the model component has the parameters: *Symbol* (input), *getRTQuoteResponse* (output), *stock_quote* (output), *symbol* (output), *time* (output), *last* (output), *change* (output), *postchange* (output), *bid* (output), and *ask* (output).

The names of the services (*getRTQuote* and *getRTQuoteResponse*) are ignored. Thus the user can see at this point that they are required to provide input in the form of a stock symbol, for which they will receive the outputs listed above, including *time*, *last value*, *change*, etc.

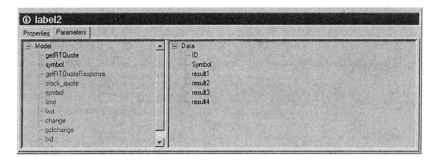

Figure 9. The Component Parameters

Populating the Solver Component To populate the solver, the user follows steps similar to populating the model, because the model and the solver are in fact derived from the same Web Service (in this case). The stock quote Web Service, therefore, acts a distributed model, because it is self-describing in that it lists the input and output parameters required to operate it. These inputs and outputs are translated into parameter objects by the DDSSG. The parameters then form the description of the model component.

The stock quote Web Service also acts as a distributed solver, in that when the inputs are sent to it, it will return the outputs. Thus, models and solvers are very similar in the DDSSG, differing mainly in that a model is simply the passive collection of the parameters of a Web Service, whereas a solver is active, utilizing the parameters to send and receive data to and from the Web Service in question.

5.5   Phase Five: Mapping Heterogeneous and Distributed Components Together

Design Guideline 5   The system should support the decision maker in connecting distributed and heterogeneous data, model, solver and visualization components together to form a scenario.

To map populated components together for the purposes of integration, the user selects them on the Canvas, and invokes the mapping function from the toolbar. A blue line representing the mapping between these two components will then appear on the Canvas, linking the two icons together graphically. Figure 10 depicts the three components after they have been mapped together.

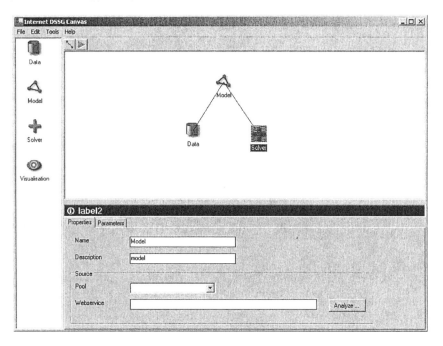

Figure 10. Mapping the Components Together

Mapping components together is an important first step towards integration. The real test of the integration capabilities of the DDSSG, however, is the ability to map the parameters of the components together, thereby fusing them into an integrated process chain.

5.6   Phase Six: Mapping Parameters of Heterogeneous and Distributed Components

> **Design Guideline 6**
> The system should support the decision maker to specify which parameter of the components should exchange data when a scenario is run.

Once all of the components in the sample session scenario have been populated and mapped together, it is necessary to create mappings between the parameters of each component. Mappings are made between parameters that represent the same data item. To instantiate the solver's *symbol* parameter with data from the data's *symbol* parameter, it is necessary to map the two equivalent parameters together. Since there is a model component that needs to fit between the data and solver components, we need to take the following steps to achieve this.

In the *Parameters* tab of model component, we can see the mapping between the data and solver components (on the right) and the model component (on the left). By dragging and dropping the model's *symbol* parameter (as in Figure 11) onto the *symbol* parameter in the data component, a mapping between the two parameters is created. This is represented in the user interface by a blue line between the two parameters.

A similar sequence is used to map the model's *symbol* parameter with the solver's *symbol* parameter. At this point the user has a mapping among the *symbol* parameters of the data, model, and solver components. This means that the solver's *symbol* parameter will be able to access the data's *symbol* parameter via the model. It will be thus able to retrieve the data it needs to give the solver's parameter a value to send to the Web Service for processing when the solver is run.

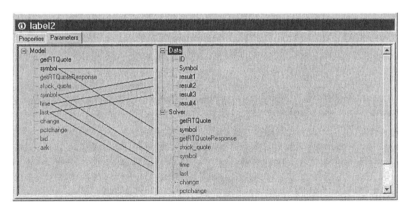

Figure 11. Mapping the Parameters

Once the user has created a mapping between two parameters in the user interface by dragging and dropping one parameter onto another, the DDSSG creates a new *Mapping* object for each of the parameters involved, populates it with the parameters being mapped. The *Mapping* object is then added to the *Mappings* collection that already exists for those parameters. This process allows the user to make flexible mappings between any parameters of distributed and heterogeneous decision making components, thereby integrating them.

5.7 Phase Seven: Running a Distributed Solver to Execute a Distributed Scenario

> *Design Guideline 7*
> The system should allow the decision maker to run the scenario by 'pulling' data from distributed components, and 'pushing' data to distributed components.

When all of the necessary components have been mapped together, populated, and their parameters mapped together, the user is able to execute the scenario. When a solver is selected and executed, the DDSSG instantiates each of the parameters that are mapped to other parameters, retrieves their values, and sends those values via a SOAP message to the Web Service. Figure 12 displays this process. A progress bar shows how much of the solver has executed. A record of the messages being sent between the DDSSG and the Web Service server is written to a SOAP Log window.

The DDSSG executes the solver by creating a SOAP request that contains an envelope, a header, and a body containing all of the parameters of the Web Service and their current value (pulled from the data component). This message is then sent to the Web Service, which interprets it, executes its own methods accordingly, and then sends a SOAP response back to the DDSSG.

5.8 Phase Eight: Analyzing the Results

> *Design Guideline 8*
> The system should allow the decision maker to analyze the results that are generated through the execution of the solver.

The process of updating the data received from a Web Service to the component's DataSet and client database allows the user to see a preview of the updated data in the *Preview* tab of the Editor Panel on the main window. This allows the user to analyze the results of the solver they have executed, albeit to a very primitive degree. True support for flexible analysis of data should be achieved through plugging in distributed visualization components.

Once the solver is executed, all of the mapped output parameters in the solver proxy component are updated with the data returned by the Web Service. This data is then "pushed" back to the data component via the model. Once there, the DataSet in the data component is synchronized with the database. The database is updated with the values of the memory resident DataSet, thereby "saving" the data returned by running the scenario.

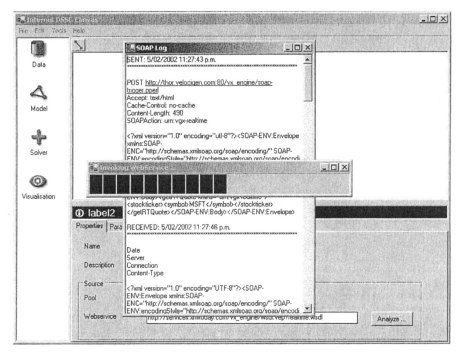

Figure 12. Executing a Scenario

5.9 Phase Nine: Storing the Distributed Scenario

> *Design Guideline 9*
> The system should support the decision maker to store the distributed scenario including its structure, details of distributed components, and so forth.

Once a scenario (such as the stock value scenario) has been created, it is possible to save it to an XML file. This allows the user to save scenarios that they have created, and then load them again whenever they are needed. The XML file stores the information required to regenerate distributed components within a scenario.

5.10   Phase Ten: Retrieving the Distributed Scenario

> ***Design Guideline 10***
> The system should support the decision maker to retrieve stored scenarios for further use.

Once a scenario has been saved, it can be loaded again, as shown in Figure 13. The ability to retrieve stored scenarios allows decision makers to share scenarios and incrementally develop them as they require new functionality or changes to existing functionality.

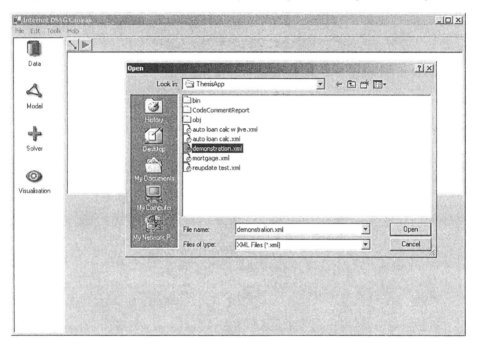

Figure 13. Loading a Saved Scenario

5.11   Support for Pipelining Between Models

Pipelining is the ad hoc integration that occurs when results from one model are fed to another model [4, 7]. The implementation of the DDSSG architecture allows the decision maker to pipeline between decision making components. Pipelining allows the decision maker to use a component as a temporary data store, improving performance in some cases over using a database connection. Figure 14 is an example of a scenario that employs pipelining between two models. The first model returns the number of days left in a year, and the second model returns the monthly payments required to pay off a loan of a certain amount, within a certain period of time, and with a specified rate of interest. In this case, once the solver has been run to determine the amount of days left in the year, instead of returning that data to the database, the data is stored temporarily in the model component's DataSet object. The second solver (the loan calculator) accesses the data by using the mapping between the 'loan calculator' model and the 'days left in the year' model.

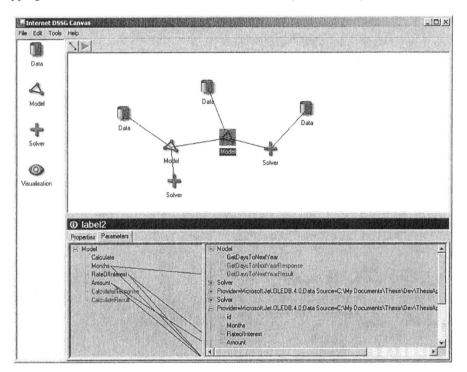

Figure 14. Pipelining Between Components

Since in the DDSSG any model becomes instantiated once it is run (i.e., filled with values), the data in the instantiated model can be used as a temporary data store for providing data to any other component. This feature is implemented in the DDSSG by the *GetData* (to be described later) method, which when running a solver, returns the first instantiated parameter value it finds. Normally, this would be a data parameter, but so long as its value has been instantiated, the data could just as easily come from a model parameter, as is the case in this pipelining scenario.

In the scenario just described, the 'days left in year' model acts as the input into the monthly payment calculator model. However, the value that is being input into the monthly payment calculator's *Months* parameter is actually a value that represents day. This type of problem is a very common one in business interoperability scenarios. Often, the data available to one company, for example, is in a format that is similar but not compatible with the data required for another company (in a supply chain, for example) to utilize appropriately. To solve this problem, the DDSSG lets the user easily plug in components that they have created themselves that can act as data transformers.

6 Conclusion

A distributed decision making lifecycle and the system to support it can be applied and integrated into a variety of inter-organizational and global scenarios. We present a few examples below of the use of web service technologies. All of these examples are situations where our approach to implementing distributed lifecycle support can be fruitfully employed.

- With over 80 Web Services in production or development, Sun Microsystems has designed services which are used by employees, suppliers, partners, and customers [1]. An example of this is ePayment, an application that was configured to provide credit card processing facility. It is made up of other web services that support financial transactions, including a currency converter and a zip code verifier and also shares a set of core Web Services for authentication, authorization, management, monitoring, measurement, and reliable messaging.

- The FreightMixer application [15] was designed to offer an end-to-end freight service to customers by combining services of other freight service providers. Using this application service, providers can interact directly with customers or with each other based on the supervision of and composition logic decided by FreightMixer. In FreightMixer various services are orchestrated together in an ad-hoc fashion to achieve customers' needs. The entire workflow of providing freight services spans several organizations and in fact is based solely on services provided by external organizations with FreightMixer acting as an intermediary between these organizations and the customer.

- Yellow Corporation [9] offers a wide range of shipping services for moving industrial, commercial, and retail goods. Three Web Service applications to track shipments, automatically create purchase orders, and get rate quotes were developed. In all three cases Web Services were front end wrappers to existing back-end legacy systems.

- General Motors is deploying web services to upgrade existing software and integrate applications across its many systems (Business Week Online, June 24, 2003). The technology is being used to act as a bridge between a diverse set of systems within the organization. Another useful application that GM sees for the technology is to connect its parts and inventory data in flexible ways with its suppliers.

Traditional DSS architectures and frameworks face significant hurdles in meeting the challenges of the modern business environment. Increasingly, integration with decision making tools that cross geographical, organizational and system boundaries is required. Existing architectures that attempt to overcome these hurdles have several limitations, but by synthesising their key benefits with emerging technological opportunities progress can be made. Distributed Decision Support requires an environment that supports manipulating, analyzing, integrating, executing, and storing distributed decision making components. The DDSSG represented by our work attempts to provide such an environment. The implementation was conducted with Microsoft's C#, in the .NET framework. It uses Web Services, technologies like SOAP and WSDL, and OO constructs such as encapsulation and late binding to overcome the limitations of existing architectures for distributed decision support.

The DDSSG addresses distributed decision making process issues by supporting all phases of the Distributed Decision Making Lifecycle including manipulating, analyzing, integrating, executing, and storing distributed decision making components. Issues such as heterogeneity and distribution that characterize typical distributed environments have been pointedly addressed by the implementation. Distributed decision making in modern organizations presents a unique set of requirements. The approach that we have taken in our work attempts to address these issues. We identify the main ones below.

- Extended independence – including location and platform independence.
- Extended flexibility – the ability to integrate components through flexible independent mappings.
- Interoperability through minimizing the requirements for shared understanding – supported by the use of both the workflow interface and OO constructs like late binding and encapsulation.
- Ad-hoc integration – allowing components to be added at runtime without prior knowledge of the components.
- Reduced complexity through encapsulation – allowing increased interoperability with other systems, supported through the use of Web Services.
- Increased interoperability of legacy applications – allowing already built functionality to be integrated and reused.

References

1. Aldrich, S. E.: Sun Microsystems, Inc.: Sun transforms its business with the Sun One platform and Architecture and java Web Services, Boston, Patricia Seybold Group (2003)
2. Brown, K.: SOAP for Platform Neutral Interoperability, XMLMag.COM, http://www.xmlmag.com/upload/free/features/xml/2000/04fal00/kb0004/kb0004.asp (2000)
3. Curran, T., Keller, G.: Chapter 15: New Age Enterprise, SAP R/3 Business Blueprint: Understanding Business Process Reference Model, NJ, Prentice Hall (1998) 267-269
4. Dolk, D. R., Kotteman, J. E.: Model Integration and Modelling Languages. Information Systems Research 3(1) (1992) 1-16

5. Fremantle, P., Weerawarana, S., Khalaf, R.: Enterprise Service, Communications of the ACM, 45(10) (2002) 77-82
6. Geoffrion, A.: Integrated Modelling Systems. Computer Science in Economics and Management 2(1) (1989) 3-15
7. Geoffrion, A.: Reusing Structured Models via Model Integration, Proceedings of the Twenty-second Annual Hawaii International Conference on System Sciences, IEEE Computer Society Press (1989)
8. Gottschalk, K.: Web Services Architecture Overview: The next stage of evolution for e-business, IBM developerWorks, http://www-106.ibm.com/developerworks/library/w-ovr/ (2000)
9. Gralla, P.: Deployment Profile: Yellow Transportation delivers three Web services, The Web Services Advisor (2003)
10. Hurlimann, T.: Linear Modelling Tools, Working Paper No. 187, Institute for Automation and Operations Research, University of Fribourg, Switzerland (1991)
11. Hurlimann, T.: Modelling Tools, Working Paper No. 200, Institute for Automation and Operations Research, University of Fribourg, Switzerland (1992)
12. IBM.: Web Services Case Studies: Defense Information Systems Agency, IBM, http://www-306.ibm.com/software/ebusiness/jstart/casestudies/disa.shtml. Accessed 27 November 2005 (2003)
13. Langley, A, Mintzberg, H., Pitcher, P., E. Posada, E.: Opening up Decision Making: the View from the Black Stool. Organization Science 6(3): 260-279 (1995)
14. McKeen, J. D., Smith, H. A.: New Developments in Practice: Managing the Technology Portfolio, Communications of the AIS, 9(5), (2002) 1-25
15. Piccinelli, G., Williams, S. L.: Workflow: A Language for Composing Web Services, Lecture Notes in Computer Science, H. A. Reijers. Berlin, Springer-Verlag (2003)
16. Sprague, R. H.: A Framework for the Development of Decision Support Systems. MIS Quarterly 4(4) (1980) 1-25
17. Stal, M.: Web Services: Beyond Component-based Computing, Communications of the ACM, 45(10), (2002) 71-7.

Management of Knowledge Transfer in Distributed Software Organizations: The Outsourcers' Perspective

Anuradha Mathrani[1], David Parsons[1]

[1] Institute of Information and Mathematical Sciences,
Massey University, Auckland, New Zealand

{A.S.Mathrani, D.P.Parsons}@massey.ac.nz

Abstract. Software development is a complex iterative process, where knowledge builds as work progresses, requiring an ongoing awareness by all participants of the changing definitions and relationships in the development effort. This has resulted decentralized decision making, where knowledge workers distributed across development centers are involved in making or breaking decisions. Outsourcers who develop for overseas clients have realized the need for some measures of control to manage distributed project tasks, while at the same time motivating their knowledge workers. A study of how knowledge capital is managed in a decentralized and distributed environment during the offshore software development processes forms the basis of this study. The issues are illustrated using two case studies of offshore outsourcers in New Zealand, an 'up and coming' outsourcing nation. The study reveals that both firms emphasize monitoring and management of knowledge transfer processes, but also raises questions about the future for New Zealand outsourcers.

Keywords: Offshore outsourcing, software development processes, outsourcer, knowledge transfer, decision making

1 Introduction

Distributed and outsourced software development projects are becoming more common, resulting in a symbiotic relationship where one nation has the money for the products and services that the other can provide. As a consequence, frontiers between nations are fading as knowledge, values and practices move freely from one nation to another. This impacts the boundaries within the organizations (the so called "silos") which are dismantled to ensure a free flow of knowledge between both nations and enterprises [1]. One example of the increase in interconnection between different societies is cross border software outsourcing, facilitating a continuous software development cycle. Thus software development is now increasingly a multi-site, multicultural, and globally distributed undertaking [2].

The role of knowledge in software development is widely recognized [3, 4, 5]. Software development is conceptualized as a knowledge intensive activity of organizing and integrating the specialized expertise, skills, and perspectives of various project stakeholders into an appropriate, coherent, and practical solution [6, 7] within the "knowledge" or "network" society [8]. It is a complex and iterative process, where knowledge builds with the progression of software development work, further requiring an ongoing awareness by the distributed team members of all the changing definitions and relationships in the development effort. The complexity can be traced to two attributes of knowledge that bear on the development process i.e. its fragmentation and its 'stickiness' (i.e. how knowledge is held in the minds of individuals) [5]. The relevant knowledge is fragmented amongst various project stakeholders, which makes its embodiment or stickiness in the design of the software a challenge [9]. This results in the decentralization of decision making amongst the stakeholders distributed across development centers.

This is an opportune time to understand how these knowledge-based industries achieve division of knowledge-based tasks, with more team members now being involved in decision making and decision breaking. These global multinational organizations prefer consistency in decision making in their knowledge transfer processes across distributed offices because this simplifies management command and control [10]. However, the integration of knowledge continues to be a chronic problem for software development [3, 9].

2 Background

The late 1990s saw an increase in the outsourcing of software development, particularly, offshore. Recent offshore development of software has changed from being highly structured to less structured with changing requirements, requiring more client contact and process management skills [11]. The diversity of software development is expected to increase, with various predictions on the offshore software market presenting a healthy picture of growth, attracting new software providers.

In the light of this background, a study on how real practitioners solve real problems of knowledge transfer in real environments will have implications for both researchers and practitioners. The transfer of knowledge does not happen easily in situations where knowledge is inter-organizational, let alone inter-national [12]. How knowledge flow is controlled by offshore outsourcers, across the silos, involving large scale development therefore needs to be viewed objectively.

At the 2004 Gartner Outsourcing and IT Services Summit, New Zealand was ranked an 'up and coming' overseas business development destination [13]. Gartner also reported that some high-value niche IT disciplines exist where New Zealand could be a potential provider for off-shored jobs, but consultancy businesses will have to change their business models to succeed [14]. However, New Zealand is still not perceived to be a major destination for global outsourcing with some companies having had limited success [13]. Another study of 32 New Zealand organizations over a four-year period shows an ad hoc approach to system development practices, with a low emphasis on mature disciplined processes [15].

Little is known about the role of standard methods in IS development within New Zealand organizations. Given their age and restricted nature, prior surveys reveal only limited information [16, 17]. However, many of the New Zealand software organizations are ISO 9001 certified, with EDS being the first organization to have CMM Level 3 certification. EDS also presently dominates the outsourcing marketplace in New Zealand [18].

The purpose of this research study is to determine and describe the key influences involved in the control and implementation of decentralized decision making in offshore software development processes from the New Zealand outsourcer's perspective. What is the emphasis on enforcing standards, project management solutions, and change management during knowledge transfer? Also, what are the practices for management and control of these processes? We consider current practice and consider whether this practice is likely to enable New Zealand to move from an 'up and coming' outsourcer to a leading outsourcing provider.

3 Software Development Processes

The field of software engineering in the offshore domain is relatively new and procedures for quality control and project management, though developing very fast, have yet to evolve fully [19]. These procedures have evolved during the client and outsourcer's offshore learning curve based upon their past experiences. For offshore sourcing to assume its rightful place in the IT sourcing portfolio, stakeholders need to swiftly move through the learning curves with best practices institutionalized [20]. These practices refer to the various socio-cultural processes inherent in the process of knowledge transfer, including the manner in which clients and outsourcers draw upon and apply different forms of explicit-implicit, formal-informal knowledge [8].

The procedures involved in the outsourcing process are very complex, and are further complicated by the non-determinism of most methods as they continually change in the business environment, since the requirements are fluid. They cannot be simply handed to team members at distributed locations as a comprehensive document without a good interactive development environment. Each project deliverable is evaluated for new value addition by team members within different geographical boundaries. Knowledge builds with the progression of software development work as software modules go through an iterative process of design, creation, test, distribution, deployment, utilization, and revision [21]. Knowledge transfer can be delayed by problems such as over-engineering or 'featuritus' [22]. Featuritus may result from over knowledgeable and interfering customers [23] or over enthusiastic developers, and often requires senior management mediation.

There is a need for development team members in the globally interconnected environment to have proper knowledge integration mechanisms put in place across their boundaries. Some mechanisms proposed in previous research are: ongoing interaction with stakeholders, formal and planned communication, project reviews, refining of requirements with each iteration, prior domain experience, automated tools to facilitate the coordination of pre-defined work flows, synchronized test fixtures by dispersed teams, integration of new tools and technologies, activation of change management agents, and use of mature software processes (e.g. CMM, ISO 9001) [5, 8, 11, 21, 24, 25, 26, 27, 28]. Good knowledge management will allow for many reuse opportunities, saving on cost and time [2]. Some frameworks related to the managing of the software development process for offshore outsourcing have been developed in previous research studies [24, 29, 30].

However, once a common model is established, maintaining it is a challenging task requiring commitment from the organization and a proper teamwork culture. The development teams are under continuous pressure from project deadlines, as they slip in and out of different technical, social, and cultural experiences [26]. These pressures take on a different form and level of complexity when looked at within the context of the temporal and spatial conditions of separation that are inherent in offshore software development processes.

Domain skills relating to technologies, specifications, processes, methodologies, skills, objectives, and management systems are transferred across the distributed teams. They all have informational components consisting of two parts: the explicit knowledge that can be laid out formally and the tacit knowledge regarding customer, design and programming choices, and working practices that cannot [30]. Unfortunately, the knowledge held by software developers has more of a tacit nature, and transferring it across distributed teams is not problem-free.

4 Research Questions

This research will explore the knowledge transfer process to answer the following questions within the offshore software development domain:
1. Do team members adhere to the standards laid down for knowledge transfer in a distributed software development environment to achieve benefits?
2. How is the effect of distributed decision making within the offshore software development processes monitored and controlled?
3. What are the implications of current practice in New Zealand for the future of outsourcing providers?

5 Methodology

The aim of this research is to explore the real life processes of knowledge management in a distributed environment in the light of the existing theory. It is appropriate that this research employs qualitative research methods because the research will takes place within an organizational setting. Multiple interactive and humanistic methods were used with participants' stories being interpreted in the context of the existing literature to build theory as stories emerged and evolved [31]. Walsham [32] states that interpretive studies emphasize those theories which suggest that the world is socially constructed, and such studies try to gain some understanding of that reality. Klien and Myers [33] argue that interpretive studies enable the researcher to gain deeper insights into information systems development. Sahay et. al [8, p. 36] also suggest the use of an interpretive study for distributed software development which emphasizes the epistemology of practice due to the subjective nature of knowledge and the social, organizational and individual nature of processes adopted, requiring a "shared understanding of each other's products, processes and work practices" across geographical boundaries.

Both practitioners and academia would benefit from a study that determines how knowledge transfer is linked with technology and the project management framework of outsourcers in their offshore software development processes. Two case studies were undertaken to understand how practitioners work with such complex, dispersed, and inter-related offshore software development projects. Project managers and developers belonging to these organizations were interviewed to provide insight into the knowledge transfer processes that can be effectively monitored and controlled in conditions of globalization. Observations and semi-structured interviews were used because they allow participants to speak with their own voices and control their responses and yet have the space to introduce and reflect on issues that they perceive as relevant [34]. Interviews also permit the development of a personal narrative [35] which gives context to the particular work events. Interviews were therefore an appropriate method for this research which focuses on individual understandings.

6 Case Narratives

This section describes the two mini cases to reveal how these organizations have institutionalized certain procedures for distributed software development based on their past experiences. Care has been taken to keep the identities of these organizations disguised as much as possible, with use of pseudonyms to protect the privacy of informants and the organizations. These organizations will be hereby referred to as HiTech and TopNet. Qualitative research depends on the presentation of descriptive data, so that the reader is led to an understanding of the meaning of experience under study [36]. However, there should exist a balance between description and interpretation [37], as "endless description is not useful if the researcher has to present a powerful narrative" [36].

6.1 Organization 1

HiTech is a small New Zealand IT software provider, having 15 employees based in Auckland. HiTech already has an established name in the local market and has been in the offshore outsourcer market since 2003. It has had some mixed experiences and has used these to guide its current direction.

HiTech had its first offshore outsourcing project experience with a client based in Australia. The client was an intermediary service provider (hereby referred to as ClientSP), who had application development contracts with many clients. ClientSP had isolated a part of one of their project's business function which was then outsourced to HiTech. Project deliverables were passed daily from the outsourcer (HiTech) to the client team (ClientSP) through a virtual private network and the client was required to validate each deliverable. Thus knowledge was meant to be transferred between team members, with ClientSP being responsible for testing each deliverable, tracking new issues, and communicating them back to HiTech. However HiTech complained that ClientSP's testing team implemented their own decisions on fixes needed in the source code without informing the developer team at HiTech, which made the developers feel a loss of ownership for their code.

Moreover, the only means of communication between HiTech and ClientSP was through email. When the HiTech team project manager raised these issues of lack of adherence to the source control standards laid down for knowledge building and refinement by the testing team, the testers sometimes did not respond to these email messages. Borchers' [38, p. 544] experiment across US, Indian and Japanese teams also supports the view that daily build updates announced via email were not considered a "good thing by developers from any culture". HiTech proposed the use of an automated project and change management tool called StarTeam (by Borland) to resolve these code infringement issues. However, in spite of repeated requests by the development team, the use of the automated tool was not encouraged by the testing team. The variation in configuration management practices between the two teams brought a sense of anxiety to the whole development exercise. The project lasted for 3 months, leaving some bitter memories with the HiTech developers. A telling comment from the outsourcer was "I can discuss rugby with them for hours, but when it comes to company culture – NO WAY".

The second offshore development project was completed with another service provider client based in the United Kingdom (UK). This time both the client and HiTech used a customized solution of StarTeam, which gave good results. The client had also stationed a project manager in the outsourcer's country. Weekly meetings between the outsourcer's project manager and the client's project manager were held and problems were resolved amicably across the table. This job has now been completed, and HiTech is presently involved with a third development project with the same client.

6.2 Organization 2

TopNet is a large New Zealand IT services provider having about 230 employees, with its main software development centre in Wellington, and another centre in Auckland. They are one of the leading IT service providers in New Zealand and have ambitious plans for further offshore software development. They have completed many local and offshore projects, for example in the UK and Singapore, and are major industry participants in outsourcing discussion groups.

TopNet was previously an ISO 9001 certified company, but let the certification lapse due to the extensive documentation requirements. As the general manager said, "The more you document, the slower you become at changing, as it is extremely hard to change the documentation – and so you don't change." Such resistance to documentation by developers has also been highlighted in previous studies [2]. The use of internal audits using the Malcolm Baldridge model is their way of coordinating processes rather than through international audits. The Malcolm Baldridge criteria have been used by businesses since 1987 to measure the maturity of their organizational performance practices, capabilities, and effectiveness in making organizations successful. TopNet felt that it was twice as good as an average company, having scored more than double the points of an average company on the Baldridge scale, but it was nowhere near world class.

The TopNet project manager emphasized exercising control on decisions made by their young team of developers as they previously had difficulty enforcing standards for knowledge transfer across distributed teams. Many times, the developer team members situated at the client site had delayed projects because they changed decisions without informing the development team in New Zealand. This resulted in many last minute changes, often leading to missed deadlines. Now they have a project manager with strong technical and managerial skills responsible for the project, at each development site. The team members regularly interact with each other over an internally developed communication tool called Clux or through open source tools for blogging like discussion forums and wikis. The interactive nature of blogging moves it from a "broadcast publishing mode to something closer to a conversation or a community-building and coordinating tool" [39, p. 20]. These wikis/discussion forums were used extensively by the teams to resolve issues. The project manager was a major participant in these discussions and could informally monitor changes within the knowledge processes. The management of TopNet is very appreciative of the use of such tools and they have set up special interest groups (SIGs), which have their own electronic editorial boards. These SIGs report some interesting past project experiences and also provide some excellent documentation components of the wikis to provide new insight into how certain project issues were resolved. This also provides a strong motivational push to the knowledge workers, who had helped to resolve some of these issues.

TopNet further emphasized the use of automated tools such as ProjectPlus and Microsoft SharePoint as a common frame of reference for sharing documents, tracking changes, and overall good software configuration management. These tools brought in a level of awareness of any changing relationships in the development effort. TopNet did not, however, believe in too much standardization of policies and procedures for development, testing or change implementation.

7 Comparison of Field Survey

Examination of the literature focusing on the processes involved in offshore software development helped to formulate semi-structured questions for each case study, with a consistent basis to enable cross case comparison. Data were collected at each site through interviews, observations, documents, and field notes. The data gathered from the two cases were then analyzed in view of the knowledge transfer practices.

Empirical data from research interviews has been briefly compared in Table 1 to highlight the work practices associated with the management of software knowledge transfer in the two cases. It is interesting to observe some of their experiences and methods in dealing with knowledge transfer issues, as categories evolved from the field data. These categories emerged by disseminating findings and keeping close to the field data, and are supported by direct quotations from notes and interviews.

Some of the categories which emerged were communication patterns between team members, domain experience, change management procedures, and requirement volatility involved with the transfer of tacit knowledge. Other categories involved quality accreditations, documentation standards, use of collaboration tools, number of status meetings, and reporting standards for management of explicit knowledge between distributed development teams.

A brief view of the organization culture and structure is also listed in Table 1, to provide the reader a larger view of the field settings, as qualitative field study is also "focused on understanding given social settings" [36].

Table 1. Empirical Observation of Case Data Variables

HiTech	TopNet
1.Organization Culture & Structure	**1.Organization Culture & Structure**
1.1 Team - Team members are New Zealanders/ European mix.	**1.1 Team -** Team members are a mix of New Zealanders/ Europeans and Asians/ Indians.
1.2 Levels - Flat organization, where no one is designated team leader in the project group.	**1.2 Levels -** Fewer levels defined, but a small hierarchy exists within the project groups.
1.3 Developers - Preference for developers with good interpersonal skills. Technical certifications are not considered relevant.	**1.3 Developers -** Preference for developers with good project management skills. Technical certifications are not considered relevant. '
2.Knowledge Transfer Management	**2.Knowledge Transfer Management**
2.1 Communication between team members – Informal means of communication was mainly used, with email alone being used between the development teams for knowledge transfer in the first project. However, HiTech has now realized the need for a more interactive interface, and started	**2.1 Communication between team members** – Communication is done on a regular basis between teams for knowledge transfer, at a semi-formal level, involving project leaders. E-mail, instant messaging, wikis/discussion forums were created for separate project groups between the developers for

some regular face-to-face means of communication between project leaders. transferring knowledge. Videoconference facilities are mainly used by management and generally used for key meetings.

2.2 Prior Domain Experience - Developers develop new skills on the job as the need arises per project.

2.2 Prior Domain Experience - Developers are given training on new language/ platform skills before being put on the job.

2.3 Requirement Volatility - No formal procedure, but work is passed on regular basis and changes are generally absorbed.

2.3 Requirement Volatility - Encountered problems with expectation management both from client and over enthusiastic developers. Intervention of senior management is often required, if deadlines are not met.

2.4 Change Procedures - Changes are not documented. Earlier project had encountered problems with ambiguity in source control, resulting in developer overtime and stress.

2.4 Change Procedures - All changes are placed in a central data repository – no paper documentation used. No minutes taken, unless essential. This ensures awareness of all changing relationships in the development effort, for smooth knowledge transfer.

2.5 Rules - No formal rules are prescribed for project groups. Decisions are made with the consensus of the group.

2.5 Rules - Rules are decided by the project manager. He/ She is responsible for ensuring decisions are sent to concerned team members.

2.6 Test Environment - No standardization of the test cases. The team felt that each project was different, and needed to have its own new tests.

2.6 Test Environment - No standardization of the test cases. The team did not believe in having too much of standardization, as this reduced the developer's flexibility.

2.7 Attrition rate – In the last 2 years, the attrition rate has been zero. The family like atmosphere was very conducive to the working environment.

2.7 Attrition rate - In the last 1 year, the attrition rate has risen from 5 to 15 percent (as per a recent newspaper and TV report on TopNet).

3. Monitoring and Control

3. Monitoring and Control

3.1 Quality Certification - No external

3.1 Quality Certification - No external

certification, no standards for internal quality audits laid down, but HiTech was keen to understand simple measures to control quality of code by enforcing some standards.

quality certifications (earlier an ISO 9001 certified organization, but felt the immense documentation reduced their flexibility to change), internal audits, use of Malcolm Baldridge criteria to measure its maturity and quality processes.

3.2 Documentation - No documentation. In the words of the director "Our job is programming, not taking minutes".

3.2 Documentation - Very minimal documentation (earlier an ISO 9001 certified organization, but felt the documentation required reduced their flexibility).

3.3 Number of status meetings - None in the first offshore project. Now, weekly or fortnightly face-to-face meetings are held with other team representatives.

3.3 Number of status meetings - Depends upon the project team leader and is project dependent.

3.4 Tools used by teams - centralized Web-based tool called Borland StarTeam.

3.4 Tools used by teams - Internally developed Web-based tool called Clux.

3.5 Management Involvement - One project leader is recruited to handle all projects. He/ She reports to the Director.

3.5 Management Involvement - The project team manager is involved in finalizing decisions made by its team members. He/ She reports to the General Manager.

8   Discussion

This paper proposed an exploration of the real life processes linked with knowledge transfer and integration within a distributed software development environment. Three research questions were posed:

1. Do team members adhere to the standards laid down for knowledge transfer in a distributed software development environment to achieve benefits?
2. How is the effect of distributed decision making within the offshore software development processes monitored and controlled?
3. What are the implications of current practice in New Zealand for the future of outsourcing providers?

The first question, whether team members adhere to the standards laid down for knowledge transfer, was addressed in the two organizations. The respondents' narratives helped identify common categories of communication, experience of developers, requirement volatility, change management, testing procedures and definition of any pre-defined rules for project groups.

It is interesting to note that neither organization used standardization in software testing processes, or defined a set of standard rules for knowledge transfer by development teams. Also, the communication levels between the distributed team members were not very formal. However, HiTech felt the need to change its informal and irregular communication pattern to a more regular basis on completion of its first project. TopNet realized the benefit of trained developers being put on the project, rather than developers being trained alongside the project development work processes. Some of the ad-hoc processes involved with HiTech could also be attributed to the small size of the organization.

The second question to understand how decision making is monitored and controlled within the offshore software development process was first identified by emerging categories of formal accreditation or certifications, documentation of processes, status meeting, automated tools, and level of senior management involvement. Again it is interesting to note that neither of these organizations had external quality accreditations, or used much documentation or standardized templates for project management. Both organizations agreed on holding regular project status meetings, good source control practices, and the use of automated tools to enforce controls in the software development effort, as they had each encountered problems in the absence of these measures. Based on their past experiences, both organizations are now taking remedial steps to control decision making involved in knowledge transfer.

Another emerging factor in the cases was the low level of hierarchy defined within the project groups. Too many checks on the development process were not encouraged, as it hindered the knowledge sharing process of their young software developers, and reduced their autonomy. With each developer having a unique approach to knowledge sharing, both the organizations identified alignment of good automated communication tools for effective management of their processes, rather than strict and formal procedures, which reduced the developer's flexibility.

With regard to the third question, we identified that current practice in New Zealand implies on ongoing learning curve for outsourcing providers, who have had some problematic experiences where knowledge transfer was not adequately controlled or supported. Our research suggests that such providers cannot rely on ad-hoc methods or tacit assumptions about how offshore development will work. Whilst such learning curves based on individual experience are useful, they are also dangerous in terms of project risk. It may be preferable for New Zealand providers to look to more successful outsourcing nations in order to evaluate their practices and consider whether their approaches are yet robust enough to compete at the highest level.

9 Conclusion

The aim of this paper has been to understand how knowledge is transferred in a distributed and decentralized environment during offshore software development processes, by exploring the real life processes of two case studies. The case data revealed that the procedures associated with knowledge management practices differed slightly in each of the two cases. While there has been no general consensus on appropriateness of methods used for different processes, the discussions on case study results revealed that for offshore software development, a significant challenge perceived by these outsourcers was in building an effective knowledge transfer process across the silos, as knowledge workers made and broke decisions at distributed centers.

To summarize the findings, the selected outsourcers consider drivers like informal and semi-formal means of communication, minimal documentation involving use of automated tools to capture changes, new testing processes for each project, and internal quality checks rather than external agency quality accreditations, important to successful offshore knowledge transfer processes. Outsourcers have realized the need for some measures of control on management of distributed project tasks, but at the same time continue to motivate their knowledge workers. The two outsourcers in the study had a low attrition rate, and attributed their content and enthusiastic workforce to a flat hierarchical organizational structure and some of its informal ad-hoc processes. However, the attrition rate has increased three-fold in one year for one of the cases under study, so this inference is speculative and raises some doubts.

As to the question of whether current practice is likely to lead New Zealand into the higher league of international outsourcing, some interesting themes have emerged. The study shows some of the ad-hoc nature of knowledge transfer processes of the two New Zealand outsourcers. This finding is in agreement with a previous study on 32 New Zealand firms [15], and is also supported by Gartner's view that New Zealand software businesses will need to change their business models to compete as an overseas outsourcing destination [14]. A tremendous amount of detailed management is required to effectively manage knowledge transfer, as clients look at outsourcers to increase their business agility and software quality, as well as competing on cost in the maturing offshore software market [28]. Outsourcers need to move up the learning experience curve, institutionalizing mature processes of best practices, rather than using an ad-hoc approach. These outsourcers may be using such ad-hoc processes for project management and monitoring because they are well within their competency zone. However, staying in the competency zone implies a need for improvement in skills, maturing of processes, and learning of new skills, or complacency will creep in. Given the growing number of the emerging world class providers from other countries [13, 40, 41, 42], a complacent nature will not lead to finding the best business opportunities as software providers/outsourcers.

Lack of organizational strategy and infrastructure has been shown in our study to have a negative impact and organizations have had to change. It may be that New Zealand organizations need to also consider their global standing in terms of international certification, and the rigorous processes that go with it, if they are to compete successfully in the international outsourcing marketplace.

The findings reported in this study are the result of only two cases. The risk of forming conclusions from this small sample may lead to generalizations which may not hold true for all cases. Additional exploratory studies of this type are required with outsourcers in other 'up and coming' nations such as Australia and Egypt [13], as well as leading outsourcing nations, so that the software community understands how practitioners can successfully work with knowledge transfer in offshore software development projects. Further research is in progress to analyze some of the methods adopted in dealing with the knowledge processes involved in the offshore software development process.

References

1   Garelli S. Competitiveness of Nations: The Fundamentals. IMD World Competitiveness Yearbook (2005) 608-19.
2   Herbsleb J, Moitra D. Global software development. IEEE Transactions on Software Engineering (2001) 18(2): 16 - 20.
3   DeSouza K. Barriers to Effective Use of Knowledge Management Systems in Software Engineering. Communications of the ACM (2003) 46(1): 99-101.
4   Rus I, Lindvall M. Knowledge Management in Software Engineering. IEEE Software (2002) 26-38.
5   Tiwana A. Knowledge Partitioning in Outsourced Software Development: A Field Study. International Conference on Information Systems, Seattle, Washington (2003) 259-70.
6   Faraj S, Sproull L. Coordinating Expertise in Software Development teams. Management Science (2000) 46(12): 1554-68.
7   Constantine L, Lockwood L. Orchestrating Project Organization and Management. Communications of ACM (1993) 36(10): 31-43.
8   Sahay S, Nicholson B, Krishna S. Global IT Outsourcing - Software Development across Borders, First ed. Cambridge University Press (2003) (285 pp.).
9   Ramesh B. Process Knowledge Management with Traceability. IEEE Software (2002) 50-55.
10   Heales J, Cockcroft S, Raduescu C. The Influence of national Culture on the Level and Outcome of IS development Decisions. Journal of Global Information Technology Management (2004) 7(4): 3 - 28.
11   Jennex ME, Adelakun O. Success Factors for Offshore Information System Development. Journal of Information Technology Cases and Applications (2003) 5(3): 12-31.
12 Macharzina K, Oesterle MJ, Brodel D. Learning in multinationals. In: Dierkes M, Antal A, Child J, Nonaka I Handbook of Organizational Learning and Knowledge. London: Oxford University press (2000) 631-56.
13   Kumar S. New Zealand Trade and Enterprise - Strategic Capabilities Assessment. Software Development Conference 2004, Wellington, New Zealand (2004).
14   Greenwood D. BPO Boom a boon for Kiwis - Gartner PCworld. Auckland: PCworld, July, (2004).
15 Taylor H. Information Systems Development Practice in New Zealand. 13th Annual Conference of the National Advisory Committee on Computing Qualifications, Wellington, New Zealand (2000) 367-72.

16   Groves L, Nickson R, Reeves G, Utting M. A survey of software requirements specification practices in New Zealand software industry. Working Paper 08/99 Hamilton; University of Waikato (1999).
17   Urban JLP, Whiddett RJ. The relationship between systems development methodologies and organizational : a survey of New Zealand organizations. Information Systems Conference of New Zealand (1996).
18   Longwood J, Caminos M, Chon M. Survey/Overview: New Zealand IT Services Provider Market, Report M-19-5474. Gartner (2003).
19   Aman A, Nicholson N. The Process of Offshore Software Development: Preliminary Studies of UK Companies in Malaysia. In: Korpela M, Montealegre R, Poulymenakou A Information Systems Perspectives and Challenges in the Context of Globalization: Kuuwer (2003).
20   Rottman J, Lacity M. Twenty Practices for Offshore Sourcing. MIS Quarterly Executive (2004) 3(3): 117 - 30.
21   Ptak R. White Paper on Managing IT Infrastructure for Business Success. Ptak, Noel and Associates (2005).
22   Endres A, Rombach D. A Handbook of Software and Systems Engineering - Empirical Observations, Laws and Theories, 1 ed. Pearson Education Limited (2003) (327 pp.).
23   Kirsch L, Sambamurthy V, Ko D, Purvis R. Controlling Information Systems Development Projects: The View from the Client. Management Science (2002) 48(4): 484 - 98.
24   Gopal A, Mukhopadhyay T, Krishnan M. Virtual Extension: The Role of Software Processes and Communication in Offshore Software Development. Communications of the ACM (2002) 45(4): 193-200.
25   RajKumar TM, Mani RVS. Offshore Software Development: The View from Indian Suppliers. Information Systems Management (2001) 18(12): 62-72.
26   Sahay S, Nicholson B, Krishna S. Global IT Outsourcing - Software Development across Borders, First ed. Cambridge University Press (2003) (285 pp.).
27   Gustavo AC, Wilson J. The "soft" dimension of organizational knowledge transfer. Journal of Knowledge Management (2005) 9(2): 59-74.
28   Rottman JW, Lacity MC. Proven Practices for Effectively Offshoring IT Work. MIT Sloan Management Review (2006) 47(3): 56-63.
29   Smith MA, Mitra S, Narasimhan S. Offshore Outsourcing of Software Development and Maintenance: A Framework and Issues. Information and Management (1996) 31: 165-75.
30   Heeks R, Krishna S, Nicholson N, Sahay S. 'Synching' or 'Sinking': Trajectories and Strategies in Global Software Outsourcing Relationships. IEEE Software 2001;18(2): 54-62.
31   Marshall C, Rossman GB. Designing qualitative research Sage Publication (1999).
32   Walsham G. Interpreting Information Systems in Organizations John Wiley & Sons, 1993.
33   Klien HK, Myers MD. A Set of Principles for Conducting and Evaluating Interpretive Field Studies in Information Systems. MIS Quarterly (1999) 23(1): 67-94.
34   Mishler EG. Research Interviewing: Context and narrative University Press (1986).
35   Cochran LR. Narrative as a paradigm for career research. In: Young RA, Borgen WA Methodological approaches to the study of career. New York: Praeger (1990).
36   Janesick VJ. The Choreography of Qualitative Research Design: Minuets, Improvisations and Crystallization. In: Denzin NK, Lincoln YS Strategies of Qualitative Inquiry. California: Sage Publications (2003) 46-79.
37   Patton MQ. Qualitative Evaluation and Research Methods Sage Publications (1990).
38   Borchers G. The Software Engineering Impacts of Cultural Factors on Multi-cultural Software Development Teams. 25th International Conference on Software Engineering, Portland, Oregon (2003) 540 -45.

39   Herman J. Blogs for Business. Business Communications Review (2003) 33(4): 20-23.
40   Gifford A. US $15 billion pie vanishing fast New Zealand Herald. Auckland (2004).
41   Jalote P. CMM in Practice: processes for executing software projects at Infosys Addison Wesley Longman (1999).
42   Kobitzsch W, Rombach D, Feldman R. Outsourcing in India. IEEE Software (2001) 54-60.

II. MEETING CHALLENGES:
Empirical Studies

A Longitudinal Study of Information Exchange in Computer-Mediated and Face-to-Face Groups

Ross Hightower[1], Lutfus Sayeed[2], Merrill Warkentin[3]

[1] College of Business, University of Central Florida, Orlando, Florida, USA
[2] College of Business, San Francisco State University, San Francisco, California 94132, USA
[3] College of Business & Industry, Mississippi State University, Starkville, Mississippi, USA

ross.hightower@bus.ucf.edu[1], lsayeed@sfsu.edu[2], mwarkentin@acm.org[3]

Abstract. Recent research has suggested that groups do not exchange information effectively. This is particularly true of groups using computer-mediated communication systems (CMCS). However, generalizing the findings of these studies to real groups is difficult because they used *ad hoc* groups and/or the groups did not have experience with the CMCS and were working on novel tasks. In this study face-to-face groups and groups using two types of CMCS completed three information exchange tasks. Information exchange performance and relational links were collected for each task. The results suggest that CMCS groups are not able to exchange information as effectively as face-to-face groups, even as they become familiar with the task and CMCS. In addition, although relational links were slightly related to information exchange performance, they were not as important as communication mode in explaining differences in information exchange performance.

Keywords: Information exchange, information sharing, virtual groups, computer-mediated communication, TIP Theory

1 Introduction

One of the most important changes brought about by the Internet has been the widespread adoption of computer-mediated communication systems (CMCS). While the most obvious example is electronic mail (few remember how little the average worker relied on e-mail before this decade) there are a variety of technologies that are being adopted by users. For example, a recently introduced technology is instant messaging. Instant messaging adds to a traditional text-based chat system features that facilitate building user communities. Despite the advantages of such tools, a growing body of research has shown that groups often do not exchange information effectively [10, 19, 22] especially when using CMCS [6, 7, 11, 12, 24]. Groups often do not discuss all of the information available to them leading to sub-optimal decisions. As organizations become increasingly reliant on CMCS, understanding the effects of these technologies on information exchange becomes increasingly important. However, while previous studies have provided useful insights into the group information exchange process, the studies suffer from limitations that make it difficult to extrapolate the findings to real groups. The present paper addresses two of these limitations.

The first limitation is that previous studies, with one exception, used *ad hoc* groups tackling a novel task. Groups develop over time, passing through phases during which group dynamics may vary dramatically [14]. Another problem with previous studies is that the participants were relatively inexperienced with the CMCS medium used in the studies. Recent evidence suggests that groups are able to adapt to the technology and to overcome its limitations with experience [2, 3]. In this study, face-to-face groups and groups using two types of CMCS tackled a series of information exchange tasks. Their performance and relational development are tracked over time in an effort to shed some light on how information exchange changes as groups gain experience with each other and the technology.

1.1 Group Information Exchange

The impact of information exchange on the outcome of a group's deliberation depends in part on how information is distributed among the group members. Information items available to a group can be distributed in three ways: common, partially common, or unique. All members of the group know common information, partially common information is known only to a subset of group members and only one member knows unique information. The extent to which information exchange affects the group's performance depends on how much of the information is unique and how important the unique information is to the group's performance.

The information exchange literature reveals that group discussion concentrates on common information [25]. Effective information exchange requires not only pooling the unique information so that all group members are aware of it but processing the information so that it becomes part of the shared information pool.

1.2 Computer-Mediated Communication Systems

Computer-mediated communication systems (CMCS) include a variety of computer-based systems designed to support communication. CMCS can be characterized along the three continua of time, space, and level of group support [1, 9]. Teams can communicate synchronously or asynchronously; they may be located together or remotely; and the technology can provide task support either for the individual team member or for the group's activities. Asynchronous CMCS such as electronic mail and computer based bulletin boards have been a standard feature in many organizations for some time. Synchronous CMCS such as video or text conferencing have been less popular but are becoming increasingly so in recent years especially with the growing popularity of instant messaging.

Researchers have identified a number of characteristics that are likely to affect information exchange in groups. These characteristics include constrained communication channels [11, 12], anonymity [6, 12], parallelism [6], and group memory [6].

Table 1. Summary of CMCS Characteristics

	SCS	ACS	GSS
Constrained Communication Channels	Most constrained since discussion takes place in real time, participants must read and type quickly to keep pace with the discussion	Not as constrained as SCS since participants can take their time to read and compose comments	Least constrained because CMCS communication can be supplemented by face-to-face discussion
Anonymity	Can be completely anonymous	Can be completely anonymous	Anonymous contributions to CMCS but non-anonymous face-to-face discussion
Parallelism	All contributions can be made in parallel but there is little time to read comments that appear quickly	All contributions can be made in parallel and there is plenty of time to read and absorb comments	Contributions to CMCS can be made in parallel but face-to-face discussions follow typical face-to-face sequencing
Group Memory	Transcript created but participants have little time to review it and it can be very disorganized	Transcript created and although there may be little organization, participants have time to review it carefully	CMCS, usually in the form of an outliner, organizes comments but group members may find it difficult to extract specific information

Three types of CMCS have been used in information exchange studies, text-based synchronous conferencing systems (SCS), asynchronous conferencing systems (ACS), and group support systems (GSS). Table 1 summarizes the effects of the four characteristics described in the previous section for the three CMCS.

All but one of the previous studies used *ad hoc* groups and in all of the studies the groups were encountering the task and technology for the first time. Longitudinal studies of groups have shown that task performance and use of available technologies changes with time [14]. Thus, it's difficult to extrapolate the findings of past studies to real groups. The next section describes theories, which might help predict how group information exchange will evolve over time.

1.3 Effects of Time on Information Exchange

Groups evolve over time as the group members become familiar with one another and with their task. The changes that take place in a group are likely to affect how the group exchanges information as well. One theory of groups that incorporates time is Time-Interaction-Processing Theory [14].

According to McGrath's TIP theory, groups produce outcomes by continuously engaging in three functions: task production (problem solving and task performance), group well being (interaction, member roles, power and politics) and member support (member inclusion, participation, loyalty and commitment). The group accomplishes these functions through activities in four modes: I) inception of the project, II) solution of technical issues, III) resolution of conflict, and IV) execution of performance requirements for the project. A group may be required to engage in one or more modes in each of the three functions to accomplish their objectives.

CMCS represent part of the technology that a group must use to accomplish their task. Thus, according to TIP theory, the group will become more efficient with the technology as they become accustomed to it. The validity of this assertion has been the subject of much of the CMCS research for the past three decades. Two opposing perspectives emerged from this literature. The first has been called the media characteristics perspective and the second has been called the time-based interaction perspective [2].

Media Characteristics Theories: Media characteristic theories suggest the capacity and type of information that a medium can transmit is an invariant characteristic of the medium. Media richness theory and social presence theory are examples of media characteristic theories.

Media richness is defined as "the ability of information to change understanding within a time interval [5]." Rich media, such as face-to-face discussion, allow multiple information cues (the words spoken, tone of voice, body language, etc.) and feedback. Lean media, such as synchronous conferencing systems, restrict the amount and type of information that can be transmitted.

According to social presence theory, media vary in their ability to convey to participants the presence of others with whom they are communicating. The richness and social presence of a medium tend to coincide since they both rely on the amount and type of information that can be transmitted as well as the ability to provide prompt feedback. Media with low social presence may increased self-absorption, reduced awareness of others and reduced awareness of status differences [18].

If the media characteristics perspective is correct, groups would find it very difficult to exchange enough social information to accomplish the group well being and member support functions in lean media. Thus, they would never be able to reduce ambiguity enough to accomplish the task production function as efficiently as groups using richer media. Groups using rich media such as face-to-face discussion would always be able to exchange more task related information than groups using lean media. The results of previous information exchange studies that compared novice groups would also apply to experienced groups. Yet, empirical support for media characteristics theories has not been overwhelming

Time-Based Interaction Theories: Time-based interaction theories assume that communication outcomes are not necessarily fixed by the characteristics of the medium but evolve over time [2]. One such theory is social information processing (SIP) theory.

According to SIP group members develop personal impressions and interpersonal relations through the exchange of social information. A lean medium reduces the amount of social information that can be transmitted in a given time. However, SIP theory suggests that relationships develop through the accumulation of social information processing over a series of exchanges. Relationships may take longer to develop with lean media but will eventually reach the same level as groups using rich media.

According to the time-based interaction perspective groups using lean media will eventually be able to exchange enough social information to develop the group relationships necessary to accomplish the group well being and member support functions. As with the media characteristics theories, evidence for SIP theory has been mixed.

2 Hypotheses

Most of the studies that have compared face-to-face groups with SCS groups have reported that face-to-face groups exchanged more information and made higher quality decisions [11, 12]. The one study that compared face-to-face groups with ACS groups found no difference between the groups [24]. Therefore our first two hypotheses are:

> *H1a: There will be no difference in the quantity of information exchanged between face-to-face and asynchronous groups.*
>
> *H1b: Face-to-face and asynchronous groups will exchange more information than synchronous groups.*

For the cases used in this study, groups can only reach optimal decisions if they exchange sufficient information, therefore:

> *H2: Groups that exchange more information will make higher quality decisions.*

As groups develop over time they will develop stronger relational links. TIP theory suggests that initially groups devote significant time to member support and group well being functions. These functions help the group develop relational links, which facilitate information exchange [24] and allow group members to evaluate the task-related capabilities of other group members. Face-to-face groups will report stronger relational links after the initial meeting since the richer medium allows them to exchange social information more quickly [2]. However, over time, as the synchronous and asynchronous groups are able to exchange more social information, the difference between face-to-face and CMCS groups will decrease.

H3a: Face-to-face groups will initially report stronger relational links than CMCS groups.

H3b: The relational links of CMCS groups will increase relative to those for face-to-face groups over time.

Stronger relational links reduce the level of uncertainty that group members have about one another. This has two effects. First, it reduces the amount of intragroup coordination and information exchange required and allows the group to devote more time to the task production function. Second, groups are more likely to process unique information contributed by group members whom they know and trust.

H4: Groups with stronger relational links will exchange more information.

Relational links will increase over time and stronger relational links are associated with more effective information exchange. Also, groups will become more skilled in the requirements of the task over time.

H5: All groups will exchange information more effectively over time.

3   Method

The method used was similar to that used previously by many researchers [24]. The only difference is that the experiment was repeated three times for each group.

One hundred and sixty-two juniors and seniors in MIS at three large universities participated in the experiment as part of a course requirement. In all cases, the grade the participants received depended, in part, on their performance on the task. Fifty-seven percent of the participants were male. The students were randomly assigned to three person groups and groups were randomly assigned to treatments.

Asynchronous groups consisted of a member from each of the three universities. All of the face-to-face and synchronous sessions were conducted at one university. There were 20 ACS groups, 17 SCS groups and 14 face-to-face groups. One face-to-face and two ACS groups were eliminated from the study because a participant did not contribute to the discussion at least a day before the post test.

3.1   Tasks

The tasks were murder mysteries for which the groups had to choose the most likely suspect from among three alternatives. Each task consisted of a description of the murder and information items on three suspects. The participants were told that their group was meeting after individually conducting preliminary investigations. They were told to compare notes and come to a consensus as to whom they thought was the most likely suspect given the information they had gathered.

The complete information set included 24 items of information, eight for each suspect. The information items tended to incriminate or to exonerate the suspects. The information was distributed such that it would be difficult to choose the correct alternative unless the participants pooled all of the available information. Either 33% or 66% of the information was common and the remainder unique. No statistical differences were found between the groups that received the two distributions so this factor was left out of the analysis.

3.2 Procedures

The experimental procedures were similar to those developed by Stasser and Titus [20] and used extensively in subsequent information exchange research. Participants first read the task and made an individual decision. The information was then removed and groups met. The groups were instructed to work together to reach a consensus as to which alternative they thought was the most likely suspect. Asynchronous groups had five days in which to exchange comments while face-to-face and synchronous groups were allowed up to 45 minutes although none of them took this long. The groups participated in one meeting a week for three weeks.

After meeting, the groups were given a post-test that measured following items: the group choice, their own choice, all information they could recall about each suspect, and relational variables. The groups were not given feedback about the cases before the end of the third meeting and they were asked not to discuss the cases outside of their meeting times.

3.3 Measurements

Data were analyzed at the group level because individual responses within a group may be correlated. Dependent variables include Unique Information Pooled during discussion, Unique Information Processed, and Decision Quality. Independent variables include Communication Mode, Satisfaction with Outcome, Satisfaction with Group Process, and Group Cohesiveness.

Unique Information Pooled: Transcripts were obtained from the group meetings. For the CMCS groups, the systems created the transcripts. For face-to-face groups, tape recordings were made of the sessions. Prior to discussion, each group member said their name so judges who coded the conversations could tell the participants apart.

Two judges reviewed the transcripts and counted each correct unique and common information item that was mentioned by the group. Nine groups were chosen at random to determine inter-rater reliability. The raters agreed on 0.93 of the ratings (1 − [number of disagreements/information pooled]). [14]

Unique Information Processed: Participants completed a post-test questionnaire on which they recorded all the information about each suspect that they could remember. Group members would be more likely to remember information items if they had processed the information [14]. Two judges counted the number of correct information items reported by the participants. Information items were classified as unique to the participant if they could not have known the information prior to the group meeting. The participants must have learned this information during group discussion. Interrater reliability was 0.95.

Communication Mode: Communication mode was asynchronous, synchronous or face-to-face. Asynchronous groups used a web based conferencing system called MeetingWeb. MeetingWeb is a proprietary system, which allows separate conferences to be established for each group. Each participant was provided a userid and password. The interface of the system is similar to many web based applications that students encounter frequently and they were able to use it easily after a brief introduction.

The ACS groups had five days to meet for each case. We felt this was sufficient time to illustrate the unique characteristics of asynchronous systems. Participants had time to consider and compose responses and the ability to attend to the task at a convenient time. The groups also had time to exchange a number of comments so that they could consider the issues sufficiently.

Table 2. Distribution of Final Group Choices

	Suspect 1	**Suspect 2**	**Suspect 3**	**Deadlock**
Synchronous	5	17	17	12
Asynchronous	9	15	27	9
Face-to-Face	3	13	23	3

Synchronous groups used an Internet Relay Chat (IRC) based system. The system allows comments to be entered and edited in a small window at the bottom of the screen before being submitted to the group. Comments submitted to the group appear in a larger window at the top of the screen. Older comments scroll off the top of the screen but can be reviewed using the page up and page down keys. The participants were given an introduction to the system prior to the first session. The system can be operated with a few simple keystroke commands and the students found the system familiar and easy to use.

Face-to-face group discussions were tape-recorded. To ensure that the tape recorder was able to capture the conversation, the groups were widely separated with two or three groups meeting in a large classroom. Face-to-face groups were allowed paper and pencil during the discussion.

Decision Quality: The quality of the groups' decisions was determined by the accuracy of their choice. In 24 of 153 sessions (15%) the groups were not able to reach a consensus. Twelve of these were synchronous groups, nine were asynchronous and three were face-to-face groups. The distribution of group choices is shown in Table 2.

Relational Variables: We measured three relational variables after each session: Group Cohesiveness, Satisfaction with Outcome and Satisfaction with Group Process. Warkentin, et al. [24] and Chidambaram [3] also used these variables.
1. Group Cohesiveness was measured using the Seashore's [17] Index of Group Cohesiveness updated by Chidambaram [3]. The instrument contains five questions

and scores can range from 5 to 25 with higher scores indicating high cohesiveness. Mennecke and Valacich [15] found group cohesiveness was positively related to information exchange. This measure had a Cronbach's α of 0.87.

2. Satisfaction with Outcome was measured using an instrument developed by Chidambaram [3]. It consists of four Likert-type questions that range from one to seven. The answers are coded such that high values indicate higher levels of satisfaction. This measure had a Cronbach's α of 0.93.

3. Satisfaction with Process was also measured using an instrument developed by Chidambaram [3]. The measure consists of five Likert-type questions that range from one to seven. The answers were coded such that higher values indicate higher satisfaction. Warkentin, et al. [24] found this measure was positively related to amount of information exchanged. The measure had a Cronbach's α of 0.94.

4 Results

Information exchange effectiveness was analyzed using repeated measures MANOVA followed by repeated measures ANOVAs for each dependent variable. Means were compared using Tukey's test. Table 3 shows the results of the MANOVA and the ANOVAs. All three show a significant communication mode effect. Figure 1 shows plots of the dependent variable cell means as a function of time for the three communication modes and Table 4 shows the actual cell means. Table 5 shows the Tukey's tests of the differences between the means. The results do not support H1a since face-to-face groups exchanged more information than asynchronous groups. H1b was partially supported. Face-to-face and asynchronous groups pooled more information than synchronous groups in sessions 2 and 3 but asynchronous groups did not pool more information than synchronous groups in session 1. Face-to-face groups processed more unique information than synchronous groups in all three sessions but asynchronous groups only processed more unique information than synchronous groups in session 3.

Table 3: Results of Communication Mode Analysis

Factor	Degrees of Freedom		Wilks' Lambda	F-Statistic	p-Value
	Num.	Den.			
Results of Repeated Measures MANOVA:					
Communication Mode	4	94	0.0976	51.71	0.0001
Time	4	45	0.4600	13.20	0.0001
Time*Com Mode	8	90	0.4009	6.51	0.0001
Results of Repeated Measures ANOVA with Unique Information Pooled:					
Communication Mode	2	48		24.06	0.0001
Time	2	47	0.7705	7.00	0.0022
Time*Com Mode	4	94	0.7551	3.54	0.0097
Results of Repeated Measures ANOVA with Unique Information Processed:					
Communication Mode	2	48		177.01	0.0001
Time	2	47	0.5767	17.25	0.0001
Time*Com Mode	4	94	0.4852	10.24	0.0001

H2 was analyzed using a MANOVA with Unique Information Pooled and Unique Information Processed as dependent variables and group choice as the only independent variable. The MANOVA was significant (Wilks' Lambda = 0.7407, F=7.99, p-value=0.0001, Num. Df=6, Den. Df=296). Individual ANOVA on the dependent variables were both significant (Unique Information Pooled: F = 3.25, p-value = 0.0236, Num. Df=3, Den. Df=152; Unique Information Processed: F = 16.05, p-value = 0.0001, Num. Df=3, Den. Df=152). Table 6 shows the results of Tukey's comparisons of means for the two ANOVA. The deadlocked groups were included on the assumption that groups that deadlocked did not exchange enough information to reveal the correct choice. The Tukey results show that groups that chose Suspect 3 (the correct choice in all cases) processed significantly more unique information than those that chose either of the other two suspects or that deadlocked. This supports H2.

Table 4: Means for Unique Information Pooled and Processed

Mode	Session 1	Session 2	Session 3
Synchronous	0.45	0.56	0.38
	(0.18)	(0.20)	(0.13)
Asynchronous	0.66	0.73	0.66
	(0.17)	(0.21)	(0.28)
Face-to-Face	0.77	0.95	0.99
	(0.44)	(0.50)	(0.79)

Values in parentheses are proportion of unique information processed during group discussion.

H3a was tested using a MANOVA with the three relational variables at session 1 as dependent variables and Communication Mode as the single independent variable. H3b was tested using a MANOVA on the session 3 relational variables and adding the three session 1 relational variables as covariates. The results are shown in Table 7 and Tukey's comparisons of means are shown in Table 9. At first glance, the MANOVA results seem to support both H3a and H3b; the Communication Mode variable is significant after session 1 but it is not after session 3. However, a closer examination of the cell means in Table 8 and Figure 2 reveals that the hypotheses were not supported. As expected, face-to-face groups had higher values on all three variables than the CMCS groups after session 1 however the difference between face-to-face and synchronous groups was not significant. All the relational variables converge over time with face-to-face and synchronous groups decreasing slightly over time and asynchronous increasing slightly. However, significant differences remain after session 3. Asynchronous groups are significantly lower than face-to-face and synchronous groups on Satisfaction with Outcome and Satisfaction with Process and significantly lower than face-to-face on Cohesiveness.

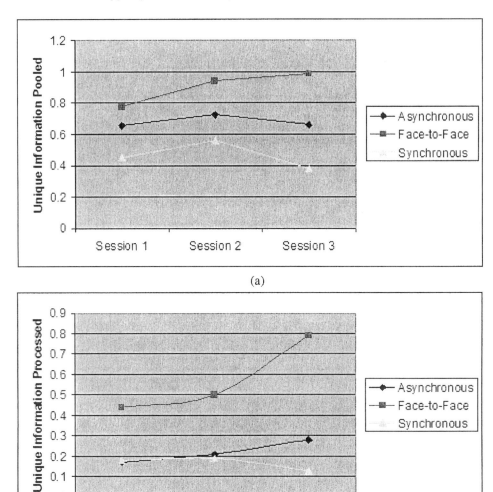

(a)

(b)

Figure 1. Information exchanged over time

Table 5. Tukey's Comparison of Means for Communication Mode

	Factors	**Difference in Means**	
		Unique Information Pooled	Unique Information Pooled
Session 1:	F-A	0.1180	0.2729 ***
	F-S	0.3230***	0.2613 ***
	A-S	02049	0.0115
Session 2:	F-A	0.2160 ***	0.3243 ***
	F-S	0.3785 ***	0.3373 ***
	A-S	0.1625 ***	0.0130
Session 3:	F-A	0.3257 ***	0.5138 ***
	F-S	0.6019 ***	0.6667 ***
	A-S	0.2762 ***	0.1529 ***

*** Significant at the 0.05 level
A – Asynchronous, F – Face-to-face, S – Synchronous, Degrees of freedom = 48

Table 6. Tukey's Comparison of Means for Decision Quality

Factors	**Difference in Means**			
	Unique Information Pooled		Unique Information Exchanged	
Choice 3 – Choice 2	0.1868	***	0.1578	
Choice 3 – Choice 1	0.2036	***	0.3485	
Choice 2 – Choice 1	0.0168		0.1907	
Choice 3 – Deadlocked	0.2678	***	0.4551	***
Choice 2 – Deadlocked	0.0810		0.2973	
Choice 1 – Deadlocked	0.0642		0.1066	

*** Significant at the 0.05 level
Degrees of freedom = 149

Table 7. Results of MANOVA to Test Difference in Relational Variables among Communication Modes for Session 1 and Session 3

Factor	Degrees of Freedom Num. Den.		Wilk's Lambda	F-Statistic	p-Value
Session 1	6	92	0.2372	16.14	0.0001
Session 3	6	92	0.5568	5.21	0.0001

Stepwise regression analyses using Unique Information Pooled and Unique Information Processed as dependent variables and using the three relational variables as independent variables were used to test H4. To account for the effect of communication mode, two dummy variables were used to represent the three communication modes. The results are shown in Table 10. Unique Information Pooled was related to Cohesiveness and Satisfaction with Process while Unique Information Processed was related to Satisfaction with Process. Although these results provide partial support for the hypothesis, the amount of variance explained is small. The relational variables accounted for only 2% of the variance in Unique Information Pooled and only 1% of Unique Information Processed. Communication mode accounts for 50 and 64%of the variance respectively.

Table 8. Cell Means for Relational Variables

	Session 1			Session 2			Session 3		
	O	P	C	O	P	C	O	P	C
Syn	26.47	32.34	19.72	25.00	31.60	20.17	23.78	30.78	18.83
Asyn	18.35	24.25	16.10	19.20	25.33	17.30	19.45	24.47	17.00
FtF	25.93	31.38	21.86	24.48	30.40	20.38	25.12	31.04	20.93

O- Satisfaction with Outcome; P- Satisfaction with Process; C- Group Cohesion

H5 was partially supported. Table 4 shows that Time was significant in the MANOVA and was also significant in both ANOVAs. This indicates that information exchange varied over time for both dependant variables. However, the significant Time*Communication Mode interaction for both ANOVAs suggests that the effect of time was not the same for all communication modes. The natures of these interactions are clear in Figure 1. The amount of information pooled increased from session 1 to session 2 for all groups although the increase was greater for face-to-face groups. However, the amount of information pooled in session 3 decreased for the CMCS groups but remained nearly unchanged for the face-to-face groups. Figure 1b shows that face-to-face and asynchronous groups improved in terms of the unique information they processed with each session. Synchronous groups actually processed less unique information each session.

Table 9. Tuley's Comparison of Means

		Cohesion	Satisfaction with Outcome	Satisfaction with Process
	F-A	5.78 ***	7.58 ***	7.13 ***
Session 1:	F-S	2.14	-0.54	-0.99
	A-S	-3.62 ***	-8.12 ***	-8.12 ***
	F-A	3.93 ***	5.67 ***	6.57 ***
Session 3:	F-S	2.10	1.34	0.26
	A-S	-1.83	-4.33 ***	-6.31 ***

***Significant at 0.05 level
A-Asynchronous, F-Face to face, S-Synchronous; Degrees of freedom 48

Table 10. Results of Stepwise Regression of Relational Variables on Unique Information Processed and Pooled

Factor	Parameter	Partial R^2	F-Statistic	p-Value
Unique Information Pooled:				
Cohesion	0.060	0.017	8.38	0.0044
Satisfaction with Process	0.027	0.010	3.05	0.0322
Unique Information Processed:				
Cohesion	0.007	0.011	4.67	0.0322

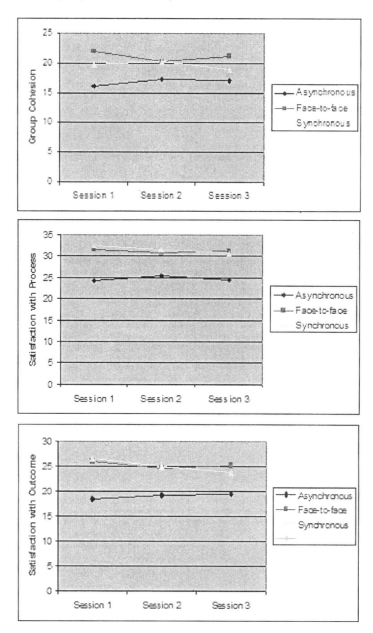

Figure 2 (a,b,c). Relational Variables over Time

5 Discussion

The central question in this experiment was whether previously identified differences in information exchange between face-to-face and computer supported groups persisted over time. Many previous studies have found that face-to-face groups usually do not exchange information effectively [10, 13, 19, 20, 21, 22, 25]. Despite the poor performance of face-to-face groups, many previous studies have found that face-to-face groups exchange more information than CMCS groups. However, all of these studies gathered data for only one session and most used *ad hoc* groups. In this experiment face-to-face groups were able to virtually eliminate information exchange deficiencies over time. However, computer supported groups did not close the gap with face-to-face groups as expected. While ACS groups improved slightly, SCS groups actually exchanged less information over time.

A secondary question was how group relationships develop over time in face-to-face and computer supported groups and whether these relationships affect information exchange. In this experiment, relationships did not change dramatically over time. Also, although they were statistically related to information exchange, the effect of these relationships on information exchange was minor compared to communication mode. One firm conclusion we can draw from this study is that factors such as task complexity and technological limitations have strong effects on information exchange independent of group relationships. The following sections discuss these findings in more detail.

As expected, face-to-face groups exchanged more information during session 1. However, contrary to expectations, face-to-face groups maintained this advantage through all three sessions. The difference between face-to-face and the CMCS groups actually increased for each session. In the last session face-to-face groups pooled nearly 100% of the unique information and processed nearly 80% of this information. Information exchanged by ACS groups increased each session but at a much slower rate than for face-to-face groups. The worst performance was turned in by the SCS groups whose information exchange performance actually decreased in the final session.

The reasons for these performance differences can be understood by examining the way the groups interacted. Almost all of the face-to-face groups learned by the second session to list all the information that each group member knew on a piece of paper. During the subsequent discussion, all group members had simultaneous access to all of the information they could recall. This simple but effective strategy helped face-to-face groups to consider all of the information and to cross-reference information from different suspects. The groups learned to pay attention to unique information. One indication that face-to-face groups considered the unique information more carefully than ACS groups is that they were far more likely to repeat unique information after it had been mentioned than either ACS or SCS groups. Face-to-face groups repeated unique information items an average of 3.2 times while the means for ACS and SCS groups were 2.5 and 1.4 respectively. Information that is repeated more often has less chance of being overlooked [16]. This helps to explain how face-to-face groups processed a high percentage of unique information pooled.

The pattern of relational variables for the three groups also showed some surprises. As expected face-to-face groups showed the strongest relationships after session 1 and these relationships remained relatively constant over the three sessions. However, unexpectedly the SCS groups had values that were statistically indistinguishable from the face-to-face groups and the ACS groups had values significantly lower than either the face-to-face or SCS groups.

The reason for the low ACS values was revealed by comments from ACS participants after the experiment was completed. Some of participants complained that their group mates were not as responsive as they wanted them to be. It wasn't that their group mates were not contributing. In only two groups did a participant not contribute to the discussion at least a day before the post test. As mentioned previously, these two groups were eliminated from the study. Some participants were ready to attack the case immediately and posted comments as soon as they received the materials. Other participants, such as group member 3 in the transcript reproduced above, took longer to contribute. This flexibility is considered to be an advantage of asynchronous systems, however, some participants found it frustrating.

6 Summary and Conclusions

What sort of generalizations can we draw from these results? It's possible that for information exchange tasks, group relationships are an insignificant factor compared to task competency and technological limitations. This would support the media characteristics view of CMCS: the effects of the media on information exchange are invariant characteristics of the media that cannot be altered with experience. This is consistent with the findings reported by Cramton [4] -- a study that followed 13 groups of graduate students over six months. The groups communicated via ACS and SCS and worked on a complex, realistic task. The groups experienced a variety of problems related to information exchange including coordination problems, difficulty in communicating the salience of information and unevenly distributed information. These problems persisted throughout the six months suggesting that experience did not change the effects of the media on information exchange.

On the other hand, it may be that in real world settings in which consequences of poor performance are greater, group relationships may have greater import. Another possibility is that the variables measured in this study were not the best variables to measure. Other variables that may be related to information exchange are trust/receptivity, formality, dominance, or similarity [23]. The transcripts of the face-to-face groups provide some evidence that changing relationships had some effect on the amount of information exchanged. During the first sessions, unique information was often greeted with comments such as "Are you sure, I didn't have that." By the third session group members were more likely to say, "I'll write what I remember and you just add your new stuff." The question is whether this represents a higher level of trust or just growing familiarity with the task.

Future DSS research should investigate additional impacts of information sharing in CMCS on group decision processes. Increasing globalization of business operations necessitates usage of CMCS features in distributed decision making environments such as virtual teams. Such undertaking will yield useful results for management of virtual teams.

Finally, the present research used student subjects in an experimental setting. Future research may use a qualitative approach with real life virtual teams such as globally dispersed software development teams.

References

1. Alavi, M. and Keen, P.W. "Business Teams in an Information Age," *Information Society*, (6:4), 1989, pp. 179-196.
2. Burke, K. and Chidambaram, L. "How Much Bandwidth is Enough? A Longitudinal Examination of Media Characteristics and Group Outcomes," *MIS Quarterly* (23:4), 1999, pp. 557-580.
3. Chidambaram, L. "Relational Development in Computer-Supported Groups," *MIS Quarterly* (20:2), 1996, pp. 143-165.
4. Cramton, C.D. "Information Problems in Dispersed Teams," *Proceedings of the Academy of Management Conference*, Chicago, 1997, pp. 298-302.
5. Daft, R.L. and Lengel, R. "Organizational information requirements, media richness and structural design," *Management Science* (32:5), 1986, pp. 554-571.
6. Dennis, A.R. "Information Exchange and Use in Group Decision Making: You Can Lead a Group to Information, but You Can't Make It Think," *MIS Quarterly* (20:4), 1996a, pp. 433-455.
7. Dennis, A.R. "Information Exchange and Use in Small Group Decision Making," *Small Group Research* (27:4), 1996b, pp. 532-550.
8. Dennis, A.R., Hilmer, K.M. and Taylor, N.J. "Information Exchange and Use in GSS and Verbal Group Decision Making: Effects of Minority Influence," *Journal of Management Information Systems* (14:3), 1998, pp. 61-88.
9. DeSanctis, G. and Gallupe, R.B. "A foundation for the study of groups decision support systems," *Management Science*, (33:5), 1987, pp. 589-609.
10. Gigone, D. and Hastie, R. "The Common Knowledge Effect: Information Sharing and Group Judgement," *Journal of Personality and Social Psychology* (65:5), 1993, pp. 959-974.
11. Hightower, R.T. and Sayeed, L. "The Impact of Computer Mediated Communication Systems On Biased Group Discussion," *Computers in Human Behavior* (11:1), 1995, pp. 33-44.
12. Hightower, R.T. and Sayeed, L. "Effects of Prediscussion Information Characteristics on Computer Mediated Group Discussion," *Information Systems Research*, Vol. 7, No. 4, December 1996, pp. 451-465.
13. Larson, J. R., Christensen, C., Abbott, A. and Franz, T. "Diagnosing Groups: Charting the Flow of Information in Medical Decision-Making Teams," *Journal of Personality and Social Psychology* (71:2), 1996, pp. 315-330.
14. McGrath, J.E. "Time, Interaction and Performance (TIP): A Theory of Groups," *Small Group Research* (22:2), 1991, pp. 147-174.

15. Mennecke, B.E. and Valacich, J.S. "Information Is What You Make of It: The Influence of Group History and Computer Support on Information Sharing, Decision Quality, and Member Perceptions," *Journal of Management Information Systems* (15:2), 1998, pp. 173-197.

16. Rao, V.S. and Jarvenpaa, S.L. "Computer Support of Groups: Theory Based Models for GDSS Research," *Management Science* (37:10), 1991, pp. 1347-1363.

17. Seashore, S.E. *Group Cohesiveness in the Industrial Work Group*, University of Michigan Press, Ann Arbor, MI, 1954.

18. Sproull, L. and Kiesler, S. "Reducing Social Context Cues: Electronic Mail in Organizational Communication," *Management Science* (32:11), 1986, pp. 1492-1512.

19. Stasser, G. and Titus, W., "Pooling of Unshared Information in Group Decision Making: Biased Information Sampling During Group Discussion," *Journal of Personality and Social Psychology* (48:6), 1985, pp. 1467-1478.

20. Stasser, G. and Titus, W. "Effects of Information Load and Percentage of Shared Information on the Dissemination of Unshared Information During Group Discussion," *Journal of Personality and Social Psychology* (53:1), 1987, pp. 81-93.

21. Stasser, G., Taylor, L.A., and Hanna, C. "Information Sampling in Structured and Unstructured Discussions of Three- and Six-Person Groups," *Journal of Personality and Social Psychology* (57:1), 1989, pp. 67-78.

22. Stasser, G. and Stewart, D. "Discovery of Hidden Profiles by Decision-Making Groups: Solving a Problem Versus Making a Judgement," *Journal of Personality and Social Psychology* (63:3), 1992, pp. 426-434.

23. Walther, J.B. and Burgoon, J.K. "Relational Communication in Computer-Mediated Interaction," *Human Communication Research* (19:1), 1992, pp. 50-88.

24. Warkentin, M.E., Sayeed, L.and Hightower, R.T. "Virtual Teams versus Face-to-Face Teams: An Exploratory Study of a Web-based Conference System," *Decision Sciences* (28:4), 1997, pp. 975-996.

25. Wittenbaum, G.M and Stasser, G. "Management of Information in Small Groups" in *What's Social About Social Cognition*, Judith L. Nye and Aaron M. Brower (eds.), Sage Publications, Thousand Oaks, CA, 1996, pp. 3-28

The Email Strategy Investigation Model (eSIM): A DSS for Analysis of Email Processing Strategies

Robert A. Greve[1], Ramesh Sharda[2], Manjunath Kamath[3], Ashish Gupta[4]

[1]Oklahoma City University, Meinders School of Business, Oklahoma City, OK 73106, USA,
[2]Oklahoma State University, William S. Spears School of Business, Stillwater, OK 74078, USA,
[3]Oklahoma State University, College of Engineering, Architecture, and Technology, Stillwater,OK 74078, USA,
[4]Minnesota State University, School of Business, Moorhead, MN 56563, USA

rgreve@okcu.edu[1], sharda@okstate.edu[2], m.kamath@okstate.edu[3], gupta@mnstate.edu[4]

Abstract. Given the prevalent use of email, intelligent decisions need to be made regarding how best to manage email workloads. The email Strategy Investigation Model (eSIM) is a decision support system with this aim in mind. eSIM provides an analysis of the effects of different email processing strategies. The strategy of continuously monitoring email messages is modeled along with alternative strategies that attempt to control the interruptive nature of email while allowing for appropriate processing of email both with and without the use of key word alarm triggers. Simulation is used to model different arrival patterns of email and the flow of the knowledge worker's focus of attention. A user of eSIM can compare various email processing strategies in deciding how best to manage his or her specific email challenges. This paper describes the eSIM decision support system in detail and provides an example of its use.

Keywords. Email, DSS, simulation, interruption

1 Introduction

Information overload is a growing problem faced by increasing numbers of knowledge workers, and email is one significant aspect of this overload. The number of email messages received per day has become a frequent subject of conversation among knowledge workers, and companies have begun to look for strategies to combat the steady stream of email messages faced by their employees [1, 2, 3, 4, 5]. In addition to the time needed to process the volume of email that is received, email's interruptive nature can have an indirect effect on knowledge worker productivity [1, 5, 6, 7, 8]. A tool is needed that allows for the analysis of knowledge workers' strategies aimed at dealing with the management of email.

Email is a technology that can interrupt primary work and cause inefficiencies if not managed properly. Some time is spent both preparing for an interruption (the interruption lag) and recovering from an interruption (the resumption lag). Trafton, et al. [9] proposed that an interruption's resumption lag is a function of the interruption lag. The interruption lag is that period of time between the interruption itself and when action is taken on the interruption. They identify the events of an interruption as those illustrated in Figure 1.

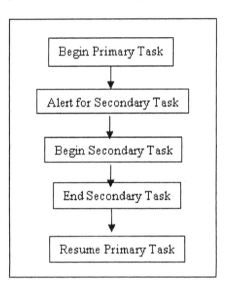

Figure 1. The Events of an Interruption [9]

Figure 2 provides an example of these events in this paper's context. An email notification occurs while the knowledge worker is engaged in a particular project, seconds or minutes elapse, and then the knowledge worker checks the email. This time between the email notification and opening the email inbox (the interruption lag) can be used to prepare for the interruption. The knowledge worker might make mental notes, save a document, or mark the page that he or she is reading. These preparations can influence the amount of time needed after the interruption to get back up to speed with the primary task (the resumption lag). Both the interruption lag and the resumption lag are needed to facilitate the interruption, but do not represent productive time with respect to the interrupted work. It is the cumulative effect of these unproductive time periods that may be reduced by employing specific email processing strategies.

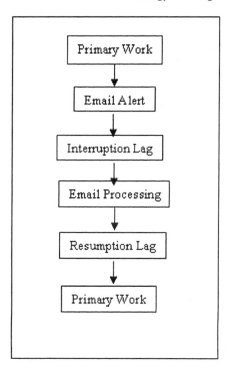

Figure 2. Interruption and Resumption Lags Resulting from an Email Interruption

Many strategies aimed at the management of email overload have been suggested. These strategies may involve reducing the email workload by eliminating any unnecessary email transmissions. This is typically done with filtering software, could take the form of policies limiting the use of the carbon copy field, or controlling the distribution of email to groups [1, 10]. Other strategies mentioned in the literature involve prioritizing messages so that time sensitive messages receive their proper attention [11, 12]. Another strategy looks at the timing of email processing. Jackson, et al. [5] suggested that a particular group limit checking email messages to every 45 minutes. The aim of this strategy was to limit email's interruptive effects. Through audible and visual notifications, email is often used much like the telephone. By treating email like the telephone, knowledge workers lose a key benefit of this "asynchronous" tool and accept additional interruptions to other important activities. A tradeoff clearly exists between interruptions and potentially slow responses. A need exists for a tool that allows us to investigate the potential benefits or drawbacks of various email (overload) management strategies and solutions.

The email Strategy Investigation Model (eSIM) is a decision support system with this aim in mind. eSIM provides a simple user interface coupled with an intricate simulation model that enables a knowledge worker to decide on the email processing strategy that best suits his or her needs. eSIM's simulation model allows a knowledge worker to define his or her "email environment" and analyze the effects of various email processing strategies within the defined environment. The email environment is described by email arrival patterns and the processing needs of the arriving messages, both in terms of the email's timeliness or urgency and the amount of time needed to process the various types of arriving email.

Currently, eSIM allows for investigation of eleven different email processing strategies. One type of email processing strategy modeled within eSIM involves only processing email during "email hours," or at a specific planned time(s) during the knowledge worker's day. These "email hours" allow us to control the number and timing of interruptions. This policy can take several forms involving both the number of controlled interruptions and the timing of the controlled interruptions. Five different schedules of email hours have been modeled, and eSIM could easily be extended to include additional variations.

Our discussions with knowledge workers from industry [13] indicate that while some knowledge workers do have preset email processing strategies, most simply do their best to respond to all email as quickly as possible, a strategy that requires continuous monitoring of all email activity. This strategy is evident in the popularity of the hand-held Blackberry device [14]. In this mode, all emails may potentially cause interruptions, despite the fact that only a few emails actually are urgent.

By categorizing or separating incoming email according to their temporal needs, and applying separate processing strategies to each category of temporal need, all incoming email need not cause interruptions in order to ensure appropriate resolution times [15]. Technology certainly exists that allows for only certain email (specific senders or subjects, for example) to trigger an audio or visual notification. Within Microsoft Outlook for example, as seen in Figure 3, creating an alert is a simple matter of creating a rule, a point-and-click operation requiring only a moment of time. Urgent alerts prompt the user when an email from a particular sender is received or when an email with a particular keyword (such as "urgent") is found in the subject heading of the email.

Each of five schedules of email hours are simulated both with and without urgent alerts; therefore, ten variations of the "email hours" strategies are simulated. The eleventh email processing strategy involves continuously monitoring and responding to email as they arrive, as is often done when using audible or visual notifications of arriving email. Because this is often the strategy prevalent among users [16, 17], it is included within eSIM for comparison against the alternative strategies mentioned above.

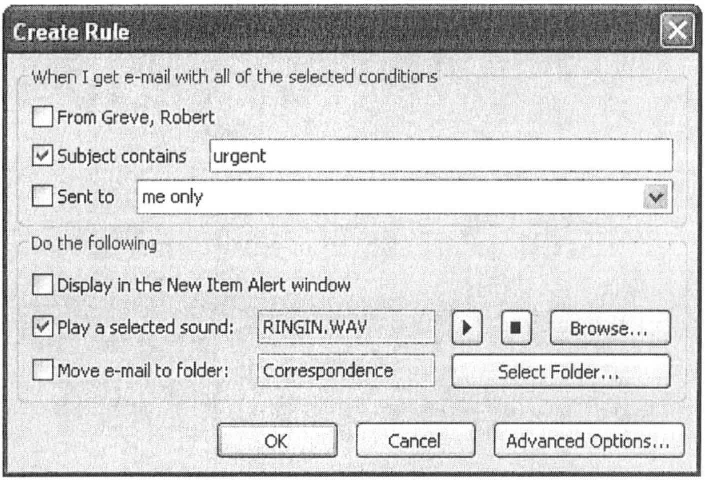

Figure 3. Screenshot from Microsoft Outlook

eSIM captures important metrics of the knowledge worker's performance. The email processing strategy's effect on the worker's ability to respond to email in a timely manner is one dimension of performance captured by eSIM. For example, moving away from continuously processing email and towards processing email only once daily will clearly affect the knowledge worker's email resolution time. On a similar note, the knowledge worker's efficient completion of ongoing work is another important dimension of performance. By work, we mean the knowledge work outside of processing emails. We also call it our primary task. eSIM can help answer the following question: To what extent do interruptions (or a lack of interruptions) affect the ability to complete ongoing work? If work is interrupted, some time is needed to reorganize one's thoughts, workspace, etc. Prior to switching tasks, some time is spent mentally preparing for an interruption. During this interruption lag the knowledge worker is not fully focused on his or her primary task. Interruptions also cause a resumption lag, the time needed to become reengaged in the work that was interrupted. Performance outcomes captured by the model include efficiency and its corollaries (daily nonproductive time and nonproductive time as a percentage of total email processing time). Efficiency represents the percentage of time that the knowledge worker is productive, and correlates to the extent of information overload experienced by the knowledge worker. Urgent email resolution time, and non-urgent email resolution time are also captured. Thus, we are able to see the tradeoffs that exist between efficiency and a quick email resolution, and we are able to see the extent to which urgent email alerts can add to our efficiency while allowing for quickly resolving those most important email messages. Thus, eSIM provides a decision support tool for analyzing the effects of alternative email processing strategies for a given knowledge work environment. In the next section, we describe the eSIM simulation model. In section 3, we describe the use of eSIM using an example. Finally, in section 4, we provide conclusions and present directions for future research.

2 The eSIM Model

eSIM was created using the Arena simulation software [18]. Arena simulation software allows for simultaneously modeling several entities including the arriving email messages and the knowledge worker's attention. Modeling the knowledge worker's attention as an entity separate from the email entities allows for manipulation of the email environment and the email processing strategy. Figure 4 depicts the top level Arena model consisting of multiple sub-models. The sub-models, seen within the top level model, can be grouped into three categories. The "Time Allocation" sub-model falls into the first category. The strategy sub-models consisting of the "Attention Initiation" sub-model, the "Strategy Simulated" module, the eleven different email processing strategy ("Attention") sub-models, and the "Attention Disposal" sub-model make up the second category. The flow of email is captured in the various "Email Arrivals" sub-models and the "Email Disposal" sub-model, which make up the third category. Each of these categories of sub-models is described in the following sections.

2.1 The Time Allocation Sub-model

The "Time Allocation" sub-model is used to track the time spent by the Attention entity on various areas of focus (email, primary work, and interruption and resumption lags). In a sense, the Time Allocation Sub-model connects the Strategy Sub-models that govern the flow of attention, to the Flow of Email Sub-models, which govern the flow of email. By tracking the time spent by the Attention entity on various tasks, the simulation model "knows" when enough attention has been spent on a particular email in order to release the email entity, i.e., treat the email as having been processed.

Figure 5 depicts the Time Allocation sub-model. The six modules within the sub-model collectively allocate time to the various areas of focus with respect to the "Attention" entity. Areas of focus include processing email messages, interruption and resumption lags, and primary work.

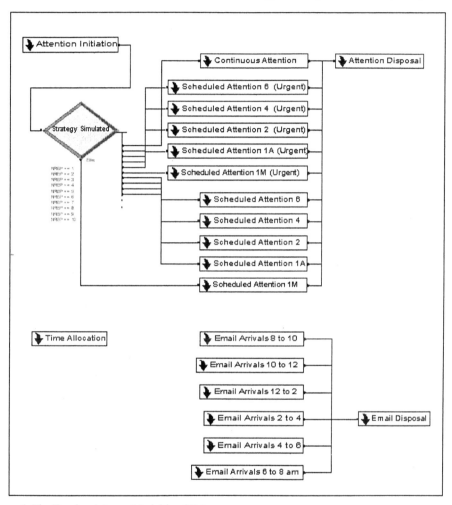

Figure 4. The Top-level Arena Model in eSIM

Module 1 in Figure 5 causes the creation of one and only one entity that will circulate within the Time Allocation sub-model throughout the entire simulation, allocating time to various areas of the Attention entity's focus. Module 2 delays this entity for four seconds for the following reason. The Time Allocation sub-model updates the amount of time spent focusing on one of the areas of attention every four seconds. Because each update represents a simulation event, choosing to update every single second causes four times as many simulation events, and therefore can cause the simulation processing time to increase dramatically. Updating every four seconds allows for reasonable accuracy, while allowing the simulations to be processed within a reasonable time frame. Module 3 routes the entity to one of four modules depending on the current area of the Attention entity's focus (the

Attention entity's focus is controlled within the strategy sub-models as described in section 2.2). The current area of the Attention entity's focus is captured by the Focus variable. Modules 4, 5, and 6 update, by 4 seconds, the time spent by the Attention entity on email, interruption or resumption lags, and primary work, respectively, before routing the entity back to module 2. If the Attention entity is not focused in one of the three areas (the Focus variable does not equal 1, 2, or 3), then the Attention entity is idle, and the time allocation entity continues to loop without allocating time to a specific activity.

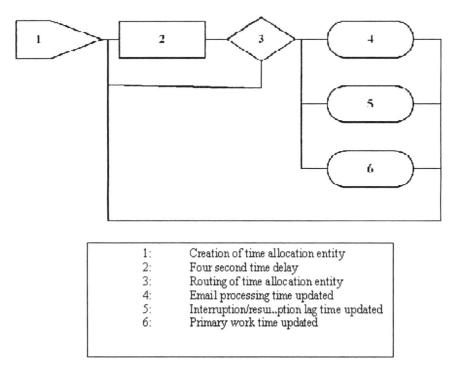

1:	Creation of time allocation entity
2:	Four second time delay
3:	Routing of time allocation entity
4:	Email processing time updated
5:	Interruption/resu..ption lag time updated
6:	Primary work time updated

Figure 5. The Time Allocation Sub-model

2.2 The Strategy Sub-models

The Strategy Sub-models consist of the "Attention Initiation" sub-model, the "Strategy Simulated" module, all of the "Attention" sub-models, and the "Attention Disposal" sub-model. The Strategy sub-models accomplish several things. First, the Attention Initiation sub-model creates one attention entity. Second, the Strategy Simulated module controls which email processing strategy is simulated by directing the attention entity to one of the eleven Attention sub-models. This module causes eSIM to cycle through all email processing strategies during one simulation run. Third, the eleven Attention sub-models simulate the flow of the knowledge worker's attention. Said differently, the Attention sub-models simulate the various email processing strategies. And fourth, the Attention Disposal sub-model resets key performance variables before disposing of the Attention entity.

The eSIM Attention sub-models and their corresponding processing strategies are each described in Table 1.

Table 1: eSIM Attention Sub-models and Their Email Processing Strategies

Continuous Attention	This processing strategy requires processing email as they arrive (giving first priority to email).
Scheduled Attention 6 (Urgent)	This processing strategy requires holding email hours 6 times daily and allows for "urgent" email messages to prompt the user for immediate processing.
Scheduled Attention 4 (Urgent)	This processing strategy requires holding email hours 4 times daily and allows for "urgent" email messages to prompt the user for immediate processing.
Scheduled Attention 2 (Urgent)	This processing strategy requires holding email hours 2 times daily and allows for "urgent" email messages to prompt the user for immediate processing.
Scheduled Attention 1A (Urgent)	This processing strategy requires holding email hours once daily (in the afternoon) and allows for "urgent" email messages to prompt the user for immediate processing.
Scheduled Attention 1M (Urgent)	This processing strategy requires holding email hours once daily (in the morning) and allows for "urgent" email messages to prompt the user for immediate processing.
Scheduled Attention 6	This processing strategy requires holding email hours 6 times daily. "Urgent" emails are not distinguished from other email messages.
Scheduled Attention 4	This processing strategy requires holding email hours 4 times daily. "Urgent" emails are not distinguished from other email messages.
Scheduled Attention 2	This processing strategy requires holding email hours 2 times daily. "Urgent" emails are not distinguished from other email messages.
Scheduled Attention 1A	This processing strategy requires holding email hours once daily (in the afternoon). "Urgent" emails are not distinguished from other email messages.
Scheduled Attention 1M	This processing strategy requires holding email hours once daily (in the morning). "Urgent" emails are not distinguished from other email messages.

The Attention entity is created once every 24 hours, beginning 8 hours into the simulation (at a simulated time of 8:00 a.m.). Each Attention entity is "disposed of" at the end of each twenty-four hour simulated day. In this way, one Attention entity arrives each morning at 8:00 a.m. and only one Attention entity will exist per day.

2.2.1 The Continuous Processing Sub-model

The Continuous Attention sub-model is illustrated in Figure 6. In the Continuous Attention sub-model, email is the knowledge worker's number one priority and will always interrupt other knowledge work.

Having been routed from the Strategy Simulated module, the Attention entity will initially enter the sub-model at module 1. Module 1 assigns the Focus variable a value of 1, indicating to the Time Allocation sub-model that the Attention entity is focusing on the processing of email. Next, the Attention entity will enter module 2, a hold module. The attention entity will stay at module 2 until all email have been processed or until noon, at which time the knowledge worker (Attention entity) is unavailable for a period of 30 minutes during the lunch break. Module 3 directs the Attention entity in one of three directions. The Attention entity is directed to module 4 if it is lunch time, to the exit point if a threshold of work has been completed for the day, or to module 6 if the Attention entity's focus is shifting towards primary work. Module 4 assigns the Focus variable a value of 4, indicating to the Time Allocation sub-model that the knowledge worker is idle. Module 5 delays the Attention entity for ½ hour, before releasing it back to module 1. Module 6 assigns the Focus variable a value of 2, indicating to the Time Allocation sub-model that the attention entity has shifted its focus to what will be a resumption lag, that time during which, having been interrupted, the knowledge worker prepares to resume his primary work. Module 7 simulates the resumption lag, and delays the Attention entity for a randomly determined time period following the exponential distribution with a mean of one minute [5]. Occasionally a knowledge worker might encounter an interruption at a "natural breaking point" in his or her work. If the interruption were to occur during a natural break, then the resumption lag would not be relevant. This possibility is captured within the model using the Natural Breaks sub-model.

The Natural Breaks sub-model, seen in Figure 7, simulates the occurrence of natural breaks throughout the knowledge worker's day. Module A creates an entity that will then exist indefinitely in modules B through E. Module B assigns a value of zero to the "Naturalbreak?" variable. A value of zero corresponds to the occurrence of a natural break. The "Naturalbreak?" variable is multiplied by the resumption lag, so that if an interruption occurs during a natural break, the resumption lag will be zero. Module C holds the entity (and therefore the "Naturalbreak?" variable value of zero) for one to five minutes (uniform distribution). Module D changes the "Naturalbreak?" variable to one, indicating that a natural break is no longer occurring. Module E holds the entity (and therefore the "Naturalbreak?" variable value of one) for ½ hour to 2 hours (uniform distribution) before the entity's return to module B. These parameters may be manipulated depending on the typical duration of tasks performed by the knowledge worker.

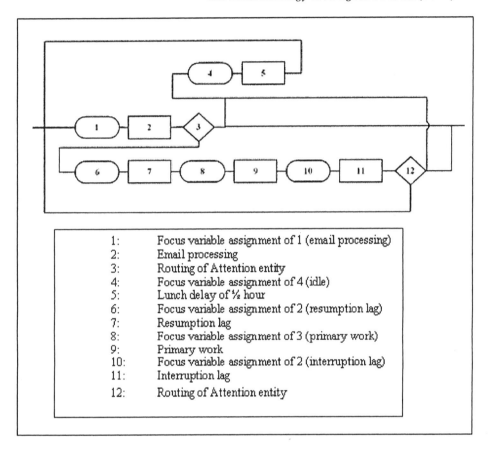

1:	Focus variable assignment of 1 (email processing)
2:	Email processing
3:	Routing of Attention entity
4:	Focus variable assignment of 4 (idle)
5:	Lunch delay of ½ hour
6:	Focus variable assignment of 2 (resumption lag)
7:	Resumption lag
8:	Focus variable assignment of 3 (primary work)
9:	Primary work
10:	Focus variable assignment of 2 (interruption lag)
11:	Interruption lag
12:	Routing of Attention entity

Figure 6. The Continuous Attention Sub-model

Turning our attention back to the Continuous Attention sub-model, module 8 assigns the Focus variable a value of 3, indicating to the Time Allocation sub-model that the Attention entity has shifted its focus to the knowledge worker's primary work. The Attention entity is held at module 9, corresponding to primary work, until an email arrives, it is lunch time, or a threshold of work has been completed for the day. Module 10 shifts the Focus variable back to a value of 2, indicating to the Time Allocation sub-model that the Attention entity has shifted its focus to what will be an interruption lag, that time between the interruption stimulus and the response to the interruption, during which the knowledge worker is preparing for the interruption, and therefore is not fully engaged in his primary task [9]. The interruption lag is simulated in module 11. The attention entity is held for a delay following a triangular distribution with a minimum of zero seconds, a mode of 6 seconds, and a maximum of 2 minutes. This results in an average interruption lag of approximately 42 seconds. This lag is again multiplied by the Naturalbreak? variable to account for the fact that the interruption may have occurred during the knowledge worker's natural break. Jackson, et al. [5] indicated that 70% of workers reacted to an email interruption within 6 seconds, and that workers reacted to an email's interruption on average within 1 minute and 44 seconds. A maximum of two minutes was used in the triangular distribution to cause a conservative average interruption lag of 42 seconds. This was done, because we do not know the proportion of that 1 minute 44 seconds that was spent preparing to be interrupted (the interruption lag), and the proportion of that time that was spent on the primary task. Module 12 then directs the Attention entity to either the exit if a threshold of work has been completed, to lunch if it is 12:00, or back to email in need of processing.

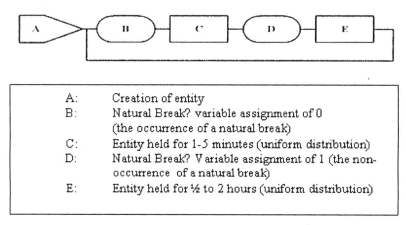

A:	Creation of entity
B:	Natural Break? variable assignment of 0 (the occurrence of a natural break)
C:	Entity held for 1-5 minutes (uniform distribution)
D:	Natural Break? Variable assignment of 1 (the non-occurrence of a natural break)
E:	Entity held for ½ to 2 hours (uniform distribution)

Figure 7. The Natural Breaks Sub-model

2.2.2 The Scheduled Attention Sub-models

The Scheduled Attention processing strategies are outlined in Figure 8. Differences in the processing strategies are captured within the logic of the modules described. Module 1 assigns the Focus variable a value of 2, indicating to the Time Allocation sub-model that the Attention entity has shifted its focus to what will be a resumption lag. Module 2 simulates the resumption lag, and delays the Attention entity for a randomly determined time period following the exponential distribution with a mean of one minute [5]. Module 3 assigns the Focus variable a value of 3, indicating to the Time Allocation sub-model that the Attention entity has shifted its focus to the knowledge worker's primary work.

Module 4 holds the Attention entity, and therefore the knowledge worker's focus on primary work, until one of a set of conditions is met. The differences between the processing strategies are captured in these differing sets of conditions. Table 2 outlines an example of differences between the five Scheduled Attention (Urgent) strategies, given a need for 2 hours and 40 minutes of email processing related activity). Time slot durations will vary according to the total email processing load being simulated. Scheduled Attention sub-models without the urgent feature differ only in that the presence of urgent email does not change the focus in module 4.

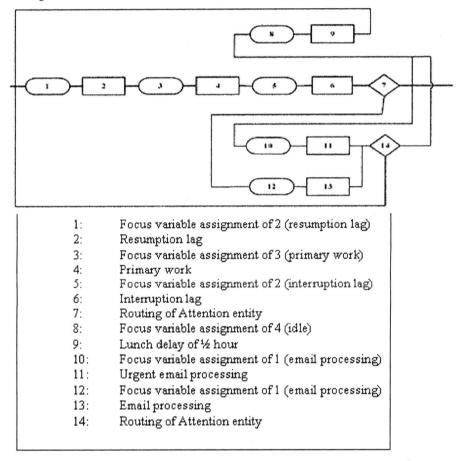

1:	Focus variable assignment of 2 (resumption lag)
2:	Resumption lag
3:	Focus variable assignment of 3 (primary work)
4:	Primary work
5:	Focus variable assignment of 2 (interruption lag)
6:	Interruption lag
7:	Routing of Attention entity
8:	Focus variable assignment of 4 (idle)
9:	Lunch delay of ½ hour
10:	Focus variable assignment of 1 (email processing)
11:	Urgent email processing
12:	Focus variable assignment of 1 (email processing)
13:	Email processing
14:	Routing of Attention entity

Figure 8. The Arena Model for Scheduled Attention (Urgent) Processing Strategies

Once a condition for leaving module 4 has been met, the attention entity moves to module 5. Module 5 shifts the Focus variable back to a value of 2, indicating to the Time Allocation sub-model that the Attention entity has shifted its focus to what will be an interruption lag. The interruption lag is simulated in module 6. As described with the Continuous Attention sub-model, the Attention entity is held for a delay following a triangular distribution with a minimum of zero seconds, a mode of 6 seconds, and a maximum of 2 minutes. Module 7 routes the Attention entity according to the condition that caused the attention's focus to shift from the primary work of the knowledge worker.

From module 7, the Attention entity will: a) exit the sub-model if a threshold of work has been accomplished, b) move to module 10 if an urgent email is awaiting processing, c) move to module 8 if it is lunch time, or d) move to module 12 to process non-priority email. Modules 8 and 9 simulate the knowledge worker's attention during the lunch break. Module 8 assigns the Focus variable a value of 4, indicating to the Time Allocation sub-model that the knowledge worker is idle. Module 9 delays the Attention entity for ½ hour, before releasing it back to module 1. Modules 10 and 11 simulate the processing of urgent email. Module 10 assigns the Focus variable a value of 1, indicating to the Time Allocation sub-model that the Attention entity is focusing on the processing of email. Module 11 holds the Attention entity's focus on email until all urgent email has been processed. Similarly, modules 12 and 13 simulate the processing of non-urgent email (Modules 10 and 11 only exist in the "Urgent" Attention sub-models). Module 14 directs the Attention entity to either module 8 (lunch time) or module 1.

2.2.3 The Attention Disposal Sub-model

The Attention Disposal Sub-model resets four variables. The Focus variable is set back to 4, corresponding to the knowledge worker being idle. Next, three variables, used to capture the daily time spent processing primary work, processing email, and in interruption and resumption lags are reset to zero, after having been recorded in the Excel file used as the user interface.

2.3 The Email Arrivals and Disposal Sub-models

Each "Email Arrivals" sub-model (Figure 9) simulates the arrival of the various types of email messages during its corresponding time frame. Each create module (1) simulates the arrival of a particular type (urgency and time needed to process) of email message. The interarrival time for each particular type is exponentially distributed. The rate of each type of arrival is derived from user inputs as described in section 3. Each assign module (2) assigns a processing time (the EPT variable) and priority (urgency) to the arriving email. Ten pairs of create and assign modules correspond to the ten different types of arriving email (combinations of urgency and time needed to process, described in section 3). The remaining two modules (3 and 4) simply dispose of the email message if it occurs outside of the sub-model's intended time frame. For example, the Email Arrivals 8 to 10 sub-model (seen in figure 4) simulates the arrival of all types of email messages that occur between 8:00 a.m. and 10:00 a.m.

Table 2. The Conditions for Stopping Primary Work, Given Alternative Email Processing Strategies

Processing Strategy	Conditions for Changing Focus (Module 4)

Scheduled Attention 5 (Urgent)	The time is between 8:00 and 8:27 a.m. & non-urgent email is present *OR* The time is between 9:55 and 10:21 a.m. & non-urgent email is present *OR* The time is between 12:30 and 12:57 p.m. & non-urgent email is present *OR* The time is between 1:44 and 2:10 p.m. & non-urgent email is present *OR* The time is between 3:38 and 4:05 p.m. & non-urgent email is present *OR* The time is between 5:33 and 6:00 p.m. & non-urgent email is present *OR* A threshold of work has been accomplished *OR* Urgent email is present *OR* The time is between Noon and 12:30
Scheduled Attention 4 (Urgent)	The time is between 8:00 and 8:40 a.m. & non-urgent email is present *OR* The time is between 11:07 and 11:47 a.m. & non- urgent email is present *OR* The time is between 2:14 and 2:54 p.m. & non- urgent email is present *OR* The time is between 5:20 and 6:00 p.m. & non- urgent email is present *OR* A threshold of work has been accomplished *OR* Urgent email is present *OR* The time is between Noon and 12:30
Scheduled Attention 2 (Urgent)	The time is between 8:00 and 9:20 a.m. & non-urgent email is present *OR* The time is between 4:40 and 6:00 p.m. & non-urgent email is present *OR* A threshold of work has been accomplished *OR* Urgent email is present *OR* The time is between Noon and 12:30
Scheduled Attention 1A (Urgent)	The time is between 3:20 and 6:00 p.m. & non-urgent email is present *OR* A threshold of work has been accomplished *OR* Urgent email is present *OR* The time is between Noon and 12:30
Scheduled Attention 1M (Urgent)	The time is between 8:00 and 10:40 a.m. & non-urgent email is present *OR* A threshold of work has been accomplished *OR* Urgent email is present *OR* The time is between Noon and 12:30

The "Email Disposal" sub-model is seen in Figure 10. Module 1 holds the email until module 2 is empty and the Focus variable equals 1, corresponding to email processing. Holding all email until the second module is empty ensures that the Attention entity is only applied to one email at a time in the second module. Module 2 holds an individual email message until the processing of the email is complete (E Time >= EPT). The E time variable is used to capture the amount of processing time that has been applied to the current email, and it is reset after each email is processed. Recall, the EPT variable represents the amount of time needed to resolve the current email. Module 3 assigns or resets the E Time variable to zero. Module 4 directs the email to one of two modules, based on whether the email is urgent or non-urgent. Modules 5 and 6 update the daily time spent processing email for non-urgent and urgent emails, respectively. The last module, module 7, simply disposes of the email message.

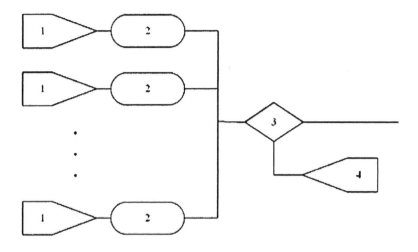

1:	Email entity creation module
2:	Email entity characteristic assignment module
3:	Routing of email entity
4:	Disposal of email entity

Figure 9. The Email Arrivals Sub-model

In the next section we describe the use of the model and provide an example that illustrates potential results.

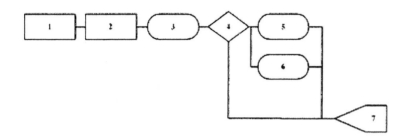

1:	Hold Email entity until module 2 is empty and until Focus variable = 1
2:	Individual Email entity held until resolved
3:	After processing an email message, module 3 reassigns the "E time" variable, corresponding to the time spent processing each individual email message, to zero
4:	Routing of Email entity
5:	Update of time spent processing non-urgent email messages
6:	Update of time spent processing urgent email messages
7:	Disposal of email message

Figure 10. The Email Flow Statistics & Disposal Sub-model

3 Using the eSIM model

Figure 11 outlines the flow of activities that occur from user input to simulation to user output. The user's inputs are manipulated within Excel, and read by the simulation model, before the simulation is run. After the simulation, the results of the simulation are written to the same Excel file, where the results are converted to several different performance charts.

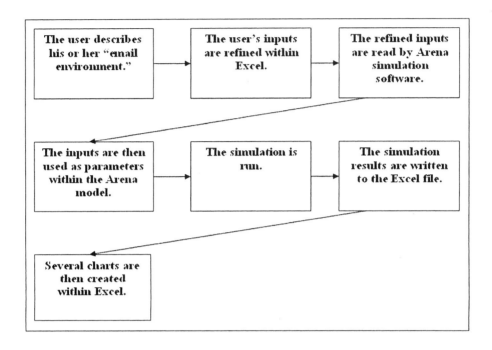

Figure 11. Flow of Activities from User Input to Simulation to User Output

A Microsoft Excel workbook serves as a user interface to the eSIM DSS. One worksheet within the workbook serves as a means of input (Figure 12), specifying the "email environment" faced by the knowledge worker. The email environment describes the email workload faced by the knowledge worker on a typical business day. The user first describes a typical day of email by completing the shaded area of the worksheet shown in Figure 12. Emails are categorized according to their acceptable resolution time (Urgent, Within Business Day, or Within one Week), the time needed to process them (< 1 minute, 1 – 10 minutes, and > 10 minutes), and the timing of their arrival (8 a.m. – 10 a.m., ..., 6:00 p.m. – 8:00 a.m.). This information is used to estimate some of the parameters for the Email Arrivals sub-models as described below.

Urgency	Time Needed	Total	8 am – 10 am	10 am – Noon	Noon – 2 pm	2 pm – 4 pm	4 pm – 6 pm	6 pm – 8 am
Urgent	< 1 Minute	4	3	1	0	0	0	0
Urgent	1 – 10 Minutes	3	0	1	2	0	0	0
Urgent	> 10 Minutes	4	1	0	1	0	2	0
Within Business Day	< 1 Minute	10	0	0	3	3	1	3
Within Business Day	1 – 10 Minutes	3	0	0	0	2	1	0
Within Business Day	> 10 Minutes	1	0	0	1	0	0	0
Within 1 Week	< 1 Minute	0	0	0	0	0	0	0
Within 1 Week	1 – 10 Minutes	0	0	0	0	0	0	0
Within 1 Week	> 10 Minutes	0	0	0	0	0	0	0
Irrelevant / SPAM	N/A	16	3	3	1	3	4	2
	Totals	41	7	5	8	8	8	5

Figure 12. Email Environment Input

The lack of an email arrival during a particular time period indicates to the model that an email arrival during this time period is impossible. In order to allow for the possibility of email arrivals during those time periods when no email arrivals were specified, each arrival rate is multiplied by 0.9, and 10% of daily arrivals of a particular type of email (one row in the worksheet above) is redistributed across all time periods. These calculations are done within a second worksheet of the Excel workbook. The following example illustrated in Figure 13 explains this further.

The first row of Figure 12 is seen in Table A of Figure 13. In Table B, these numbers are converted from total arrivals to *hourly arrival rates*. Next, in Table C, these numbers are then multiplied by 0.9. Next, in Table D, the hourly rate corresponding to 10% of the total email arrivals (0.1 * 4 = 0.4 / 24 = 0.0167) is then added to the hourly arrival rate of all time periods. In Table E, these arrival rates are then converted to inter-arrival times. The values in Table E are then read as parameters within the eSIM simulation model, specifically within the create modules of the Email Arrivals sub-models described in Section 2.3.

Table A

8am – 10am	10am – Noon	Noon – 2pm	2pm – 4pm	4pm – 6pm	6pm – 8am
3	1	0	0	0	0

↓

Table B

8am – 10am	10am – Noon	Noon – 2pm	2pm – 4pm	4pm – 6pm	6pm – 8am
1.5	0.5	0	0	0	0

↓

Table C

8am – 10am	10am – Noon	Noon – 2pm	2pm – 4pm	4pm – 6pm	6pm – 8am
1.35	0.45	0	0	0	0

↓

Table D

8am – 10am	10am – Noon	Noon – 2pm	2pm – 4pm	4pm – 6pm	6pm – 8am
1.367	0.467	0.017	0.017	0.017	0.017

↓

Table E

8am – 10am	10am – Noon	Noon – 2pm	2pm – 4pm	4pm – 6pm	6pm – 8am
.732	2.143	59.996	59.996	59.996	59.996

Figure 13. The Establishment of Email Arrival Pattern

Once the user has described his or her email environment within the Microsoft Excel workbook, the workbook is saved and closed, and the simulation model is run. The eSIM simulation model automatically reads the user's parameters from the Excel file and cycles through each of the email processing strategies, recording performance information along the way. This performance information is automatically written to the same Excel workbook, and performance charts are generated within the Excel file for users to view the differences between imate some of theail as having been processed.We also call it our primary task. er to your offic,day around 9 or 10, that wou the various email processing strategies.

Once the Excel worksheet seen in Figure 12 is completed, the Excel file is closed, and the Arena simulation is run. The simulation automatically pulls the email arrival parameters from the updated Excel file, runs the simulations, and writes the statistics back to the Excel file, where performance charts are generated. Using the input from Figure 12, the following performance charts (Figures 14 – 18) were generated.

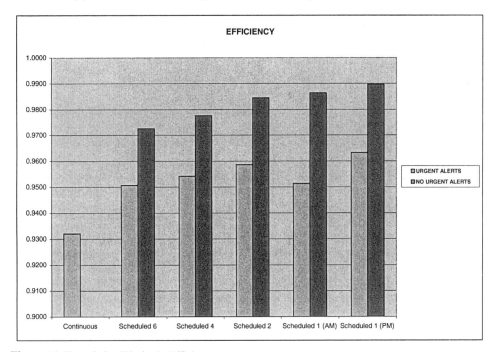

Figure 14: Knowledge Worker's Efficiency

In Figure 14, we see the impact different email processing strategies have on knowledge worker efficiency, defined as the knowledge worker's productive time (time spent processing email messages and performing primary work) divided by total time (time spent processing email messages, performing primary work, in interruption lags, and time spent in resumption lags). As one would expect, continuously processing email messages was the least efficient. For this particular knowledge worker, differences of 3% to 6%, representing more than 1 to 2 hours per week, are possible with other email processing strategies, but at what cost to appropriate email resolution times?

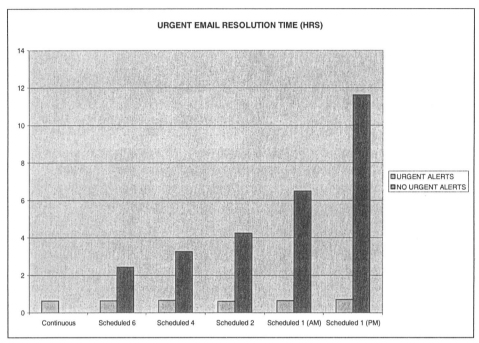

Figure 15: Urgent Email Resolution Times

Figure 15 illustrates the average resolution time for urgent email messages. For this knowledge worker, the results of applying an email processing schedule, without prompting the user of urgent messages, are less than satisfactory. Even processing email six different times during the day resulted in an average response of more than 2 hours for urgent messages. Depending on the user's interpretation of "urgent", this may or may not be satisfactory. What is perhaps more interesting, in this example, is the impact of using technology that prompts the user of urgent email arrivals. Because urgent alerts prompt the user for immediate response, it is possible for this user to maintain appropriate urgent email resolution times, while enjoying a significant increase in efficiency. Essentially, the knowledge worker is able to separate truly asynchronous communications from urgent communications, and adapt his or her behavior to each type of communication independently. eSIM provides the knowledge worker with decision support allowing him or her to make an intelligent decision regarding how best to manage their email workload.

Figure 16 illustrates the average resolution times for priority 2 email (those email in need of processing within one business day). Although a response within one business day is deemed to be appropriate, quicker responses are still desirable. Processing email twice daily while allowing urgent alerts might be best for this particular knowledge worker. Using the "Scheduled Attention 2 (Urgent)" email processing strategy, both urgent and non-urgent emails were responded to within an appropriate timeframe, and an efficiency gain of close to 3% was achieved when compared to processing email continuously.

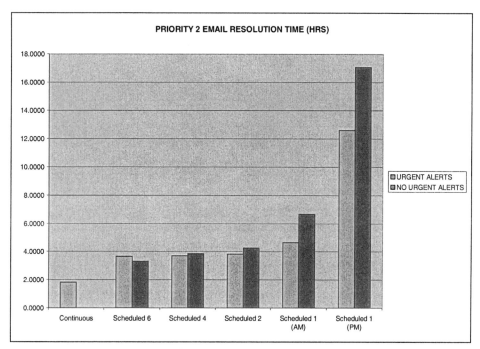

Figure 16: Email Resolution Times for Email in need of Processing within 1 Business Day

Figures 17 and 18 drive home the effect of inefficiency by illustrating the number of minutes wasted in interruption and resumption lags each day. Roughly 17 minutes can be gained each day when comparing continuous processing to processing email only twice daily while allowing for urgent alerts. Though this time may seem rather small in comparison to a knowledge worker's day, consider its application on an organization level. If even 50 workers with similar email environments adopted a strategy to reduce their interruptions, this would be equivalent of having more than one new worker employed by the organization. Interruption and resumption lags accounted for roughly 23% of the time spent due to email activity. In other words, only 77% of the time spent in activities related to email actually pertained to processing email. When this knowledge worker employed a strategy of continuously processing email; close to ¼ of the time spent because of email was unproductive time.

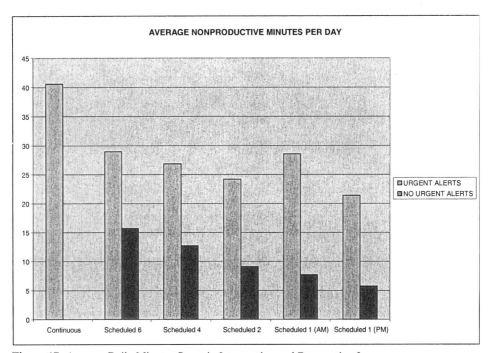

Figure 17: Average Daily Minutes Spent in Interruption and Resumption Lags

4. Conclusions

The eSIM model provides a decision support tool for testing the effectiveness of alternative email processing strategies, given individual knowledge workers' email environments. The eSIM model is especially useful, given that the results obtained from eSIM would be difficult at best to collect from the real environment. By modeling the knowledge worker's attention as an entity that flows from one area of focus to another, we are able to simulate and capture the effects of email processing strategies on various email environments. The model easily accommodates different email workloads, and can easily be extended to include additional email processing strategies. Initial use of the DSS with the simulation of one knowledge worker's email environment pointed out potential gains in efficiency, while allowing for appropriate responses to email messages. This same illustration points to the potential need for and value of the use of urgent alerts. Any knowledge worker, by reviewing a typical 24 hour time period from his or her email inbox, can easily define his or her email environment. They may then simulate their environment using various email processing strategies. The results generated from eSIM will then provide guidance for the decision of how best to manage the individual's email overload challenge. The results of these analyses might have implications for organizations wishing to minimize the burden that email imposes on their employees' productivity. Policies could be established enforcing the use of key words in the subject field, allowing for urgent alerts, and knowledge workers could be encouraged to adopt specific email processing strategies. These potential benefits begin with a tool for analyzing alternative strategies or an email Decision Support System. Future work will include testing the various email processing strategies within various email environments and extending the model to include additional email processing strategies. If you would like to receive your own individual eSIM results, go to: http://iris.okstate.edu/REMS/eSIM.

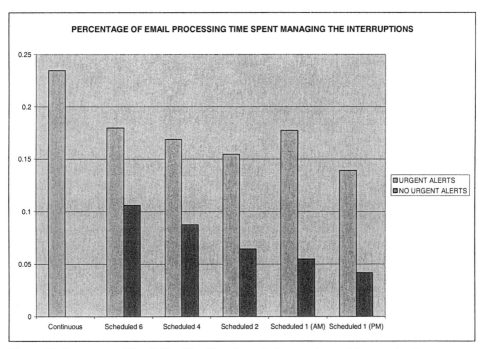

Figure 18: Percentage of Email Handling Time Spent in Interruption and Resumption Lags

References

1. Jackson, T.W., Burgess, A. and Edwards, J. (2005) "Optimising the Email Communication Environment", Managing Modern Organizations With Information Technology, Khosrow-Pour, M. (ed.), IRMA, San Diego, California, USA, May 2005, 819-820.
2. Macklem, K. (2006) You've Got Too Much Mail. http://www.macleans.ca/topstories/business/article.jsp?content=20060130_120699_120699
3. Kennedy, C. (2006) The High Cost of Email Interruptions. http://jointcommunications.blogspot.com/2006/01/high-cost-of-email-interruptions.html
4. CNN.com (2005) E-mails 'Hurt IQ More than Pot'. http://www.cnn.com/2005/WORLD/europe/04/22/text.iq/
5. Jackson T. W., Dawson R. and Wilson D. (2003) Understanding Email Interaction Increases Organizational Productivity, Communications of ACM, 46 (8), 80-84.
6. Gupta, A., Sharda, R., Greve, R., Kamath, M., Chinnaswamy, M. (2005). How Often Should We Check Our Email? Balancing Interruptions and Quick Response Times. Presented at the Big XII IS Research Symposium, University of Oklahoma, Norman.
7. Russell E., Purvis L. M. and Banks A. (in press) Describing the Strategies Used for Dealing with Email Interruptions According to Different Situational Parameters, Computers in Human Behavior
8. White G. and Zhang L. (2004) Sender-Initiated Email Notification: Using Social Judgment to Minimize Interruptions, Microsoft Research Technical Report MSR-TR-2004-126
9. Trafton J. G., Altmann E. M., Brock D. P., and Mintz F. E. (2003) Preparing to Resume an Interrupted Task: Effects of Prospective Goal Encoding and Retrospective Rehearsal, International Journal of Human-Computer Studies, 58, 583-603.
10. Sharda R., Frankwick, G., & Turetken, O. (1999) Group Knowledge Networks: A Framework and an Implementation, Information Systems Frontiers 1:3, pp. 221-239.
11. Losee, R. (1989) Minimizing Information Overload: The Ranking of Electronic Messages. J. Inform. Sci. 15, 3, 179–189.
12. Horvitz, E., Jacobs, A., and Hovel, D. (1999). Attention-Sensitive Alerting. In Proceedings of UAI '99, Conference on Uncertainty and Artificial Intelligence (pp. 305-313).
13. Greve, R. (2005) Modeling and Simulation of Knowledge Worker Attention for Evaluation of Email Processing Strategies, PhD dissertation, Oklahoma State University, Stillwater.
14. Krakow, G. (2006) BlackBerry Lives! Long Live BlackBerry.
15. http://msnbc.msn.com/id/11660067/
16. Tschabitscher, H. (2006) Spend Less Time on Email and Get More Done
17. http://email.about.com/od/netiquettetips/qt/et033105.htm
18. Hymowitz, C. (2004) Missing From Work: The Chance to Think, Even to Dream a Little. The Wall Street Journal, March 23, 2004
19. D'Antoni, H. (2004) Email: Workers' Constant Companion. Information Week, March 8, 2004, http://www.informationweek.com/story/showArticle.jhtml?articleID=18202012
20. Kelton, W.D., Sadowski, R.P., and Sadowski, D.A. (2002) Simulation with Arena. The Mc-Graw Hill Companies, Inc. NY.

Effects of Knowledge Management Capabilities on Perceived Performance: An Empirical Examination

Ting-Peng Liang[1], Yen-Ching OuYang[2], Daniel J. Power[3]

[1]Professor, Department of Information Management National Sun Yat-sen University, 70 Lien-hai Rd. Kaohsiung 804, Taiwan, R.O.C.
[2]Lecturer, Department of Information Management, Fortune Institute of Technology, 7F.-4, No.73, Jiouru 1st Rd., Sanmin District, Kaohsiung 807, Taiwan, R.O.C.
[3]Professor, Department of Information Systems and Management, College of Business Administration, University of Northern Iowa, Cedar Falls, Iowa 50614-0125 U.S.A

tpliang@mail.nsysu.edu.tw[1], lina@center.fotech.edu.tw[2], Daniel.Power@UNI.edu[3]

Abstract. Many business consultants and strategy theorists consider Knowledge Management (KM) critical to the success of an organization. While a few empirical studies have investigated the relationships among KM capability and various measures of performance, it is still not known what KM capabilities actually affect organization performance. Also, some research has examined contingency factors related to KM and performance, but industry type has not been examined as a possible moderator. This study explored two major questions: (1) Do KM capabilities impact perceived organization performance? and (2) Do KM capabilities have different effects in different industries? The results indicate that activities for knowledge documentation, acquisition and creation positively impact business performance and that the type of industry moderates the relationships. From a resource-based and knowledge-based view of the firm, the results indicate that in some circumstances KM creates a capability that results in improved performance. In general, the results help understand the complex role of knowledge management capabilities in firms.

Keywords: Knowledge Management, Knowledge Management Capabilities, Competitive Advantage, Organization Performance, Decision Support.

1 Introduction

For more than 10 years, an influential group of strategic management and organization theorists as well as many business consultants have advocated the importance of managing knowledge in organizations [20, 61, 62, 70]. Knowledge management (KM) is viewed as especially important in multinational and global enterprises. Proponents of knowledge management argue that because knowledge is difficult to create and imitate, it can be an important source of sustainable competitive advantage [66, 69, 80] and hence positively impact the success of individual corporations [44, 23, 52].

Knowledge can be defined as information that is relevant, actionable, and linked to meaningful behavior and information that is especially characterized by its tacit elements that are derived from firsthand experience. It is generally accepted that knowledge, or intellectual capital, has become an important source for wealth creation and may provide organizations with the only lasting basis for a sustainable competitive advantage [25, 53]. The basic proposition is that in a knowledge-based economy it is important to expand the focus of managers from exploiting natural resources to creating and using knowledge. For example, service industries should be conceptualized as providing knowledge-based "products". Even managers in traditional manufacturing businesses are encouraged to compete using their knowledge of customer needs, supply chain management and production processes instead of relying solely upon control of tangible resources like raw materials, labor, and facilities. A prescriptive focus in academic articles and in the popular business literature describing the importance of creating and using knowledge to achieve business success has encouraged executives to adopt knowledge management practices with an expectation that KM would result in competitive advantage and improved organizational performance.

Even though knowledge is an important asset and knowledge management may ultimately be related to better business performance, attempts to measure KM capabilities, especially the contribution of knowledge management to business performance has been difficult. KM hypothesized relationships are poorly understood and the relationships between KM and performance have not been adequately examined using empirical data (cf., [41]). Most prior KM articles have focused on defining KM concepts, the processes of KM, prescriptive guidance and case study examples of successful implementations [1, 72, 45]. Recently, some articles have addressed the theoretical issue of whether KM can create competitive advantage and hence improve firm performance. Despite the fact that many companies recognize the importance of the relationship between KM capabilities and business performance, thus far, research has not established an explicit causal link and direct or indirect effects upon business performance, regardless of how variables are measured.

Knowledge management efforts have included developing new applications of information technology to support the capture, storage, retrieval, and distribution of explicit knowledge [35]. Before 2001, most organizations had not taken a conscious process-oriented approach to KM. The limited published research has used multiple competing theoretical frameworks and various measures of constructs. Few researchers have investigated KM from an enabler-strategy-performance perspective. Although prior research provides some insight into the relationship between KM capability and performance, it is still poorly understood why the same KM capability may result in different results in different organizations. More specifically, additional research is needed to answer the questions: (1) Do KM capabilities impact perceived organization performance? And (2) Do KM capabilities have different effects in different types of industries?

The following sections briefly review the relevant theory and research, propose and define the research framework, summarize results from data collected using a survey questionnaire, discuss implications of the results and explain conclusions for practice and future research.

2 Relevant Theory and Research

The classic approach to strategy formulation begins with an appraisal of organizational competencies and resources [4, 39]. Knowledge is viewed as a strategic asset with the potential to be a source of sustainable competitive advantage for an organization. Managers implement knowledge management programs to gain advantage, increase productivity, and remain competitive. The Resource-Based View (RBV) of the firm [7] [59] provides an explanation of why firms can obtain strategic advantage from information technology [58].

To understand why knowledge management activities are important, it is useful to consider KM programs in the context of the Resource-Based View of the firm. From this perspective, organizations are studied in terms of how their resources can predict their performance in a dynamic, competitive environment [17]. Resources which are distinctive or superior relative to those of rivals may become the basis for competitive advantage if they are matched appropriately to environmental opportunities [4, 66].

The Resource-Based View of the firm has had a significant impact on how information systems and strategy are understood [16]. The RBV is closely linked with strategy and sustainable competitive advantage [7]. For example, Bloodgood and Salisbury [10] use the theory to identify how information technology can best be used with different types of change strategies. They suggest that different change strategies focus on different combinations of tacit and explicit knowledge that make certain types of information technology more appropriate in some situations than in others.

The Resource-Based View (RBV) of the firm [7] identifies four more stringent characteristics that a "resource" like KM must have to create a capability and a competitive advantage and hence positively impact a firm's performance. Assuming that KM process activities are viewed as potential strategic resources, then RBV requires the constellation of KM activities must be rare, valuable, imperfectly imitable, and non-substitutable to create a competitive advantage. One can reasonably argue that although KM activities are valuable, they are no longer rare. One can also argue that in many cases KM activities are socially complex and much more than the information technology and people that perform them [59]. In which case, KM activities could create a competitive advantage.

In a Knowledge-Based View (KBV) of organizations, the focus is on managing knowledge resources and the associated human and material resources that have capabilities for governing, operating on, and otherwise deploying knowledge [64]. The KBV of the firm, foreseen by Drucker [25], is a special case of the RBV with a focus on knowledge as an organizational resource [33, 34, 77]. A Knowledge-Based View (KBV) of organizations provides the conceptual foundation for much of the research and design efforts that link information technology (IT), organizational learning, and KM systems. The KBV has shaped the discussion of Knowledge Management Systems and the role of information technology in gaining competitive advantage [58, 49].

In general, knowledge management activities occur throughout a firm's value chain activities. To highlight the idea that competitive advantage grows fundamentally out of the value a firm is able create, Holsapple and Singh [40, 41] proposed a Knowledge Chain model. Shin et al. [74] describe KM capabilities as a simple KM value chain. Wilson [83] concluded KM has been used as an "umbrella term for a variety of organizational activities" concerned with managing information and work practices. Rather than debating the various concepts of KM, it seems more productive to identify and study specific activities in the operational dimension of KM [13]. The knowledge chain model identifies and characterizes KM capabilities that an organization can focus on to achieve competitiveness.

Some prior studies have examined the effect of enablers impacting performance through KM capabilities [8, 32]. Seven empirical studies in the literature seem most relevant to the current project (see Table 1). In the business strategy literature, many factors are identified that can affect firm performance and KM capabilities are potentially only one of them. Nevertheless, some empirical studies have examined the impact of integrated KM capabilities on business performance [9, 15, 32, 55, 56, 73, 79].

In a major study related to the current study, Lee and Choi [55] examined what they argued was an integrative framework for studying knowledge management. An intermediate outcome, creativity was introduced in the interaction process that transforms knowledge into business value. Their study attempted to provide insights about which enablers are critical for knowledge creation and which can subsequently improve organizational performance. They assert the direct relationship between knowledge processes and organization performance had not been explored prior to their study.

More recently, Chuang [15] reported a study to assess the impact of KM resources on competitive advantage. He asserted firms leverage their KM resources to create unique KM capabilities that determine a firm's overall effectiveness. The survey study used a relatively homogeneous sample of larger manufacturing firms and he argued that would alleviate moderating effects of the economy and industry. His dependent variable was a perceptual measure of competitive advantage with 4 items focused on innovativeness, market position, mass customization, and difficulty to duplicate. Performance was not measured.

Prior process-based knowledge management studies have emphasized viewing knowledge as a critical business resource. That approach seems sound, but it does not explain how so-called "enablers" such as industry characteristics are relevant. Also, hypothesizing causal relationships between KM capability and performance without considering type of industry implies the effect of KM activities on business performance is potentially the same across all types of organizations and industries.

This project was grounded in a Resource-Based view (RBV) of competitive strategy [7] that links a firm's resources and capabilities to sustained competitive advantage and superior performance. Knowledge management activities are conceptualized as a constellation of related resources embedded in a firm's value chain that creates a KM capability.

Table 1. Summary of Relevant Empirical Studies

Study	Sample Characteristics	Respondents	Independent Variables	Dependent variables
[8] Becerra-Fernandez & Sabherwal (2001)	1 organization; N=200 respondents in 7 subunits	Survey of Kennedy Space Center employees: 50% senior managers	KM processes (Externalization, Combination, Socialization, Internationalization)	Knowledge Management satisfaction with availability, sharing, management
[15] Chuang (2004)	N = 177 larger manufacturing firms in Taiwan	Survey R&D managers	Structural, Cultural, Human and Technical KM	Competitive advantage mea-sured with 4 items
[55] Lee & Choi (2003)	N=58 firms, 426 questionnaires; 3 industries manufacturing, finance, service in Korea	Survey middle managers	Culture, Structure, People, Information Technology, Knowledge Creation, Processes	Organizational creativity: novel ideas (5 items), organizational performance: (5 items)
[14] Choi & Lee (2003)	N=51 firms, 1290 questionnaires; 3 industries in Korea	Survey middle managers	4 KM styles: Dynamic, system-, human-oriented, and passive	Corporate performance
[32] Gold et al. (2001)	N = 323 with 58% finance and manufacturing firms; larger firms.	Survey senior managers (86%).	Technology, structure, culture, KM acquisition, KM conversion, KM application, KM protection	Organizational effectiveness
[56] Liu et al. (2004)	102 Taiwanese high technology manufacturers	Survey anonymous respondents	KM capability (obtaining, refining, storing, sharing)	Competitiveness: Forecasting ability, Sales ability, financial capability
[73] Sher & Lee (2004)	142 Taiwanese companies: 94 manufacturing, 48 service & finance	Survey respondents not specified	Management of endogenous and exogenous knowledge; IT applications	Enhancement of dynamic capabilities: learning, quality of decisions (10 items)

3   Research Framework

This study extends and refines Gold et al.'s work [32] and explains and tests a more parsimonious framework than that used by Lee and Choi [55]. Specifically, the current framework eliminates the vague concept of organizational creativity as a distinct intermediate outcome and recognizes that a number of subjective, perceptual measures are intermediate outcomes that may determine observed performance.

According to Alavi and Leidner [1], six different perspectives on knowledge management have been used in the literature. They concluded that knowledge management is "largely regarded as a process involving various activities ... At a minimum, one considers the four basic processes of creating, storing/retrieving, transferring, and applying knowledge (p. 114)". These processes have been described using a variety of labels to define KM capability.

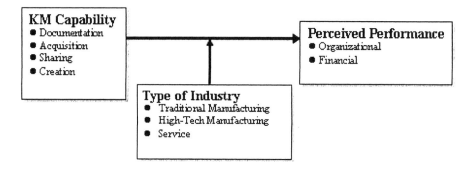

Figure 1. Research Framework

Three major constructs are included in the framework (see Figure 1). The major independent variable under investigation is KM capability, which includes four dimensions derived from Alavi and Leidner [1] and others, documentation, acquisition, sharing and creation. Industry type is included as a moderator that can cause KM activities to be more or less effective at improving performance. The dependent variable is perceived performance and it is measured by perceived organizational and financial performance indicators. A direct relationship is assumed between perceived and observed performance.

3.1   Impact of KM Capability on Business Performance

Early studies of knowledge management systems (KMSs) viewed them as applications of IT to improve the information value chain. Our review elaborates on this KM value chain model and focuses on four basic capabilities in knowledge work: documentation, acquisition, sharing, and knowledge creation. This conceptual model views KMSs as systematic attempts to make visible the collective and individual knowledge in an organization.

Reports of performance benefits have included both improved organizational and financial performance. These benefits may be direct or indirect. Direct benefits are those associated with each KM capability. Some indirect benefits are antecedents to direct benefits: knowledge documentation, acquisition, sharing and new knowledge creation can improve firm performance, and knowledge documentation, acquisition, and sharing can increase new knowledge creation, and so on. KM capability is an interrelated multidimensional construct. In order to investigate KM success, we have investigated process capability [32, 44]. The four KM process dimensions have been fragmented in the literature and they are summarized in the following sections.

3.2 Effects of Knowledge Documentation

In identifying KM capabilities, one of the basic approaches to knowledge documentation is called codification [46]. The codification approach focuses on how structured knowledge can be captured, codified, and stored. Knowledge codification means converting tacit knowledge to explicit knowledge [84, 36]. Explicit knowledge can be expressed in words and numbers and shared in the form of data and scientific formula [28]. Davenport et al. [21] categorized knowledge as: (1) external knowledge; (2) inside knowledge; and (3) informal information.

Knowledge can be codified or articulated in manuals, computer programs, training tools, and so on. This kind of knowledge is stored in databases where it can be easily accessed and used. Sharing explicit knowledge is easier through visible and embodied procedures. Explicit knowledge is organized, categorized, indexed and accessed. Codification must be done in a form/structure which will eventually build the knowledge base. On the other hand, if knowledge is highly tacit so the underlying structures are not well understood, learning is limited because that knowledge cannot be as systematically applied [80]. Therefore, the codification strategy can capture, create, and store knowledge so it can be applied to more contexts.

Codification seems to affect the speed of knowledge creation and innovation by improving the reliability of information storage and retrieval [22]. Also, codification may facilitate the emergence of new forms of innovation in a learning organization [3]. Codification may therefore be used as a management strategy to structure information and decision-making, to achieve deep understanding of an issue, or to support capabilities of knowledge diffusion (e.g. *knowledge sharing*) and accumulation. Nevertheless, despite the fact that codification may be a tool for the production and accumulation of knowledge, it may not lead to the production of radically new knowledge (e.g. *knowledge creation*) [18, 19].

The goal of a codification strategy is promoting reuse and involves building knowledge repositories to store knowledge and then make it available for workers. Teece [80] pointed out that codification of tacit knowledge has a direct relation to the degree of knowledge transfer (e.g. *knowledge sharing*). Foray and Steinmueller [30] suggest knowledge representations are devices to screen and classify information and to open new opportunities for codification, but their benefits depend on the capabilities to manipulate and transform the knowledge that it represents. When knowledge is less documented, transfer (e.g. *knowledge sharing*) is more difficult [84]. Codification refers to knowledge structured for transmission (e.g. *knowledge sharing*) purposes [76].

3.3 Effects of Knowledge Acquisition

Many terms have been used to describe knowledge acquisition capabilities, including knowledge seeking, capturing, retrieval, learning, discovery, and collaborating. Knowledge discovery is the nontrivial extraction of implicit, previously unknown, and potentially useful information from data. Often employees use structured knowledge learning strategies to increase knowledge acquisition. With the growing amount of codified knowledge in organizational memories, KMSs face the challenge of helping users find pertinent and needed knowledge. Knowledge retrieval is a core component to access knowledge items in a knowledge repository [51, 29]. Knowledge capture is employed to identify and extract knowledge from internal [60] or external sources [41]. Knowledge discovery identifies information from a knowledge-base to make recommendations to different stakeholders in the organization [6].

Knowledge can be acquired using information technology or non-technological sources. As a technology example, Web technologies can help identify, evaluate, analyze, synthesize, qualify, and accumulate externally created knowledge content [48]. As a non-technological example, employees engage in external training to acquire knowledge [40].

Nonaka and Takeuchi [62] thought individuals through their use of information technology tools would bring knowledge into a knowledge base and promote knowledge sharing. Zander and Kogut [84] argued that prior accumulated knowledge is the critical factor for understanding new knowledge (e.g. knowledge creation). Employees use their acquired knowledge to generate other knowledge (cf., [40]).

Supposedly the amount of knowledge acquisition activity affects business performance. Davenport and Prusak [20] also note that the only sustainable competitive advantage for a firm comes from what its members collectively know, how efficiently it uses what it knows, and how readily it acquires and uses new knowledge. Laurie [54] argued that the fortunes of companies in different industries can rise or fall meteorically, depending on how well they acquire, create, capture, and leverage their knowledge.

3.4 Effects of Knowledge Sharing

Knowledge sharing capabilities include knowledge dissemination, distribution, contribution, and transfer. In identifying KM capabilities, one of basic approaches is called personalization [46]. The personalization approach, concentrates on facilitating the sharing and transfer of tacit or unstructured knowledge. Knowledge transfer occurs in various ways. Knowledge transfer can be informal or formal, personal or impersonal [42]. Knowledge transfer and sharing occurs at various levels including transfer of knowledge between individuals, from individuals to explicit sources, from individuals to groups, between groups, across groups, and from the group to the organization [1].

Wasko and Faraj [82] concluded knowledge sharing often occurs without regard to expectations of reciprocity from others or with high levels of commitment to the communication network. Therefore, individuals connected through a network of practice may never know or meet each other face to face, yet they are capable of sharing a great deal of knowledge [11]. The literature suggests that knowledge transfer capabilities can bring many advantages to organizations [63] and now knowledge transfer capabilities are part of organizational life [20]. Knowledge that is effectively transferred within an organization can significantly affect business performance [78]. An organization's ability to create knowledge is rooted in its ability to synthesize and apply its existing knowledge [49] and in its ability to recognize the value of knowledge and assimilate it. To be useful, knowledge must be distributed and shared; only in that way can knowledge increase company performance in the market place [24].

3.5 Effects of Knowledge Creation

The phenomenon of knowledge creation involves creating capabilities for knowledge generation, construction, derivation, and production. Knowledge is created inside an organization [27] and organizational knowledge creation involves developing new content or replacing existing content within the organization's tacit and explicit knowledge framework. Nonaka and Takeuchi [62] proposed that knowledge could be created through the interaction of explicit knowledge and tacit knowledge. Knowledge creation is a capability that produces knowledge by discovering it or deriving it from existing knowledge, where the latter has resulted from codification, acquisition, and sharing. Creating knowledge is closely related to innovation. The generation of new knowledge is a critical determinant of organizational effectiveness (e.g. *performance*). Industry performance depends upon how well firms in the industry create knowledge [54, 24, 31].

There is a general consensus that knowledge creation and performance are positively and significantly related and, furthermore, that the application of knowledge creates competitive advantages for firms.

3.6 Industry Type

From a structural, competitive forces perspective [67]; industry factors like availability of product substitutes, jockeying for position, and bargaining power of suppliers determine performance of firms in an industry. Porter's [68] Value Chain model suggests that if KM capabilities add value to a product or service, then they will improve the competitive position of the firm (cf., [40]). These theoretical perspectives suggest that the relationship between KM capability and performance will vary among firms and that industry factors may moderate the relationship.

Besides studying KM capabilities, researchers have investigated factors influencing effective KM. The main factors or enablers identified are organizational culture, organizational leadership, types of IT, industry characteristics and knowledge characteristics. Researchers are particularly interested in how these enablers affect knowledge transfer capabilities [36, 78, 84]. In this research stream, industry characteristics are an enabler of KM capability rather than moderators of the relationship with performance.

One can speculate that the same KM capability would have different utility for service, traditional manufacturing, and high-tech industries. The three industries are facing very different operating complexities and different degrees of competition. This structural variable is a surrogate for factors like the degree of competition, the speed of technology change, and operating complexity.

3.7 Business Performance

Business performance can be analyzed in two categories. One is financial performance. The other is non-financial measures including operating performance outcomes and direct measures of learning. Strategic management research on performance effects has mainly conceptualized business performance in terms of financial and management performance goals. The finance-based measures of performance are often categorized as accounting and market-based measures of performance. The industry adjusted return on assets (ROA), return on sales (ROS), return on equity (ROE), and return on investment (ROI) are accounting-based measurement of performance. A typical approach is to use financial measures such as return on assets or earnings per share (cf., [9, 75]). For knowledge management research, however, the direct impact of KM on financial performance may not adequately reflect the total value of KM in an organization. Hence, the existing literature also uses a broader concept of organizational performance or organizational effectiveness as a dependent variable [14, 55].

Organizational performance is either an objective or subjective measure of output or results that is often compared to intended outputs, goals, and objectives. Common dimensions include: product/service innovation, number of patents and customer satisfaction. In this project, we followed Lee and Choi [55] and included perceptual measures of both financial and organizational performance. This approach is similar to assessing a Balanced Scorecard of metrics [47].

3.8 Hypotheses

Our hypotheses are derived from the above discussion of the framework. We conceptualized KM capabilities as consisting of four interrelated capabilities: knowledge documentation, knowledge acquisition, knowledge sharing, and knowledge creation. The framework focuses on the strategic resources that firms develop and nurture. Based on this framework, we formulated two major hypotheses:

H_1: Adoption of KM capabilities will have a positive effect on organizational performance and financial performance.

H_2: Industry type moderates the effects of KM capabilities on organizational performance and on financial performance.

4 Methodology

To empirically test this research framework, a survey instrument was constructed to measure both a firm's involvement in KM capabilities and the perceived historical performance of the firm. Existing instruments in the literature were used to help identify items. Since prior instruments were built for different frameworks and sometimes contained conflicting items, revised measures were needed to accurately capture the richness of the four KM activities and measure perceived performance.

4.1 Survey Development and Distribution

The survey instruments were pre-tested with a focus group of 3 academic domain experts and 5 practicing managers. The pretest assessed the face and content validity of the operational measures and ensured that informants would understand instructions, questions, and response scales of the study in the intended ways.

The constructs employed in the research model were measured using multi-item scales. A version of the questionnaire translated into English (a Chinese version is available upon request) is in Appendix I. The translation is a composite of machine and human translation. In the first wave of data collection, questionnaires were distributed by mail to large enterprises in Taiwan. The cover letter requested the CKO (Chief Knowledge Officer) or CIO (Chief Information officer) to fill out and anonymously return the questionnaire. The second wave of data was collected at a KM conference. The third wave was collected by email. Relying upon retrospective reports of key informants always has limitations (cf., [43]), but this study design attempted to minimize them.

4.2 Measuring Variables

The operational definitions of the major variables in this research framework are summarized in Table 2. For each variable the construct is defined and relevant literature is indicated in the table.

Informants assessed the extent of their firm's documentation, acquisition, sharing, and creation activities across business units using a five point Likert scale ranging from 1 = very low to 5 = very high. Industry type was measured using fixed categories. Business performance was measured by asking respondents: "What is your assessment of the following outcomes over the past three years on a scale where 1 = significantly decreasing, 3 = no change and 5 = significantly increasing." Financial assessments included ROA (Return On Assets) and ROS (Return On Sales). The other questions asked about non-financial measures including operating performance outcomes, innovation, and customer satisfaction.

4.3 Response Rates

Of the 1116 questionnaires initially mailed, 161 usable questionnaires were returned (effective response rate of 15.7%). At approximately the same time, 778 questionnaires were distributed at a KM conference with 74 usable questionnaires returned (effective response rate of 9.5%). In a third wave, 39 usable questionnaires were collected through email. Result from the Chi-squared test shows that responses collected from different channels does not have significant heterogeneity in company profiles (such as industrial type). That is, data from different channels can be viewed as equally representative of the population (cf. [5]). Table 3 shows the demographic data for the final set of 252 responding companies in three industry categories.

Table 2. Operational Definitions and Related Literature

Variables	Operational definition	Related Literature
Knowledge Documentation	Acts to record, store, write down, convert, cite, externalize or annotate actions, knowledge and conclusions. Capabilities include: categorizing documents, creating manuals.	Alavi & Leidner (2001); Gold et al. (2001); Holsapple & Singh (2001); Lee & Choi (2003), Demarest (1997); Davenport et al. (1998); Hansen et al. (1999)
Knowledge Acquisition	Acts to locate, retrieve or obtain facts, information and knowledge. More specific capabilities include: internal training, collecting experiences of experts, external training.	Alavi & Leidner (2001); Gold et al. (2001); Holsapple & Singh (2001); Lee & Choi (2003)
Knowledge Sharing	Acts involving joint use of resources, transferring and distributing information, and exchanging knowledge. Capabilities include using email and computer supported work flows.	Alavi & Leidner (2001); Gold et al. (2001); Holsapple & Singh (2001); Lee & Choi (2003); Hendriks (1999)
Knowledge Creation	Acts to assemble, combine, construct, or design knowledge and solutions. Capabilities include using databases, using Internet, using data mining and decision support systems.	Alavi & Leidner (2001); Gold et al. (2001); Holsapple & Singh (2001); Lee & Choi (2003)
Industry Type	A categorization describing a company's primary business capability. Industries have been classified in various ways including traditional manufacturing, high-technology manufacturing and service.	Kusunoki et al. (1998); Cardinal et al. (2001)
Financial Performance	An objective or subjective measure of competitive or historical outcomes such as total revenue and profit.	Lee & Choi (2003); Harel & Tzafrir 1999; Pelham (2000)
Organizational Performance	An objective or subjective measure of output, effectiveness or results of an organization against its intended outputs (or goals and objectives).	Gold et al. (2001); Holsapple & Singh (2001); Lee & Choi (2003); Harel & Tzafrir 1999; Drucker (1986); Kaplan & Norton, 2000

Table 3. Sample Demographics (n=252)

Industry	Number (%)
Traditional Manufacturing	131 (52.0%)
High-Tech Manufacturing	41 (16.3%)
Services	80 (31.7%)
Assets (US$)	**Frequency**
< 0.6 million	60 (23.8%)
0.6 – 3 million	58 (23.0%)
3 – 30 million	62 (24.6%)
> 30 million	62 (24.6%)
Missing values	10 (4.0%)

4.4   Validation of the Instrument

Confirmatory Factory Analysis (CFA) results are shown in Table 4. The scales are assessed in terms of item loadings, discriminant validity, and internal consistency. Table 5 provides the means, standard deviations, reliabilities (Standardized Cronbach alphas), and zero-order correlations among the research variables. In general, item loadings and internal consistencies greater than 0.6 are considered acceptable for exploratory research [71]. Scales used in this study largely met these guidelines. All items except for two related to knowledge acquisition (KAC) exhibit high loading on their respective constructs. Furthermore, all constructs in the model exhibit good internal consistency as evidenced by their composite reliability scores.

Reliability and convergent validity of the factors was estimated by composite reliability, and by the average variance extracted (see Table 4). The average extracted variances were all above the recommended 0.50 level, which meant that more than one-half of the variance observed in the items, are accounted for by the hypothesized factors. To examine discriminant validity, we compared the shared variances between factors with the average variance extracted for the individual factors. This analysis shows that the shared variances between factors were lower than the average variance extracted for the individual factors, thus confirming discriminant validity. In summary, the survey instrument demonstrated adequate reliability, convergent validity, and discriminant validity.

Table 4. Results of Rotated Factor Matrixes with Varimax Rotation

Factors / Variables	Documentation	Acquisition	Sharing	Creation	Organizational Performance	Financial Performance
DOC1	.824	.171	.220	.082	.162	.035
DOC2	.769	.127	.168	.234	.212	.017
DOC3	.739	.177	.109	.205	.114	.192
DOC4	.690	.247	.247	.059	.099	.099
OP1	.045	.162	.263	-.046	.776	.227
OP2	.159	.228	.226	.008	.768	.165
OP3	.183	-.103	.045	.163	.720	.021
OP4	.203	.319	-.122	.189	.599	.235
KMC1	.171	.158	.183	.861	.105	.062
KMC2	.152	.183	.222	.842	.043	.111
KMC3	.245	.226	.414	.513	.158	.148
KSH1	.203	.022	.718	.245	.165	.106
KSH2	.260	.131	.630	.395	.098	.099
KAC1	.342	.736	.128	.224	.132	.099
KAC2	.196	.715	.103	.405	.198	.199
KAC3	.393	.576	.479	.071	.132	.038
KAC4	.336	.551	.474	.053	.163	-.019
FP1	.124	.083	.070	.098	.177	.890
FP2	.085	.095	.105	.104	.219	.878

5 Research Results

The 2 major hypotheses were tested in a number of ways. The following sections report both descriptive statistical analyses and more sophisticated path analyses.

5.1 Descriptive Statistics and Correlations.

Table 5 summarizes descriptive statistics and correlations among the constructs used in this research study. As hypothesized, KM capability has significant positive associations with the measures of firm performance.

Table 5. Descriptive Statistics and Inter-Correlation Matrix for the Measures (All Firms)

	Mean	S.D.	No. of Items	Reliability	(DOC)	(KAC)	(KSH)	(KMC)	(OP)
Documentation	3.38	0.86	4	.85					
Acquisition	3.33	0.89	4	.87	.673***				
Sharing	3.28	0.98	2	.62	.546***	.616***			
Creation	2.69	0.93	3	.84	.500***	.600***	.671***		
Organizational Performance	3.42	0.64	4	.78	.443***	.475***	.384***	.345***	
Financial Performance	3.10	1.00	2	.85	.298***	.310***	.282***	.295***	.449***

*** $p \leq 0.001$ (n=252)

5.2   Test of Hypotheses H1

Path analysis was used to test hypothesis H1. It allows us to explore how the independent variables directly and indirectly influence the dependent variables. Direct effects are the effects remaining when intervening variables are held constant. Indirect effects tell us how much of a given effect occurs because the manipulation of the antecedent variable of interest leads to changes in other variables which in turn change the consequent variable (cf., [2]). The direct and indirect effects can be combined to examine the total effect that one variable may have, thereby enhancing understanding of relationships among the variables.

Table 6 presents the results of this path analysis which support the proposed hypotheses H1 and H2. However, not all the KM capability variables have direct, positive effects on performance.

As shown in Figure 2, documenting has a positive impact on organizational performance but not on financial performance, creating knowledge has a positive impact on financial performance but not on organizational performance, acquiring knowledge has a positive impact on both organizational and financial performance, and finally sharing knowledge has no effect on firm performance but it is positively associated with creating knowledge.

Table 6. Results of Stepwise Regression Analysis (All Firms)

Dependent / Independent	Performance		KM capabilities			
	Organizational Performance	Financial Performance	Creation	Sharing	Acquisition	Documentation
Documentation	.223**			.242***	.675***	-
Acquisition	.325***	.199**	.302***	.452***	-	-
Sharing			.486***	-	-	-
Creation		.192*	-	-	-	-
R^2	0.253	.122	.509	.411	.456	

*$p \leq 0.05$, ** $p \leq 0.01$, *** $p \leq 0.001$ (n=252)

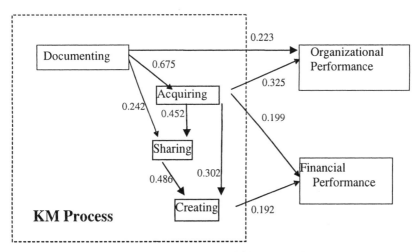

Figure 2. Inter-Relationships among KM Capabilities and Performance

5.3 Test of Hypotheses H2

Table 7 shows the means and standard deviations for the four independent and two dependent variables for the three types of industries in the study. ANOVA tests show that the degree of documentation is significantly greater in the high-technology manufacturing industry than in the service industry. Also, the degree of acquiring knowledge is higher in the high-technology manufacturing industry than in traditional manufacturing.

Table 7. Descriptive Statistics by Industry Type

	Traditional Manufacturing (n=131)		High-Tech Manufacturing (n=41)		Service (n=80)		ANOVA	
	Mean	S.D.	Mean	S.D.	Mean	S.D.	F value	Scheffe
Documentation	3.39	.85	3.76	.64	3.18	.92	6.48**	HT>S
Acquisition	3.18	.88	3.65	.69	3.42	.94	4.86**	HT>T
Sharing	3.12	.99	3.52	.77	3.44	1.01	3.89*	HT>T
Creation	2.58	.89	2.96	.85	2.74	.99	2.76	
Organizational performance	3.42	.63	3.54	.67	3.37	.62	1.32	
Financial performance	2.99	.91	3.45	.95	3.14	1.13	3.33*	HT>T

Levene test for ANOVA $p \geq 0.05$; * $p \leq 0.05$, ** $p \leq 0.01$, *** $p \leq 0.001$; (n=252)

Tables 8-10 show the path analysis results for the three industry groups. The results indicate that there exists an interaction effect between type of industry and performance. The results for the traditional manufacturing industry are most similar to those of the overall sample. Noticeable differences in the path analyses exist for all three industry types. The results show that in all three industries acquiring knowledge is significantly related to documenting knowledge. Likewise acquiring and sharing knowledge are significantly related. Finally, in all three industries acquiring knowledge was significantly related to organizational performance.

Table 8. Results of Stepwise Regression Analysis (Traditional Manufacturing)

Dependent ⟍ Independent	Performance		KM Capabilities			
	Organizational Performance	Financial Performance	Creation	Sharing	Acquiring	Documentation
Documentation	.276*			.391***	.687***	-
Acquisition	.234*	.296*		.371***	-	-
Sharing			.730***	-	-	-
Creation		.206**	-	-	-	-
R^2	.220	.198	.533	.490	.472	

* $p \leq 0.05$, ** $p \leq 0.01$, *** $p \leq 0.001$ (n=131)

Table 9. Results of stepwise Regression Analysis (High-Tech Manufacturing)

Independent / Dependent	Performance		KM Capabilities			
	Organizational Performance	Financial Performance	Creation	Sharing	Acquiring	Documentation
Documentation			.301*		.652***	-
Acquiring	.478***			.557***	-	-
Sharing			.579***	-	-	-
Creation			-	-	-	-
R^2	.229		.589	.311	.425	

p≤0.05, ** p≤0.01, *** p≤0.001 (n=41)

Table 10. Results of Stepwise Regression Analysis (Service)

Independent / Dependent	Performance		KM Capabilities			
	Organizational Performance	Financial Performance	Creation	Sharing	Acquiring	Documentation
Documentation		.346**			.706***	-
Acquiring	.558***		.470***	.549***	-	-
Sharing			.289**	-	-	-
Creation			-	-	-	-
R^2	.311	.120	.453	.301	.499	

* p≤0.05, ** p≤0.01, *** p≤0.001 (n=80)

6 Discussion and Conclusions

Knowledge management capability is an important organizational variable, but apparently all KM capabilities are not equally important. This study has begun examining the link between KM capabilities and firm performance. This new KM framework makes a number of key contributions. It integrates concepts from prior studies, it focuses on knowledge capabilities and it is anchored in the knowledge-based view of the firm. The exposition of the framework and this exploratory study should ground knowledge management strategy on a more theoretically sound foundation. By looking at knowledge capability in a new light, we have tried to show how KM capabilities and business performance can be related.

Results indicate that documentation and acquisition capabilities have direct positive effects on organizational performance while acquisition and creation activities have direct positive effects on financial performance. Knowledge sharing only has an indirect effect on firm performance. Also, moderating effects were found for type of industry. These results indicate KM capabilities have different effects on performance for firms operating in different environments.

From a competitive forces perspective, industry type influences what capabilities are most important for improving performance. KM capabilities have different utility for service, traditional manufacturing and high-tech industries. The three industries are facing very different operating complexities and different degrees of competition. The knowledge acquisition capability significantly impacts organizational performance for each industry. The knowledge creation capability only seems to affect financial performance for traditional industry environments. That implies firms in a traditional industry environment need more new knowledge creation activities to improve financial performance.

This framework is just a beginning, but it highlights a number of areas for further research. First, the model points to the need for an empirical study to test the linkages between knowledge capabilities and their impact on actual firm performance. Second, further understanding of how industry type moderates business performance is needed. This research might unveil closer linkages between knowledge capabilities and business performance in more specific industry environments.

Finally, there are possibilities for expanding beyond these initial variables to show that a firm's performance is enhanced by deploying combinations of knowledge capabilities in particular industry situations.

A few limitations should be kept in mind in interpreting the findings and implications of this study.

6.1 Limitations

Although the direction of the relationships is strong and positive, this study still has limitations. A major limitation of the study is the focus on business firms in three industries in Taiwan, which is a reasonably homogeneous cultural context. Another limitation is that this study focuses on explicit knowledge and identifiable KM capabilities. Also, many of the capabilities and activities involve the use of information technology. Most of the capabilities associated with documenting, creating and sharing knowledge have integrated information technologies in them.

Another limitation is that the study focuses on perceptual measures of performance rather than upon more objective measures. A number of studies have demonstrated a link however between perceptual and objective performance measures. Also, there is no reason to believe the key informant who responded to the survey would be motivated to distort or misrepresent his/her organizations past performance on the six items in the survey. A final limitation is the cross sectional research design.

6.2 Conclusions for Practice

We need to better understand how knowledge management activities and decision support systems can impact individual, group and enterprise performance. Alavi and Leidner [1, p. 115] note "management reporting systems, decision support systems, and executive support systems have all focused on the collection and dissemination" of codified, explicit organizational knowledge. We need to improve upon and better understand the use and differential deployment of these technologies.

Also, we need to understand when it is most appropriate and cost/effective to use Information Technology to help identify people who have knowledge that is needed, when to share knowledge, when to store structured knowledge in expert systems that make decisions and when to keep people as decision makers and build knowledge-driven DSS, and when to build model, data and document-driven DSS.

In general, periodically assessing knowledge management capabilities may highlight very useful information for evaluating and compensating knowledge workers and for allocating and developing human capital depending upon business needs. Our goal should be deploying appropriate knowledge management capabilities rather than just deploying more knowledge management capabilities.

References

1. Alavi, M., Leidner, D.E.: Review: Knowledge Management and Knowledge Management Systems: Conceptual Foundations and Research Issues. MIS Quarterly. 25, 1 (March 2001) 107-136
2. Alwin, D.E., Hauser, R.M.: Decomposition of Effects in Path Analysis. American Sociological Review. 40 (1975) 37-47
3. Ancori, B., Bureth, A., Cohendet, P.: The Economics of Knowledge: the Debate about Codification and Tacit Knowledge. Industrial and Corporate Change. 9, 2 (June 2000) 289-313
4. Andrews, K.R: The Concept of Corporate Strategy. Homewood, IL: Dow Jones Irwin, 1971
5. Armstrong, J.S. and Overton, T.S. Estimating nonresponse bias in mail surveys. Journal of Marketing Research. 16 (August 1977) 396-402
6. Balasubramanian, P., Nochur, K., Henderson, J.C., Kwan, M.M.: Managing Process Knowledge for Decision Support. Decision Support System. 27, 1-2 (November 1999) 145-162
7. Barney, J. B. Firm resources and sustained competitive advantage. Journal of Management, 17, 1 (1991), 99-120
8. Becerra-Fernandez, I., Sabherwal, R.: Organizational Knowledge Management: a Contingency Perspective. Journal of Management Information Systems. 18, 1 (Summer 2001) 23-55
9. Bierly, P., Chakrabarti, A.: Generic Knowledge Strategies in the U.S. Pharmaceutical Industry. Strategic Management Journal. 17, 10 (Winter 1996) 123-135
10. Bloodgood, J.M., Salisbury, W.D.: Understanding the Influence of Organizational Change Strategies on Information Technology and Knowledge Management Strategies. Decision Support Systems. 31, 1 (May 2001) 55-69
11. Brown, J.S., Duguid, P.: Knowledge and Organization: a Social Practice Perspective. Organization Science. 12, 2 (2001) 198-213
12. Cardinal, L.B., Alessandri, T.M., Turner, S.F.: Knowledge Codifiability, Resources, and Science-based Innovation. Journal of Knowledge Management. 5, 2 (2001) 195-204
13. Carlucci, D., Marr, B., Schiuma, G.: The Knowledge Value Chain: How Intellectual Capital Impacts on Business Performance. International Journal of Technology Management. 27, 6/7 (2004) 575-590

14. Choi, B., Lee. H.: An Empirical Investigation of KM Styles and their Effect on Corporate Performance. Information and Management. 40, 5 (2003) 403-417
15. Chuang, S. A.: Resource-based Perspective on Knowledge Management Capability and Competitive Advantage: an Empirical Investigation. Expert Systems with Applications. 27 (2004) 459-465
16. Clemons, E.K.: Corporate Strategies for Information Technology: a Resource-based Approach. Computer. 24, 11 (November 1991) 23-32
17. Collis, D.J., Montgomery, C.A.: Competing on Resources: Strategy in the 1990's. Harvard Business Review. (July -August 1995) 118-128
18. Cowan, R., Foray, D.: The Economics of Knowledge Codification and Diffusion. Industrial and Corporate Change. 6, 3 (1997) 595-622
19. Cowan, R., David, P.A., Dominique, F.: The Explicit Economics of Knowledge Codification and Tacitness. Industrial and Corporate Change. 9, 2 (June 2000) 211-253
20. Davenport, T.H., Prusak, L. Working Knowledge: How Organizations Manage What They Know. Boston: Harvard Business School Press, (1998)
21. Davenport, T.H., De Long, D.W., Beers, M.C.: Successful Knowledge Management Projects. Sloan Management Review. 39, 2 (Winter 1998) 43-58
22. David, P. A., Foray, D.: Information Distribution and the Growth of Economically Valuable Knowledge: a Rationale for Technological Infrastructure Policies. In Technological Infrastructure Policy: An International Perspective, eds. Teubal M., M. (1996)
23. De Long, D.W., Fahey, L.: Diagnosing Cultural Barriers to Knowledge management, The Academy of Management Executive, 14, 4 (November 2000) 113-127
24. Demarest, M.: Understanding Knowledge Management. Long Range Planning. 30, 3 (1997), 374-384
25. Drucker, P.F. The coming of the new organization, Harvard Business Review, (January-Fevruary 1988), 45-53
26. Drucker, P.F. Management challenges for the 21th Century. New York: Harper Business, (1999)
27. Duffy, J.: Knowledge management: to be or not to be? Information Management Journal. 34, 1 (2000) 64-7
28. Emin, C.: Knowledge Management as a Competitive Asset: a Review. Marketing Intelligence & Planning. 18, 4 (2000) 166-174
29. Fenstermacher, K.D.: Process-Aware Knowledge Retrieval Proceedings of the 35th Hawaii International Conference on System Sciences. Big Island, Hawaii USA, (2002) 209-265.
30. Foray D., Steinmueller, W.E.: The Economics of Knowledge Reproduction by Inscription. Industrial and Corporate Change. (2002)
31. Francisco J.F., Guadamillas, F.: A Case Study on the Implementation of a Knowledge Management Strategy. Oriented to Innovation Knowledge and Process Management. 9, 3 (July/September 2002) 162-171
32. Gold, A.H., Malhotra, A., Segars, A.H.: Knowledge Management: an Organizational Capabilities Perspective. Journal of Management Information Systems. 18, 1 (Summer 2001) 185-214
33. Grant, R. M.: Prospering in Dynamically-Competitive Environments: Organizational Capability as Knowledge Integration. Organization Science. 7, 4 (1996a) 375-387
34. Grant, R.M.: Toward a Knowledge-based Theory of the Firm. Strategic Management Journal. 17 (1996b) 109-122
35. Grover, V., Davenport, T.H.: General Perspective on Knowledge Management: Fostering a Research Agenda. Journal of Management Information Systems. 18, 1 (Summer 2001) 5-21

36. Hansen, M.T., Nohria, N., Tierney, T.: What's your Strategy for Managing Knowledge? Harvard Business Review. 77, 2 (March/April 1999) 106-116

37. Harel, G.H., Tzafrir, S.S.: The Effect of Human Resource Practices on the Perceptions of Organizational and Market Performance of the Firm. Human Resource Management. 38, 3 (1999) 185-199

38. Hendriks, P.H.J., Vriens, D.J.: Knowledge-based Systems and Knowledge Management: Friends or Foes? Information & Management. 35, 2 (February 1999) 113-125

39. Hofer, C., Schendel, D.: Strategy Formulation: Analytical Concepts. St. Paul, MN: West Publishing, Inc., (1978)

40. Holsapple, C.W., Singh, M.: Toward a Unified View of Electronic Commerce, Electronic Business and Collaborative Commerce: a Knowledge Management Approach. Knowledge & Process Management Journal. 7, 3 (2000) 151-164

41. Holsapple, C.W., Singh, M.: The Knowledge Chain Model: Activities for Competitiveness. Expert Systems with Applications 20, (2001) 77-98

42. Holtham, C., Courtney, N.: Developing Managerial Competencies In Applied Knowledge Management: A Study Of Theory And Practice, Proceedings of AIS Americas Conference, Baltimore. (1998)

43. Huber, G.P., Power, D.J.: Retrospective Reports of Strategic-level Managers: Guidelines for Increasing their Accuracy. Strategic Management Journal. 6, 2 (1985) 171-180

44. Jennex, M.E., Olfman, L.: A Model of Knowledge Management Success. International Journal of Knowledge Management. 2, 3 (2006) 51-68

45. Kakabadse, N., Kakabadse, A., Kouzmin, A.: Reviewing the Knowledge Management Literature: Towards Taxonomy. Journal of Knowledge Management. 7, 4, (2003) 75-91

46. Kankanhalli, K., Tanudidjafi, F., Sutanto, J., Tan, B.C.Y.: The Role of IT in Successful Knowledge Management Initiatives. Communications of the ACM. 46, 9 (2003) 69-73

47. Kaplan, R., Norton, D.: Having Trouble with your Strategy? Then map it. Harvard Business Review. 78, 5 (September/October 2000) 167-176

48. Kennedy, D. Academic Duty, Cambridge: Harvard University Press, (1997)

49. Kogut, B., Zander, U.: What Do Firms Do? Coordination, Identity, and Learning, Organization Science. 7, 5 (1996). 502-518

50. Kusunoki, K., Nonaka, I., Nagata, A.: Organizational Capabilities in Product Development of Japanese Firms: a Conceptual Framework and Empirical Findings. Organizational Science. 9, 6 (1998) 699-718

51. Kwan, M.M., Balasubramanian, P.: KnowledgeScope: Managing knowledge in context. Decision Support System, 35. (2003). 467-486

52. Ladd, A., Ward, M.A.: An Investigation of Environmental Factors Influencing Knowledge Transfer. Journal of Knowledge Management Practice. (August 2002)

53. Laszlo, K.C., Laszlo, A.: Evolving Knowledge for Development: the Role of Knowledge Management in a Changing World. Journal of Knowledge Management. 6, 4 (2002)

54. Laurie J.: Harnessing the Power of Intellectual Capital. Training & Development. 51, 12 (1997) 25-30

55. Lee, H., Choi, B. Knowledge Management Enablers, Processes, and Organizational Performance: an Integrative View and Empirical Examination. Journal of Management Information Systems. 20, 1 (Summer 2003) 179-228

56. Liu, P.L., Chen, W.C., Tsai, C.H.: An Empirical Study on the Correlation between Knowledge Management Capability and Competitiveness in Taiwan's Industries. Technovation. 24 (2004) 971-977

57. Marshall, L.: Facilitating Knowledge Management and Knowledge Sharing: New Opportunities for Information Professionals. Online, 21, 5 (1997) 92-95

58. Mata, F.J., William, L.F., Barney, J.B.: Information Technology and Sustained Competitive Advantage: a Resource-based Analysis. MIS Quarterly. 19, 4 (December 1995) 487
59. Meso, P., Smith, R.: A Resource-based View of Organizational Knowledge Management systems. Journal of Knowledge Management. 4, 3 (March 2000) 204-216
60. Nissen, M.E.: Knowledge-based Knowledge Management in the Reengineering Domain. Decision support systems,.special issue on knowledge management. Decision Support Systems. 27, 1-2 (November, 1999) 47-65
61. Nonaka, I.: Knowledge-Creating Company. Harvard Business Review. 69, 6 (1991) 96-104
62. Nonaka, I., Takeuchi, H. The Knowledge-Creation Company: How Japanese Companies Create the Dynamics of Innovation. New York: Oxford University Press, (1995)
63. O'Dell, C., Grayson, C. J.: If only we Knew what we Know: Identification and Transfer of Internal Best Practices. California Management Review. 40, 3 (1998) 154-174
64. Paradice, D. B., Courtney, J. F.: Organizational Knowledge Management. Information Resources Management Journal. 2, 3 (1989) 1-13
65. Pelham, A.M.: Market Orientation and Other Potential Influences on Performance in Small and Medium-sized Manufacturing Firms. Journal of Small Business Management. 38, 1 (January 2000) 48-67
66. Peteraf, M. A.: The Cornerstones of Competitive Advantage: A Resource-based View. Strategic Management Journal. 14 (March 1993) 179-191
67. Porter, M.E. Competitive Strategy. New York: Free Press, (1980)
68. Porter, M.E., Millar, V.: How Information Gives you Competitive Advantage. Harvard Business Review. 63, 4 (1985) 149-160
69. Prahalad, C.K., Hamel, G.: The Core Competence of the Corporation. Harvard Business Review. 68 (May-June1990) 79-91
70. Prusak, L.: Where did Knowledge Management come from? IBM Systems Journal. 40, 4 (2001) 1002-1007
71. Robinson, J.P., Shaver, P.R., Wrightsman, L.S.: Criteria for Scale Selection and Evaluation, in Measures of Personality and Social Psychological Attitudes, J.P., Robinson, P.R. Shanver, and L.S. Wrightsman (eds.) San Diego, Calif.: Academic Press, (1991)
72. Rubenstein-Montano, B., Liebowitz, J., Buchwalter, J., McCaw, D.: A Systems Thinking Tramework for Knowledge Management. Decisions Support System. 31, 1 (2001) 5-16
73. Sher, P.J., Lee, V.C.: Information Technology as a Facilitator for Enhancing Dynamic Capabilities through Knowledge Management. Information & management. 41 (2004) 933-945
74. Shin, M., Holden, T., Schmidt, R.A.: From Knowledge Theory to Management Practice: Towards an Integrated Approach, Information Support for the Sense-making Activity of Managers. Decision Support Systems. 31, 1 (2001) 55-69
75. Simonin, B.: The Importance of Collaborative Know-how: an Empirical Test of the Learning Organization. Academy of Management Journal. 40, 5 (1997) 509-533
76. Smart, P.A., Maull, R.S., Radnor, Z.J., Housel, T.J.: An Approach for Identifying Value in Business Processes. Journal of Knowledge Management. 7, 4 (April 2003) 49-61
77. Spender, J.C., Grant, R.: Knowledge and the Firm: Overview. Strategic Management Journal. 17, (1996) 5–10
78. Szulanski, G.: Exploring Internal Stickiness: Impediments to the Transfer of best Practice within the Firm. Strategic Management Journal. 17, (Winter 1996) 27-43
79. Tanriverdi, H.: Information Technology Relatedness, Knowledge Management Capability, and Performance of Multibusiness Firms. MIS Quarterly. 29, 2 (June 2005) 311-334
80. Teece, D.J.: Capturing Value from Knowledge Assets: the New Economy, Markets for Know-how, and Intangible Assets. California Management Review. 40, 3 (1998) 55-77

81. Teece D.J., Pisano, G., Shuen, A.: Dynamic Capabilities and Strategic Management. In The Nature and Dynamics of Organizational Capabilities, eds. Dosi G., R. R. Nelson and S. G. Winter, Oxford University Press, (2000)
82. Wasko, M.M., Faraj, S.: Why should I Share? Examining Social Capital and Knowledge Contribution in Electronic Networks of Practice. MIS Quarterly. 29, 1 (2005) 35-47
83. Wilson, T.D.: The Nonsense of Knowledge Management. Information Research. 8, 1 (2002), paper no. 144. Available at http://InformationR.net/ir/8-1/paper144.html.
84. Zander, D., Kogut, B.: Knowledge and the Speed of the Transfer and Imitation of Organizational Capabilities: an Empirical test. Organization Science. 6, 1 (1995) 76-92

Appendix 1: Survey Questionnaire

Items for KM Process Activities

Construct	Variable Name	Item: Assess on a scale of 1 = very low to 5 = very high, the degree to which …
Documentation Knowledge (DOC)	DOC1	Operational processes are completely documented.
	DOC2	Internal documents are categorized using a standardized classification.
	DOC3	Marketing and technical material are formally documented and well-maintained.
	DOC4	Operations follow standard management procedures (such as ISO).
Acquiring Knowledge (KAC)	KAC1	An employee suggestion system encourages employees to propose innovative ideas for solving problems.
	KAC2	Routine internal training encourages employees to learn new knowledge/skills.
	KAC3	Experience of experts is collected and organized to help employees solve problems.
	KAC4	Employees are encouraged to attend external seminars and education programs.
Sharing Knowledge (KSH)	KSH1	Operational documents and workflows are supported using information technology.
	KSH2	Employees use the Internet (e.g. e-mail or BBS) for communication and information sharing.
Creation Knowledge (KMC)	KMC1	Data mining and knowledge discovery tools are used to analyze data and documents.
	KMC2	Employees use computers to acquire information from the Internet for improving decision making.
	KMC3	Employees can find needed information/data from corporate databases.

Items for Perceived Performance

Construct	Variable Name	Item: What is your assessment of the following outcomes over the past three years on a scale where 1 = significantly decreasing, 3 = no change and 5 = significantly increasing
Financial Performance (FP)	FP1	return on assets (ROA)
	FP2	return on sales (ROS)
Organizational Performance (OP)	OP1	improvement in manufacturing and work flow processes product/service innovation.
	OP2	number of patents.
	OP3	customer satisfaction.
	OP4	

Using Social Choice Rule Sets in Multiple Attribute Decision Making for Information System Selection

Edward W. N. Bernroider[1], Johann Mitlöhner[1]

[1]Vienna University of Economics and Business Administration,
Department of Information Systems and Operations, Augasse 2-6, 1090 Vienna, Austria

{Edward.Bernroider,Johann.Mitloehner}@wu-wien.ac.at

Abstract. The evaluation of investments in information systems (IS) is usually based on conflicting criteria applied to the available alternatives, and the results are aggregated into a single ranking. The aggregation process is regularly complicated and biased through the usage of criteria weights. This article simply suggests avoiding the weighting process, and alternatively relies on a set of multiple social choice methods. This work investigates various methods of social choice voting rules for aggregation and the properties of the results they deliver in typical IS decisions. Results are compared with the outcome of traditional multiple attribute decision making, taking into account case study and simulation data. The results support our notion that weighting criteria in the context of complex IS investment appraisals does not provide a different or more comprehensive outcome than the less demanding social choice rule set applied.

Keywords: information systems selection, social choice, voting rules

1 Introduction

A well recognized area of research is characterized by the evaluation and selection problems faced in Information System (IS) investment appraisals, in particular in the context of business applications. Today IS can be seen as the central nervous system of enterprises supporting core business processes and enabling crucial business functionalities. The complexity of enterprise IS is increasing continuously, covering a wide range of different aspects. These aspects can be adequately covered by multiple criteria in decision making methods, which have been developed for the last decade to support the evaluation, selection, and follow-up controlling of IS. An important stream of research can be assigned to the concept of multiple attribute decision making (MADM), where problems are represented by several (conflicting) attributes or criteria. It was described as the most well known branch of decision making [14]. These methods appeal to management due to their intuitive, simple and cost effective application. They are relatively transparent, allowing others to see the logic of the results and enabling the inclusion of the full range of intangible consequences in terms of considered attributes. Nevertheless, many difficulties in MADM exist that lead to application errors in business practice. Model extensions proposed to avoid these errors are, in general, coupled with increased complexity that, in turn, hinders their acceptance. In this article, we seek to increase the awareness and test the applicability of well researched selection rules used in social choice theory and compare them with popular MADM techniques used in the IS field.

The remainder of this article is structured as follows: Firstly, the research background and objectives are clarified. Next, social choice methods are summarized and thereafter applied in a case study showing the selection of an enterprise wide IS in an Austrian company. This section is followed by results of a simulation comparison of social choice rules. Finally, conclusions are given.

2   Research Background and Objectives

This article draws on two independently developed research streams, namely MADM and Social Choice Theory.

MADM refers to making preference decisions over a finite number of alternatives that are characterized by multiple, usually conflicting, attributes. A MADM problem can be expressed by a matrix, where columns indicate the attributes considered and rows denote the competing alternatives. Each MADM problem needs to be solved by one of the numerous MADM methods available. It is essential for many compensatory MADM methods to obtain comparable scales by normalization of attribute ratings. Solving the MADM problem can imply the aggregation of utilities into an overall evaluation for each alternative leading to a final ranking. In many applications a weight vector describing the relative importance values of each attribute is used to aggregate the alternative evaluations.

In this paper we focus on MADM in a finite IS selection problem, where usually the number of alternatives is limited and a wide choice of selection attributes are considered. In the field of IS evaluation the MADM approach 'Information Economics' received considerable attention [10]. The model gives the decision makers the means to identify and assess a comprehensive set of evaluation attributes in the IS evaluation problem setting, therefore it primarily assists in the important generation of attributes. Other more general concepts provide assistance to identify places where important criteria, especially benefits, might be found, e.g. [7]. Usually frameworks used in systematic IS selection for MADM are based on additive value models. Probably the most well known are the Analytic Hierarchic Process [12] (AHP) or some kind of utility ranking models (based on the so-called "Nutzwertanalyse" - NWA) [16]. In both cases the decision maker tries to maximize a quantity called utility or value. This postulates that all alternatives may be evaluated on a single scale that reflects the value system of the decision maker and his preferences. To generate this super scale, multiple single-attribute value functions are aggregated, most regularly by a simple additive procedure. In the mentioned methodologies the assessment of attribute weights and single-attribute value functions is needed. The value aggregation per alternative is in the case of AHP undertaken by a weighted sum of those single-attribute value functions. In terms of NWA, the decision maker is allowed to choose among a set of methods and typically relies on the standard recommendation, again formally a weighted sum approach. In the weighted sum method the overall suitability of each alternative is thereby calculated by averaging the score of each alternative with respect to every attribute with the corresponding importance weighting. In business practice important pre-conditions of the NWA (and the AHP) are violated. Regularly, scale types are misused or scale transformations made are invalid, e.g., ordinally scaled values are used as if they were cardinally scaled. Another major problem lies in the necessity of defining attribute weights, which is known as major challenge for decision makers. Another, more general, nevertheless major criticism of MADM is that different methods may yield different results when applied to the same problem. This phenomenon is known as the inconsistent ranking problem caused by the use of different MADM methods [15]. The availability of a wide selection of methods for solving IS decision problems generates the paradox that the selection of a MADM method for a given problem leads to a MADM problem itself [14].

Selection rules from social choice theory should appeal to business practices since they demand less rigorous information from the decision maker. No single-attribute value functions need to be derived and no weighting of attributes is needed. MADM approaches are typically single decision maker methods, while social choice approaches are designed for multiple decision maker situations. However, the analogy between voting and multiple criteria decision support is easily found. If attributes are replaced by voters, and alternatives by candidates, a social choice problem is designed. In other words, the preferences of a voter in social choice problems play the same role as the preferences gained along a single dimension or attribute in MADM [4]. A major motivation for this analogy lies in the fact that voting theory has developed since the original works by Borda, Condorcet, and Arrow [3, 5, 1] to a large amount of results at disposal for use in MADM.

In this article we seek to compare the input demands and aggregation results, i.e. final rankings, of a standard MADM framework (NWA) to popular social choice methods for IS selection. In particular, it needs to be assessed if the data demands and relative processing complexity in the NWA are justified in terms of outputs compared to the inputs and outputs supplied by applying social choice rules. The next section gives a short overview of the social choice rules considered in this paper.

3 Social Choice Methods and Rank Aggregation

The problem of preference aggregation in social choice consists in finding an aggregate ranking $x>=y>=z$ such that the preferences stated by the individual voters are expressed. Consider a set of n voters who express preferences on a set of m alternatives, resulting in a profile consisting of n rankings, e.g., $n=4$, $m=3$, alternatives a,b,c and rankings $a>b>c$, $b>c>a$, $c>a>b$, $b>c>a$, where $a>b$ means that a is preferred to b. We assume that the profile does not contain indifferences, i.e. the voters are not allowed to state $a=b$ but must decide on $a>b$ or $b>a$; however, the resulting aggregation may contain them. As already stated, in the MADM context the voters are replaced by the dimensions or attributes considered. In contrast to the scoring methods typically used in MADM the evaluation of the alternatives is reduced to finding the n rankings of alternatives for the m dimensions or attributes, instead of defining n single-attribute value functions. It is usually much easier for experts to provide rankings such as *b>c>a* for each category instead of numeric values such as *a:18, b:25, c:22*, which are usually questionable yet fundamental for the further NWA analysis.

While there are various approaches to preference aggregation, each algorithm results in an aggregate relation, a set of pair-wise comparisons of the *m* alternatives stated in *m×m* matrix notation, encoding weak preference with Boolean values, such that *x>=y* is encoded as *1* and *x<y* as *0*.[2] A plausible aggregation of the rankings stated above is *[[1,0,0],[1,1,1],[1,0,1]]*, stating that a>=a, a<b, a<c (first line), b>=a, b>=b, b>=c (second line), and c>=a, c<b, c>=c (third line), which is equivalent to the aggregate ranking *b>c>a*. While the social choice aggregation rules are aimed at generating an ordering over all alternatives, special emphasis is on selecting the winner. If an alternative *x* exists that beats all other alternatives in pairwise comparisons, *x* is a Condorcet winner [9]. An obvious demand on an aggregation rule is that it select *x* as a winner. Another demand on an aggregation rule is that it results in an aggregate relation that can be interpreted as a preference relation, i.e., that does not contain intransitivities or cycles.

Table 1 gives a short overview of popular methods of rank aggregation from social choice theory, which will be forwarded into case study and simulation analysis. A more detailed definition is supplied by existing literature [9, 11].

While the first eight rules can be computed in polynomial time on *n* and *m,* the last four rules in the list (KE, SL, YO and DO) are computationally more costly and become impractical with larger numbers of alternatives and voters. However, in the typical IS selection the number of alternatives is not very large, and with typical values of *m<=3* and *n<=25* the computational complexity of even the Dodgson rule does not pose a problem. In the following section we will take a look at such an IS selection problem and apply the rules discussed to that situation.

Table 1. Considered methods of rank aggregation from social choice theory.

Selection Rule	Description
Simple Majority (SM)	Simple Majority is a well-known voting procedure which counts the number of rankings where alternative x is preferred to y versus the number of rankings where y is preferred to x; a positive margin means that x wins against y in pair-wise comparison and results in x>y, a negative margins leads to x<y, and a zero margin means indifference. This rule can easily result in cycles, such that x>y, y>z, z>x (drop the fourth voter from the above example to arrive at a cycle). In addition, transitivity is not guaranteed, i.e. x>y and y>z does not necessarily entail x>z. These disadvantages limit the use of the SM rule in practical applications.
Transitive	The transitive closure applies repeated matrix multiplication of the

---

2 Encoding weak preference instead of strict preference has the advantage that indifference can be encoded as well, by stating 1 both for *x>=y* and *y>=x*.

Closure (TC)	SM rule relation with itself until no more change occurs, in order to arrive at a transitive relation. This approach can result in a large winner set, again limiting the practical use of this rule.
Maximin (MM)	The Maximin rule scores the alternatives with the worst margin they each achieve and ranks them according to those scores. All scoring rules share the distinct advantage that there are never any intransitivities or cycles.
Copeland (CO)	The Copeland rule scores the alternatives with the sum over the signs of the margins they achieve and ranks them according to these scores.
Plurality (PL)	The plurality rule ranks the alternatives according to the number of times they received top place. While easily understood and commonly applied, especially in political elections, this rule often fails the put the Condorcet winner in the winning set, if one exists. This is not surprising considering the fact that this rule ignores all the preference information stated by the voters except for the top-ranked alternative.
Antiplurality (AP)	A similar rule known as the Antiplurality rule ranks the alternatives according to the number of times they did not received last place. This rule also often fails to elect the Condorcet winner if it exists.
Borda (BO)	The Borda rule assigns decreasing points to consecutive positions, such as 2 points for first place, 1 point for second and zero for third. The alternatives are then ranked according to their total score.
Nanson (NA)	The Nanson rule repeatedly calculates the Borda scores and drops the alternatives with the minimal scores, using the iteration number for the final ranking, i.e. alternatives which survive the dropping process longer are ranked higher.
Kemeny (KE)	The Kemeny rule chooses the ordering with minimal distance to all rankings in the profile, where distance is defined as the number of different pairwise relations.
Slater (SL)	The Slater rule chooses the ordering with minimal distance to the outcome of the simple majority rule, where distance is defined as the number of different entries in the aggregate relations.
Young (YO)	The Young rule ranks alternative x by the minimum number of voters which must be dropped to make x an SM winner.
Dodgson (DO)	The Dodgson rule ranks alternative x by the minimum number of switches of adjacent alternatives in the voters' rankings it takes to make x an SMR winner.

4 Case Study

This case analysis refers to Primagaz Austria, an international wholesaler of liquid and gaseous fuels and related products (SHV Holdings N.V.). It needed to replace their legacy IT environment for Enterprise Resources Planning (ERP) applications through standard software. Their independent decision making process was based on multiple attributes and alternatives. Thus, it provided an ideal grounding for ERP/IS investment appraisal analysis with multiple criteria.

The applied ERP decision making methodology was based on the NWA complemented with vendor related perceptions and a separate financial analysis. The NWA yielded an ERP utility score for each alternative (we will refer to them as A, B and C) through simple additive weighting based on a number of pre-selected attributes reflecting their specific range of targeted software specific functionalities and benefits. Table 2 denotes the defined categories with the scores of the three pre-selected alternatives.

Table 2. Scores from individual categories in the Primagaz case study.

Category	Alternative A	Alternative B	Alternative C
Controlling and Reporting	13	15	14
Accounting	14	21	16
Logistics	9	6	6
Purchasing	8	7	5
Local Divisions	12	13	9
Services and Engineering	15	18	18
Sales	24	25	27
Management	13	16	14

Source: Case study

The weighted utility scores for the three alternatives A, B, and C were 253, 288 and 252 respectively. Alternative B outranks its opponents whereas A and C seem to have a tie, i.e. they can be considered as equally good. This situation demonstrates shortcomings of the NWA: The resulting utility scores are hardly interpretable and do not provide a clear-cut ranking. Furthermore, the common mistake of using ordinally scaled utility values in a simple additive weighting model was observed.

The application of social choice rules would limit the demands placed on the data considerably. No value judgments and no weighting of attributes would be needed. Removing weights from the analysis has the implicit assumption that every attribute is of equal importance. Therefore, analyzing the robustness of the winner becomes even more important. Preference information must be gathered in terms of the alternatives for each dimension/attribute, which were derived for our ex post analysis from the supplied case study data. The aggregation rules described above were applied to the preferences resulting from the application of 8 criteria to 3 alternatives in the case study. For this purpose, the values from Table 2 were translated into rankings for each category, such as B>C>A for Controlling, B>A>C for Purchasing, and so on. The ties in Logistics and Services were broken lexicographically, i.e. A>B>C for Logistics, and B>C>A for Services. The result is shown in Table 3.

In terms of alternative B, the application of all methods validates B as the winner, i.e. as the best alternative. This remains unchanged even if the ties in Logistics and Services are resolved differently. Table 4 gives an overview of the results for all four combinations of tie resolves. In terms of the remaining alternatives, C seems to be slightly preferable in comparison to A. The results suggest further investigating the ratings of A compared to C in order to achieve a more stable ranking outcome. Similar interpretations were achieved in the NWA, where A was valued higher by one value unit in comparison with C.

Applying different voting rules (and, when necessary, tie resolves) to the same input data provides a simple way of judging the robustness of the results. In this example alternative B was always selected as the winner. This is an obvious indicator towards the reliability of the winner set. Furthermore, in some situations the Maximin, Young, and Plurality rules identified the almost identical utility values in the MADM analysis of alternatives A and C by stating an explicit indifference A=C.

Table 3. Application of the voting rules to the case study data, ties resolved lexicographically.

Rule	Relation	Ranking
SM	[[1,0,0],[1,1,1],[1,0,1]]	B>C>A
BO	[[1,0,0],[1,1,1],[1,0,1]]	B>C>A
CO	[[1,0,0],[1,1,1],[1,0,1]]	B>C>A
TC	[[1,0,0],[1,1,1],[1,0,1]]	B>C>A
NA	[[1,0,0],[1,1,1],[1,0,1]]	B>C>A
MM	[[1,0,1],[1,1,1],[0,0,1]]	B>A>C
KE	[[1,0,0],[1,1,1],[1,0,1]]	B>C>A
SL	[[1,0,0],[1,1,1],[1,0,1]]	B>C>A
YO	[[1,0,1],[1,1,1],[0,0,1]]	B>A>C
DO	[[1,0,0],[1,1,1],[1,0,1]]	B>C>A
PL	[[1,0,1],[1,1,1],[0,0,1]]	B>A>C
AP	[[1,0,0],[1,1,1],[1,0,1]]	B>C>A

Source: Case study

Table 4. Results for all four different ways of resolving the ties in Services and Logistics.

Rule	Ranking	Ranking	Ranking	Ranking
SM	B>C>A	B>C>A	B>C>A	B>C>A
BO	B>C>A	B>C>A	B>C>A	B>C>A
CO	B>C>A	B>C>A	B>C>A	B>C>A
TC	B>C>A	B>C>A	B>C>A	B>C>A
NA	B>C>A	B>C>A	B>C>A	B>C>A
MM	B>A>C	B>A=C	B>A=C	B>C>A
KE	B>C>A	B>C>A	B>C>A	B>C>A
SL	B>C>A	B>C>A	B>C>A	B>C>A
YO	B>A>C	B>A=C	B>A=C	B>C>A
DO	B>C>A	B>C>A	B>C>A	B>C>A
PL	B>A>C	B>A=C	B>A>C	B>A=C
AP	B>C>A	B>C>A	B>C>A	B>C>A

Source: Case study

5 Distances of Voting Rules

The case study shows the results of applying the twelve voting rules to a single set of input data. The question remains how these rules related to each other in a more general way, e.g., would the Simple Majority rule and the Borda rule always generate the same aggregate rankings, as in the case study, and if not, how much would the results differ. Therefore, all voting procedures described have been applied to a large number of random profiles, i.e. randomly generated rankings provided by voters[3]. As typical setting in IS selection problems, for each profile the number of alternatives was set to $m=3$. This count was identified as the (rounded) mean number of alternatives considered in ERP selection problems in an empirical study of Austrian medium and large scale enterprises [2]. Furthermore, the number of voters (attributes) was set to $n=25$, and the number of random profiles was 1000[4]. The aggregate relations resulting from the random profiles have been compared by using a distance measure on the $m \times m$ bit-wise comparisons in the relation generated by the voting rules [6], the number of different bits divided by $m(m-1)$ for normalization. These values are tabulated in Table 5. For instance, the very small distance value for Dodgson and Nanson of 0.02 signifies that those rules have generated very

---

[3] The simulation has been programmed in the Python language and is available for download at http://prefrule.sourceforge.net.

[4] Rankings are independent from each other and distributed uniformly over the $m!$ permutations; this is referred to as impartial culture in social choice literature.

similar relations from the random profiles. Note that for the small number of 3 alternatives some rules always provide identical results, such as Young and Maximin.

We visualized the relationship between the different rules using a method commonly used in phylogenetics, a biological research discipline which investigates the relationships of groups of organisms [8]. Pairwise distances were converted into a tree structure by the use of the Neighbor Joining algorithm, a clustering method described in [13]. Branch lengths are drawn proportional to distance. The neighbor tree resulting from the distance matrix above is shown in Figure 1. It is immediately visible that the Plurality and Antiplurality are distinctly separated from the other rules, while other rules such as Borda and Copeland are arranged closer to each other.

These findings are consistent with other results [6] in identifying Borda and Copeland as a core set of voting rules, with the remaining rules being placed apart in the neighbor tree. An important application of the simulation results is the support they provide for the composition of a social choice rule set for selecting among IS alternatives. We suggest choosing rules which show large distances in order to provide for a wide range of possibly different rankings. If the chosen set of social choice rules share a common winner it can be expected that no further robustness test is required.

Table 5. Distances of the relations generated by the voting rules on the random rankings.

Rule	SM	BO	CO	TC	NA	MM	KE	SL	YO	DO	PL	AP
SM	.000	.116	.050	.050	.066	.140	.033	.033	.140	.085	.211	.209
BO	.116	.000	.105	.105	.051	.107	.086	.121	.107	.052	.173	.173
CO	.050	.105	.000	.000	.074	.123	.050	.050	.123	.069	.201	.198
TC	.050	.105	.000	.000	.074	.123	.050	.050	.123	.069	.201	.198
NA	.066	.051	.074	.074	.000	.074	.051	.079	.074	.020	.179	.198
MM	.140	.107	.123	.123	.074	.000	.116	.147	.000	.054	.176	.221
KE	.033	.086	.050	.050	.051	.116	.000	.036	.116	.062	.195	.199
SL	.033	.121	.050	.050	.079	.147	.036	.000	.147	.093	.215	.206
YO	.140	.107	.123	.123	.074	.000	.116	.147	.000	.054	.176	.221
DO	.085	.052	.069	.069	.020	.054	.062	.093	.054	.000	.173	.197
PL	.211	.173	.201	.201	.179	.176	.195	.215	.176	.173	.000	.346
AP	.209	.173	.198	.198	.198	.221	.199	.206	.221	.197	.346	.000

Source: Simulation study

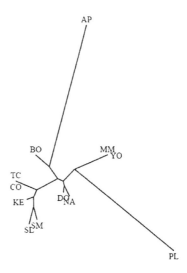

Figure 1. Nearest neighbor tree of the relation distances.

6 Conclusion

The comparison of main results from the traditional multiple attribute decision making method (NWA) and from the set of applied social choice rules are the same. We have a distinct winner, on the second rank C has a minor advantage over B which is ranked third. A main difference lies in the complexity and input data demands of both approaches. Whereas the NWA needs the definition of weights for each criteria and the determination of attribute values (on a metric scale), respectively of single-attribute value functions, for each alternative, the social choice methods are content with a set of simple preference relations. For the former, problems in quantifying weights and criteria values as well as errors in method application, e.g. wrong scale definitions and transformations, are well known as mentioned in the article. Especially in critical decisions, such as large scale IS investments, an understandable and accountable decision support is needed for all involved stakeholders.

The simulation results, especially the graphical representation, give an intuitive impression of the effect of rule choice on the outcome of the aggregation process. Borda and Copeland will generate more similar results than Plurality and Antiplurality. A possible application of this figure is to determine a choice of methods based on their disparity in these result, which can be used for decision making or validating purposes. If strongly differential rules produce the same ranking outcomes, then the validity of the results is supported, otherwise questioned. The usage of a set of methods and comparison of ranking outcomes can supply the kind of easy and intuitive MADM validation called for in practical applications.

Future work will further analyze characteristics of voting rules and consequence for MADM in IS selection, such as manipulability, Condorcet criterion, and computational feasibility. Based on the achieved results, a modified NWA based procedural model will be developed to supply business practice with the possibility of selecting a suitable aggregation rule portfolio including diverse social choice selection rules. The main goal is to apply less information demanding MADM selection approaches and also to support validation, since this requirement is often neglected in practice.

References

1. Arrow, K.J., *Social Choice and Individual Values*, Wiley, New York, 2nd Edition (1963)
2. Bernroider, E, Mitlöhner, J., "Characteristics of the Multiple Attribute Decision Making Methodology in Enterprise Resource Planning Software Decisions", *Communications of the International Information Management Association* (CIIMA), 5 (2005), pp 49-58
3. Borda, J.C., "Mathematical Derivation of an Election System", *Isis*, (1781), 44, pp. 42-51
4. Bouyssou, D., Marchant, T., Pirlot, M., Perny, P., Tsoukias, A., Vincke, P., *Evaluation and Decision Models - A critical Perspective*, Kluwer Academic Publishers, Boston (2000)
5. Condorcet, M.J.A.N.C., *Essai sur l'application de l'analyse μa la probabilité des décisions rendues à la pluralité des voix*, Imprimerie Royale, Paris (1785)
6. Eckert, D., Klamler, C., Mitlöhner, J., Schlötterer, C., "A Distance-based Comparison of basic Voting Rules", In: Joint Workshop on Decision Support Systems, Experimental Economics and e-Participation, Graz, Austria (2005), pp 131-138.
7. Farbey, B., Targett, D., Land, F., "The great IT benefit hunt", *European Management Journal*, 12(3) (1994) pp 270-279
8. Felsenstein, J., Inferring Phylogenies, Sinauer Associates, Sunderland, MA (2004)
9. Fishburn, P.C., "Condorcet Social Choice Functions", *Siam Journal of Applied Mathematics*, 33 (1977) pp 469-489
10. Parker, M.M., Benson, R.J., Trainor, H.E., *Information Economics, Linking Business Performance to Information Technology*, Prentice-Hall, New Jersey (1988)
11. Saari, D., *Decisions and Elections – Explaining the Unexpected*, Cambridge University Press (2001)
12. Saaty,T.L., *The Analytic Hierarchy Process*, McGraw Hill, New York (1980)
13. Saitou, N., Nei, M., "The Neighbor-Joining Method: a new Method for Reconstruction of Phylogenetic Trees", Mol. Biol. Evol., 4 (1987), pp 406-425
14. Triantaphyllou, E., *Multi-Criteria Decision Making Methods: A Comparative Study*, Kluwer Academic Publishers, London (2000)
15. Yeh, C.H., "The selection of multiattribute decision making methods for scholarship student selection", *International Journal of Selection and Assessment*, 11(4) (2003) pp. 289-296
16. Zangemeister, C., *Nutzwertanalyse in der Systemtechnik*, Wittemann, Munich (1976).

Individual's Response to Security Messages: A Decision-Making Perspective

Tang Qing[1], Boon-Yuen Ng[1], Atreyi Kankanhalli [1]

[1] Department of Information Systems, School of Computing,
National University of Singapore, 3 Science Drive 2, Singapore 117543

atreyi@comp.nus.edu.sg

Abstract. Individual decision making determines critical outcomes for organizations in various domains including information security, where the increase of security incidents is causing great concern to organizations. Information security awareness programs are an important approach towards educating users to prevent such incidents. However, it is unclear how to effectively design security programs and messages such that they can inform and change user behavior. This paper attempts to investigate this problem by studying the effects of security message characteristics on users, using the decision-making theory of elaboration likelihood. A 2x2 factorial design experiment was conducted to determine the influence of message repetition and message comprehensibility on user's elaboration likelihood towards a security message. Our findings indicate that message repetition enhances elaboration likelihood of users. Message comprehensibility interacts with message repetition in determining elaboration likelihood. The results have implications for designing effective security messages and for decision support systems for this purpose.

Keywords: information security, security awareness, security message characteristics, elaboration likelihood model

1 Introduction

Human decision-making behavior has received much interest in the management and information systems literature [11, 20, 21]. Decision making of individuals in various domains such as sales and marketing, strategic planning, operations and logistics, determine critical outcomes for organizations [27, 17]. One such domain is information security where the increasing frequency of security incidents is causing great concern to organizations [10]. The management of information security is vital for today's global enterprises, with the growing global interdependency and the vast amount of valuable information flowing between business partners, suppliers and customers.

According to the annual CSI/FBI survey [9], 56% of respondents indicated that their organization experienced computer security incidents within the last 12 months. Further, total financial loss per respondent amounted to US$203,606. Of all the types of attacks or misuse detected, virus attacks continue to be the most reported and the source of the greatest financial loss [9].

In the face of security threats, organizations have implemented a variety of technical measures such as firewalls and intrusion detection systems to bolster their defenses. However, deploying sophisticated security techniques is not sufficient in preventing security incidents. Many people in the security business regard the human factor as the weakest link in security solutions [22, 19]. User behavior, e.g., forgetting passwords or not installing patches, is found to play a part in many security failures. Therefore, management is beginning to realize the importance of security awareness training of users [25, 26].

Previous research on approaches to deal with human failures in security has classified the approaches into two categories, i.e., non-punishment and punishment/deterrence [23]. While some studies suggest that punishment works well [24], several adverse effects of punishment based approaches have been reported. These side effects include loss of trust, productivity and loyalty, increased dissatisfaction and stress, aggression and fear [22]. Therefore a balance of punishment and non-punishment based approaches is recommended [10].

Of the non-punishment based approaches, the most commonly used techniques are information security awareness education and training. The term information security awareness refers to a state where users in an organization are aware of and committed to the security mission expressed in their organization's end-user security guidelines. Increasing awareness towards information security should be able to minimize user-related faults [22].

Information security awareness programs need to be designed to educate users to become more aware of the risks and their responsibilities towards information security. However, it is not clear how to effectively design information security awareness programs and messages such that they can have maximum impact in terms of changing user behavior. While there are many guidelines for designing security awareness programs in practice, their effectiveness has not been investigated from a theoretical standpoint. The guidelines are mainly practices without empirical and theoretical support.

The way in which the security messages in the awareness program are framed is particularly important in determining their effectiveness. However, there is little knowledge of how to design these messages to maximize their effectiveness. Therefore, this paper attempts to investigate this problem by studying the effects of security message characteristics on users thinking.

In this regard, behavioral theories of decision-making can help elucidate how changes in behavior can be effected. One such behavioral decision making theory is the elaboration likelihood model (ELM). ELM explains the conditions under which people decide to think attentively or expeditiously [15]. When people think attentively and with effort in response to a message, they are more likely to be persuaded by the message.

Hence, this study investigates the influence of message characteristics on elaboration likelihood in the context of information security awareness. An experiment is designed to manipulate two message properties, message repetition and message likelihood, and observe their effects on elaboration likelihood in response to the message. The results of this study are expected to benefit security practitioners by assisting them in designing more effective information security awareness programs in future. Specifically it should help them understand how individual users decide to adopt security practices based on the type of message they receive. In terms of IT, it should help them implement more effective decision support systems used to design such programs. Theoretically it should provide a basis for application of decision-making theories like ELM to the security awareness domain.

While this section provided the motivation and background for the study, the rest of the paper is structured as follows. The next section contains a literature review of security awareness, ELM, and factors affecting elaboration likelihood, tuned to the context of our study. The following section describes the research model and hypotheses. Subsequently the experimental methodology is explained. This is followed by a description of the results and ending with the discussion and implications of the study.

2   Literature Review

2.1   Information Security Awareness

Information security awareness programs are considered as the essential tool to educate users. Thomson and Solms [26] suggest principles that will help improve the effectiveness of these programs. They propose that the behavior of people can be changed in three ways, i.e., directly changing their behavior, using a change in behavior to influence a person's attitude, changing a person's attitude through persuasion. The focus of this study is on changing a person's attitude through persuasion, since security messages in information security awareness programs are intended for that purpose.

Behavioral theories (e.g. [1]) suggest that a change in attitude will ultimately change people's behavior. A five-step persuasion method has been proposed i.e., exposure, attention, comprehension, acceptance, and retention [26]. First, users have to be comfortable with listening to the message, followed by paying attention to the message, understanding the message, and accepting the message. Lastly, retention deals with ensuring that the intended attitude is maintained for a long period.

2.2   Elaboration Likelihood Model

Among theories of decision-making, the elaboration likelihood model (ELM) has been used for explaining attitude change through persuasion [16]. It has been widely applied in various areas, particularly to the persuasion of consumers by advertising messages (e.g. [6, 13]). ELM provides a general framework for understanding the effectiveness of persuasive communications.

ELM posits that there are two different routes that lead to attitude change, i.e., central route and peripheral route. The central route involves effortful cognitive activity in which the message recipient carefully evaluates all the information presented in support of the advocated position. The recipient considers the quality of the message content and the merits of the arguments. In other words, the elaboration likelihood of the message is high.

The peripheral route involves the use of simple cues rather than systematically processing the message arguments. This route elicits an affective state (such as happiness) that becomes associated with the advocated position or triggers a relatively simple inference or heuristic cue that a person can use to judge the validity of the message. For example, a message from an expert can be judged by the heuristic, "experts are generally correct" without the message recipient devoting much effort to assess the actual merits and implications of the information provided [5]. Similarly, a message with many arguments can be accepted if a person thinks that "more is better" without the need to carefully evaluate the truth of those arguments [15].

The choice of the route is determined by the person's motivation and ability to elaborate, or process the arguments of a persuasive message. If both motivation and ability to elaborate are high, the central route is more likely to be taken. If the motivation and/or ability to elaborate are low, the peripheral route is more likely. As motivation and ability to process arguments decreases, peripheral cues become relatively more important determinants of persuasion. Conversely, as argument scrutiny increases, peripheral cues become relatively less important determinants of persuasion [16].

Research has shown that attitude changes that result from central route processing of issue-relevant arguments will show greater temporal persistence, greater prediction of behavior, and greater resistance to counter-persuasion than attitude changes that result from peripheral cues [16]. By increasing people's motivation and ability to process the message, their elaboration likelihood towards persuasion can be increased as it is more likely for the central route to be taken. This, in turn, leads to a more consistent and permanent change in attitude.

2.3 Factors Affecting Elaboration Likelihood

Different factors are suggested to influence a person's motivation to think about a message, such as whether the message is perceived to be personally relevant [16] or whether the person is the kind of individual who enjoys thinking [4]. Such variables are known as motivational variables i.e., they can affect a person's conscious intentions and goals in processing a message. In addition, certain variables can influence a person's ability to think about a message, such as whether the person has any prior knowledge to understand the communication [28]. These are known as ability variables i.e., they may affect the extent or direction of message scrutiny without the necessary intervention of conscious intent. If a person is both motivated and able to think about the underlying arguments in a message, the end result of this careful evaluation is a high level of elaboration likelihood level that will lead to an attitude that is well articulated and integrated into the person's belief structure [16].

Of the motivational variables, personal relevance and need for cognition are considered the two most salient factors. Variables affecting people's ability to think about the message include both message characteristics, e.g., message comprehensibility and message repetition, and individual characteristics, e.g., user's prior knowledge about the message topic. Since our objective is to improve the design of security messages, our study manipulates message characteristics and retains the other variables as controls.

3 Research Model and Hypotheses

As described in the previous section, motivational factors and ability factors are two types of variables that may affect elaboration likelihood. In this study, we will focus on two particular ability variables, i.e., message comprehensibility and message repetition. By manipulating these properties of the message, we can study whether they affect recipients' elaboration likelihood. Individual characteristics like prior knowledge, personal relevance, and need for cognition serve as control variables. Through manipulation of message properties, we will study if the central or peripheral route is taken, which in turn may lead to change in attitude and ultimately, change in behavior.

3.1 Message Comprehensibility

Message comprehensibility refers to the extent to which the message is designed for recipients' ease of understanding. In the context of security awareness, we define message comprehensibility as the property of the security message to be easily read and understood. Ratneshwar and Chaiken [18] tested the effect of message comprehensibility in their Heuristic Systematic Model. It was found that message comprehensibility positively impacted consumer's ability in systematic processing. Moreover, Eagly and Himmelfarb [8] hypothesized and found that reduced comprehension may decrease persuasion. Petty and Cacioppo [16] also stated that comprehensibility of the message might affect elaboration likelihood by increasing recipients' ability to think about the message. Based on these arguments, we propose:

H1: Message comprehensibility is positively related to elaboration likelihood.

3.2 Message Repetition

Message repetition is defined as the repeated times of exposure to a message. In the context of security awareness, we modify this concept somewhat to define message repetition as the repeated exposure to the arguments of a security message. In particular, Berlyne's two-factor theory shows an inverted U-curve relationship between message repetition and its effectiveness [2]. Increasing the number of exposure to a message from a low to a moderate level is expected to enhance its impact by give people a feeling of familiarity, whereas further exposure is expected to reduce its effectiveness. Research has shown that memorization of at least one of the message arguments caused by repetition significantly enhances attitude change [7]. Hence, we propose that repetition of message arguments should lead to greater elaboration likelihood.

H2: Message repetition is positively related to elaboration likelihood.

The resultant research model is shown in Figure 1.

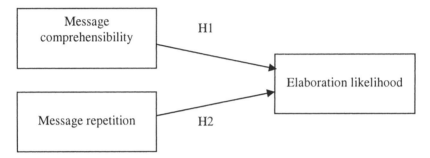

Figure 1. Research model.

4   Research Methodology

The methodology used in this study is a two-by-two factorial design experiment. In the experiment, the independent variables are message comprehensibility and message repetition and the dependent variable is the elaboration likelihood of the security message. Need for cognition, personal relevance, and prior knowledge of the information security message topic are control variables.

4.1   Operationalization of Constructs

The security message in our study was a message taken from a security awareness campaign of a university, informing students about an anti-virus software package that they could install on their computers. Based on this message, four versions of the security message were created, i.e., high / low on message comprehensibility and with / without message repetition. The items for each model construct were generated based on previous literature and modified to the context of our study. The measurement of each construct is discussed below.

The high comprehensibility messages were written in simple English and avoided the use of jargon. On the other hand, the low comprehensibility messages had complex sentence structures and vocabulary including security terminologies. Message repetition was manipulated by including the arguments once in the message without repetition and repeating the arguments several times in the message with repetition. Examples to illustrate high/low comprehensibility and message repetition can be found in the Appendix.

Elaboration likelihood is defined as extensiveness of information processing that the person engages in with respect to the message and evaluation of message quality. Methods for its assessment include self-reports of effort, argument recall, thought-listing, electrophysiological activity, and evaluation of argument quality. In this study, we used five items related to self-reports of effort and argument recall measures of elaboration likelihood from Petty and Cacioppo [16].

Need for cognition is defined as an individual's tendency to engage in and enjoy effortful cognitive endeavors. Eight items measuring need for cognition are adapted from the standard scale for this construct proposed by Cacioppo et al [3].

Personal relevance is defined as the extent that recipients perceive the message to be self-related or in some way instrumental in achieving their personal goals and values. We redefine personal relevance in the context of our study as the extent that users perceive using anti-virus software to be self-related or in some way instrumental in achieving their personal goals and values. It is represented by perceived linkage between an individual's needs, goals, and values and their computer security knowledge. Our three items for measuring this construct are derived from the scales by Zaichkowsky [29].

The measures for prior knowledge are based on the definition of the variable, i.e., the quantity and type of previous knowledge users acquired through their own experience in computer security, which influences the availability and accessibility of knowledge of the security issue at hand. Therefore, four questions such as "have you used the software before" were asked to test respondents' prior knowledge about the anti-virus software.

4.2 Pretest and Sorting

After the generation of construct items, pretest interviews were conducted with four faculty experts. To address the issue of content validity of the instrument, the experts were asked to evaluate the items and the four versions of the security message. The items and messages were refined based on the comments of the experts. Thereafter, four versions of the security message were reviewed by four students from non-computing background to provide feedback concerning the message comprehensibility and argument repetition of each version.

Subsequently, labeled sorting was done to formally validate the questionnaire items [14]. Three judges were involved in the first round and an average placement ratio of 74% was obtained. After refining the items based on the first round comments, a second round of labeled sorting was conducted with four new judges. The second round sorting results showed an average placement ratio of 87%, which is acceptable and indicates that most of the items were categorized correctly.

4.3 Experiment Design

The experimental design follows the posttest-only control group design proposed by Petty and Cacioppo [15], which is widely used in the study of ELM. In this design, elaboration likelihood is only measured after the test i.e., exposure to the message. Forty-one subjects were selected randomly from an undergraduate class consisting of students from different faculties. The subjects were randomly assigned to the four treatments i.e., high/low comprehensibility and with/without repetition. A survey was administered at the start of the experiment to measure the control variables, i.e., prior knowledge, need for cognition, personal relevance, and demographic characteristics. Six subjects with extreme scores in the pre-experiment survey were eliminated to ensure that the subjects have similar levels of motivation and ability to start with.

Upon finishing the survey, the subjects proceeded with the experiment. The experimental task involved reading the message printed on a sheet of paper about good security practices and recommending an anti-virus software. Subjects were required to answer another questionnaire after reading the message. The message was collected back before giving the questionnaire. Hence subjects could not refer to the message as they filled out the questionnaire. The second questionnaire contained items to check the manipulation of message comprehensibility as well as the items to measure elaboration likelihood (including effort and argument recall).

The experimental design and the distribution of subjects are summarized in Table 1.

Table 1. Experiment design.

	Low comprehensibility	High comprehensibility	Total
Without repetition	9 subjects	9 subjects	18 subjects
With repetition	9 subjects	8 subjects	17 subjects
Total	18 subjects	17 subjects	35 subjects

5 Data Analysis and Results

The descriptive statistics of the sample indicate that the majority of respondents were male (61%), in the age-group 20-25 (39%), and had experience of at least 5 years in using a computer (81%).

The analysis of variance (ANOVA) test was used to detect significant main and interaction effects. A five percent level of significance was used for all the statistical tests. The SPSS software was used to perform the statistical tests.

The results of statistical analysis are presented in two tables. The first table (Table 2) presents the mean and standard deviation for the dependent variable elaboration likelihood under each treatment condition. The second table (Table 3) presents the results of the ANOVA test for the dependent variable.

Table 2. Elaboration likelihood mean and standard deviation for each group

Treatment	Low comprehensibility	High comprehensibility	Total
With repetition	4.30 (0.60)	4.42 (0.44)	4.364 (0.51)
Without repetition	3.89 (0.417)	3.972 (0.491)	3.935 (0.443)
Total	4.103 (0.54)	4.196 (0.510)	

The mean analysis indicates that repetition manipulation resulted in an average difference of 0.429 in elaboration likelihood while comprehensibility manipulation resulted in an average difference of 0.093, indicating that the impact of comprehensibility is weaker than repetition. The mean difference in the dependent variable between low comprehensibility without repetition and high comprehensibility with repetition is 0.53. The mean and standard deviation values are not sufficient to conclude the effects. To test whether the impact is significant, ANOVA is required [12].

Table 3 reports the results of the ANOVA test on elaboration likelihood. Message repetition had a significant main effect on elaboration likelihood (H2 is supported). On the other hand, the effect of message comprehensibility on elaboration likelihood is not significant (H1 is not supported). The interaction effect of message comprehensibility and message repetition on elaboration likelihood is significant.

Table 3. Analysis of variance for elaboration likelihood

	Df	Sum Sq	Mean Sq	F value	Prop>F
Repetition	1	2.83	2.83	15.04	0.0005***
Comprehensibility	1	0.61	0.61	3.25	0.081
Repetition * Comprehensibility	1	0.78	0.78	4.15	0.050*
Residuals	32	6.03	0.19		

Figure 2 shows the dependent measures of the four groups. The group with low message comprehensibility and without message repetition is set as the baseline treatment group and the score is set to 100%. The other three groups have scores that are divided by the score of the baseline group, thus giving measures that are relative to the baseline group. Figure 3 presents a clearer view of message repetition and comprehensibility effects on elaboration likelihood. Starting from the baseline group of low comprehensibility and without message repetition, the group with high message comprehensibility and without message repetition exhibits a higher elaboration likelihood score than the baseline group (around 2%). The group with message repetition and low message comprehensibility expressed a larger impact on elaboration likelihood (10% more than the baseline group). The interaction effect between message repetition and message comprehensibility can also be observed in Figure 3, where the highest elaboration likelihood score is from the group with message repetition and high message comprehensibility (around 14% above the baseline group).

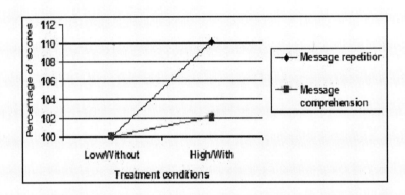

Figure 2. Elaboration likelihood level expressed as percentage of scores relative to low comprehensibility / without repetition group

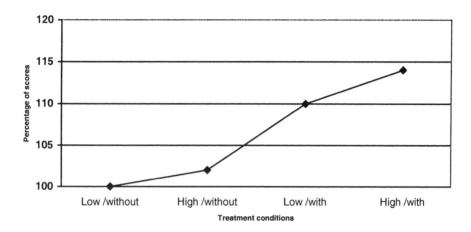

Figure 3. Elaboration likelihood level expressed as percentage of scores relative to low comprehensibility/ no repetition group

6 Discussion

6.1 Discussion of Results

Our findings provide some insights on how persuasion and decision-making theories can be applied to the area of information security awareness. The results of the data analysis indicate that message repetition has a positive relationship with elaboration likelihood, i.e., message repetition can increase recipient's elaboration likelihood towards security messages. Nevertheless, their elaboration likelihood is not affected by message comprehensibility except under conditions of message repetition. The reason for the lack of effect of message comprehensibility might be because of the subjective taste of recipients regarding message comprehensibility. Some people may prefer messages with more explanation, so that they can understand better. Yet other people may feel confused when lots of information is provided in the message. Use of jargon and terms may be helpful in technical fields such as information security. Although they make the message complex, jargon can be reassuring to readers and give precise meanings. Therefore the effect of comprehensibility of the message may depend on the type of topic and the preferences of the recipient.

The interaction effect between message comprehensibility and repetition is significant in this study. An in-depth analysis of the interaction is required because the interpretation of an interaction takes precedence over the interpretation of a significant main effect [12]. It appears that comprehensibility strengthens the effect of repetition on elaboration likelihood.

6.2 Implications

The finding that message repetition affects elaboration likelihood has implications for practitioners in the field of information security awareness program design. From a practitioner perspective, security program designers should be aware of message repetition's effect on audience elaboration likelihood. Particularly, they should repeat the arguments of message, e.g., summarize arguments at the end of each message part and repeat them in the conclusion.

From the academic perspective, this study appears to indicate that ELM can be used to explain decision-making and persuasion in the area of information systems security training and awareness. ELM can explain the effect of motivation and ability factors on the effectiveness of security messages. This helps to address the lack of previous research in this area that was theoretically based and empirically validated.

6.3 Limitations and Future Research

There are some limitations of our study that should be taken into account when interpreting the results. One limitation is that the sample size of the experiment is small. Since this study is an initial test, future studies should include larger sample sizes. Second, our study didn't measure the long-term effect of different routes of elaboration on attitude and behavior change. Future studies can perform such longitudinal analyses.

This study has addressed the effect of two variables on elaboration likelihood. There are other properties of messages that can influence elaboration likelihood, e.g., modality of message presentation. In future, more studies are needed to identify the relationships of other motivation and ability variables towards elaboration likelihood.

7 Conclusion

More and more organizations are realizing the importance of information security due to the increasing occurrence of security incidents. Conducting security awareness programs is one of the most popular approaches to educate users in conjunction with the implementation of technical security measures and deterrents. However, current security awareness program frameworks have not been assessed for their effectiveness. This calls for theoretically based, empirically validated research in this area.

In response to this need, this study investigated how security message characteristics impact elaboration likelihood of users, and thereby affect effectiveness of information security awareness programs. To test the research model, an experiment was conducted to collect empirical data. The instrument used in this experiment underwent an extensive process of refinement to ensure its reliability and validity.

The study contributes to research and practice in several ways. First, this is an initial study in the field that applied decision-making models such as ELM in the information security awareness area. Second, the results of the study indicate that security message characteristics can affect user's effort put in to understand the message. It provides empirical evidences that message repetition can enhance user's scrutiny towards security messages. Therefore, in the process of designing security awareness programs, designers need to be aware of such properties of messages. Studies of this nature can help to further our knowledge of how to design information security awareness programs, both manually and through decision support systems.

References

1. Ajzen, I.: Nature and Operation of Attitudes, Annual Review of Psychology, Vol. 52 v2001) 27-58
2. Berlyne, D.E.: Motivational Problems Raised by Exploratory and Epistemic Behavior. In: Psychology: A Study of Science (5), New York: McGraw-Hill (1963) 284-364
3. Cacioppo, J.T., Petty, R.E., and Chuan, F.K.: The Efficient Assessment of Need for Cognition, Journal of Personality Assessment, Vol. 48:3 (1984) 306-307
4. Cacioppo, J.T., Petty, R.E., and Morris, K.J.: Effects of Need for Cognition on Message Evaluation, Recall, and Persuasion, Journal of Personality and Social Psychology, Vol. 45 (1983) 805-818
5. Chaiken, S.: The Heuristic Model of Persuasion. In: Social Influence: The Ontario Symposium, M.P. Zanna, J.M. Olson, and C.P. Herman (eds.), Vol. 5, Hillsdale: Erlbaum, (1987) 3-39
6. Chebat, J.C., Charlebois, M., and Gelinas-Chebat, C.: What Makes Open vs. Closed Conclusion Advertisements More Persuasive? The Moderating Role of Prior Knowledge and Involvement, Journal of Business Research, Vol. 53 (2001) 93-102
7. Chebat, J.C., Laroche, M., Baddoura, D., and Filiatrault, P.: Effects of Source Likeability on Attitude Change through Message Repetition, Advances in Consumer Research, Vol. 19 (1992) 353-357
8. Eagly, A.H. and Himmelfarb, S.: Current Trends in Attitude Theory and Research. In: Readings in Attitude Change, S. Himmelfarb and A. Eagly (eds.), Wiley, New York (1974)
9. Gordon, L.A., Loeb, M.P., Lucyshyn, W., and Richardson, R.: 2005 CSI/FBI Computer Crime and Security Survey, Computer Security Institute, July 2005, Accessed 8 May 2006. http://www.gocsi.com/forms/fbi/csi_fbi_survey.jhtml
10. Kankanhalli, A., Teo, H.H., Tan, B.C.Y., and Wei, K.K.: An Integrative Study of Information Systems Security Effectiveness, International Journal of Information Management, Vol. 23 (2003) 139-154
11. Keen, P.G.W. and Scott Morton, M.S.: Decision Support Systems: An Organizational Perspective, Addison-Wesley, Reading, Mass. (1978)

12. Keppel, G.: Design and Analysis: A Researcher's Handbook (3rd Ed.), Prentice Hall, New Jersey (1991)
13. Laroche, M., Cleveland, M., and Maravelakis, I.: Attitude Accessibility, Certainty and the Attitude-Behavior Relationship: An Empirical Study of Ad Repetition and Competitive Interference Effects, International Journal of Advertising, Vol. 21 (2002) 149-174
14. Moore, G.C. and Benbasat, I.: Development of an Instrument to Measure the Perceptions of Adopting an Information Technology Innovation, Information Systems Research, Vol. 2:3 (1991) 173-191
15. Petty, R.E., and Cacioppo, J.T.: Source Factors and the Elaboration Likelihood Model of Persuasion, Advances in Consumer Research, Vol. 11:1 (1984) 668-670
16. Petty, R.E., and Cacioppo, J.T.: Communication and Persuasion: Central and Peripheral Routes to Attitude Change, Springer-Verlag, New York (1986)
17. Power, D.J.: A Brief History of Decision Support Systems. DSSResources.COM, World Wide Web, http://DSSResources.COM/history/dsshistory.html, version 2.8, May 31, (2003)
18. Ratneshwar, S., and Chaiken, S.: Comprehension's Role in Persuasion: The Case of Its Moderating Effect on the Persuasive Impact of Source Cues, Journal of Consumer Research, Vol. 18 (1991) 52-62
19. Sasse, M.A., Brostoff, S., and Weirich, D.: Transforming the 'Weakest Link': A Human/Computer Interaction Approach to Usable and Effective Security, BT Technology Journal, Vol. 19 (2001) 122-131
20. Sharda, R., Barr, S., and McDonnell, J.: Decision Support Systems Effectiveness: A Review and an Empirical Test, Management Science, Vol. 34:2 (1988) 139-159
21. Simon, H.A.: Administrative Behavior (4th Ed.). Free Press, New York (1997)
22. Siponen, M.T.: A Conceptual Foundation for Organizational Information Security Awareness, Information Management and Computer Security, Vol. 8:1 (2000) 31-41
23. Siponen, M.T.: Critical Analysis of Different Approaches to Minimizing User-Related Faults in Information Systems Security: Implications for Research and Practice, Information Management and Computer Security, Vol. 8:5 (2000) 197-209
24. Straub, D.: Effective IS Security: An Empirical Study, Information Systems Research, Vol. 1:3 (1990) 255-276
25. Straub, D., and Welke, R.: Coping with Systems Risk: Security Planning Models for Management Decision-Making, MIS Quarterly, Vol. 22:4 (1998) 441-469
26. Thomson, M.E., and Solms, R.V.: Information Security Awareness: Educating Your Users Effectively, Information Management and Computer Security, Vol. 6:4 (1998) 167-173
27. Todd, P., and Benbasat, I.: The Impact of Information Technology on Decision Making: A Cognitive Perspective. In: Framing the Domains of IT Management, R.W. Zmud (ed.), Pinnaflex Educational Resources (2000) 1-14
28. Wood, W., Kallgren, C., and Preisler, R.M.: Access to Attitude-Relevant Information in Memory as a Determinant of Persuasion: The Role of Message Attributes, Journal of Experimental Social Psychology, Vol. 21 (1985) 73-85
29. Zaichkowsky, J.L.: Measuring the Involvement Construct, Journal of Consumer Research, Vol. 12 (1985) 341-352

Appendix: Manipulation of Message Properties

Table A1 gives an example of how message repetition is manipulated.

Table A1. Manipulation for message repetition

Without Message Repetition	With Message Repetition
The school recommends Protect Client[5]. It can protect your computer from viruses and updates are very easy.	The school recommends Protect Client. It can protect your computer from viruses and updates are very easy. It not only protects computers from virus infection, but also makes the update of virus definition and implementation of security policy more convenient.

Table A2 gives an example of how message comprehensibility is manipulated.

Table A2. Manipulation for message comprehensibility.

High Message Comprehensibility	Low Message Comprehensibility
A virus is a harmful software program whose sole purpose is to do damage to your computer and the information stored in it.	A virus is a code fragment that copies itself into a larger program, modifying that program. The virus then replicate itself, infecting other programs as it reproduces.
The school recommends Protect Client. It can protect your computer from viruses and updates are very easy.	The school recommends Protect Client, which is an integrated client security solution that protects campus networks from viruses, Trojans, worms, hackers, and network viruses, plus spyware and mixed threat attacks.

---

[5] The name of the software has been changed for confidentiality.

III. SUCCESSES AND FAILURES:
Learning from Experience

An Analysis of ERP Decision Making Practice and Consequences for Subsequent System Life Cycle Stages: A Case Study

Edward W. N. Bernroider[1]

[1]Vienna University of Economics and Business Administration,
Department of Information Systems and Operations, Augasse 2-6, 1090 Vienna, Austria

Edward.Bernroider@wu-wien.ac.at

Abstract. Enterprise resource planning (ERP) projects are highly complex information technology (IT) based business initiatives that should be grounded on a strategic infrastructure decision adding value to the firms' IT infrastructure capability. Not every ERP project is seen in this sense and research has placed a focus on the more technical viewpoint of ERP. This article provides an analysis based on a case study of a strategy driven ERP decision with an emphasis on the organizational fit of ERP. It shows the organizational impact of the ERP project, especially pertaining to project costs and utility, in comparison with the common practice situation in terms of the stages of ERP implementation as well as ERP operation. Results show an example of a highly successful ERP project grounded on the high decision making quality observed, in particular, in terms of team building or evaluation procedures, and the positive consequences for ERP implementation and operation.

Keywords: Enterprise resource planning; Decision making quality; Implementation success; Operation success

1 Introduction

An Enterprise Resource Planning (ERP) system is a software infrastructure embedded with "best practices", respectively best ways to do business based on common business practices or academic theory. The aim is to improve the co-operation and interaction between all the organizations' departments such as the products planning, manufacturing, purchasing, marketing and customer service departments. As an enabling key technology, as well as an effective managerial tool, ERP systems allow companies to integrate at all levels and utilise important ERP applications such as supply-chain management, financial and accounting applications, human resource management and customer relationship management [6]. They represent large, complex, and integrated information systems with built-in reference models of business processes targeting all functional areas. Tailoring an ERP system to a firm's specific needs can be a complex and costly task associated with high risks.

An ERP investment can be viewed as a strategic infrastructure decision adding value to the firm's information technology (IT) infrastructure capability. The importance of a firm's

IT infrastructure capability is increasingly recognized as critical to firm competitiveness [7, 17]. The overall problem of the business of any firm is to configure and direct the resource-conversion process in such a way as to optimize the attainment of its objectives [1]. The infrastructure should provide an environment which allows the firm to meet its objectives. In this sense, infrastructure has to follow the given strategy. Thus, the rationale behind an ERP investment should be to follow and support the given strategic position of the firm.

An ERP adoption may cause major influences regarding the firm's competencies. The firm may lose a unique capability to manage its resources, therefore risking a distinctive competence. On the other side, ERP may also reinforce an existing or create a new competence, enhancing the company's long-term strategic position. The firm's distinctive competency can be viewed as a strength allowing a company to achieve superior efficiency, quality, innovation, or customer responsiveness, which can be seen as the generic building blocks of competitive advantage that companies seek to achieve [11].

Literature on ERP has focused extensively on ERP implementation issues [8], especially from a technological point of view. While this stream of research provides undoubtedly important information, studies on driving ERP as a strategic concept and considering the organizational and managerial implications of ERP decisions in a wider context are limited. Researchers call for viewing ERP as a strategic concept and important infrastructure decision [12]. The strategic value of ERP and its degree of alignment in the organizational context should have an even greater impact on a firm's competitive position.

Based on this assumption, this research provides a case-study based analysis of a strategy driven ERP decision with an emphasis on the organizational fit of ERP. The topics considered in the case-study can be connected in a process oriented, causal representation of ERP adoption in a firm, beginning with decision making, followed by implementation, and, finally, usage and maintenance. All three stages are reflected through separate sections. The last stages usually considered in product life cycle models [9], namely evolution and retirement, are not considered in this article. Decision making, specifically its quality and outcome, can be seen as pre-condition for success in subsequent stages. The article shows the consequential impact of the ERP project, in particular pertaining to project costs and utility, in comparison with the common practice situation for ERP implementation, usage and evolution. For assessing the value of ERP in operation, a framework based on the balanced score card is used to capture the most relevant dimensions and criteria. The article seeks to conclude with research findings that are specifically valid for the analyzed case for further discussion and validation.

The next section gives more information on the applied methodology. Thereafter, the initial situation covering background information on the analyzed company and the applied decision making approach are described. This is followed by the analysis of organizational impacts for ERP implementation and operation. The last section concludes the article.

2   Research Methodology

The exploratory work is based on the case study method, which allowed investigating the dynamics present within a single setting. After an examination of the data gathered through this survey, a semi-structured and individualized case study protocol was designed and used to guide the face-to-face interview in the second stage of the data collection process. Prior to the interview, the protocol questions were sent to the interviewee for the purpose of preparing and gathering missing information. The analysis of the given answers in the interview brought up new open questions, which were discussed with the companies in the third stage of contact over the telephone. In addition, this work draws on results from empirical survey conducted by the author in the years 2003 to 2004 with Austrian small-to-medium scale enterprises (SMEs) as well as large scale enterprises (LEs) as target groups [3, 4, 5]. Data from the survey allowed for the comparison of the case results with the common situation observed in Austrian companies. Since the case in this paper is a large enterprise, the latter group was explicitly considered for benchmarking.

3   Initial Situation

To qualify as a candidate for the case study the company needed to have undertaken an evaluation of ERP against the background of their strategic position, thereby deriving the fundamental objectives for the underlying decision problem in order to ensure that their IT infrastructure capability supports and enhances their distinctive competence, prior to making the decision for a system. The company had to fit to our research topics stated in the introduction. The desired candidate was the Austrian MAN Steyr AG. It manufactures motor vehicles and is a subsidiary of the German MAN AG Munich, a supplier of capital goods and systems in the fields of commercial vehicle construction, mechanical and plant engineering. Worldwide, MAN has 64,000 employees generating sales of approx. € 14 billion (75 % abroad). The Austrian MAN Steyr AG, subsequently referred to as MAN only, is an autonomous subsidiary operating flexibly in the marketplace. Table 1 summarizes the company profile.

The company showed a good fit among business strategy, organizational infrastructure and process, as well as IT infrastructure and processes. This follows the recommendations found in literature concerning the concept of strategic alignment where an emphasis is put on this multivariate property of the concept [2, 10]. In terms of ERP, MAN has reached the extension stage and has extended its ERP functionality by introducing Supply Chain Management (SCM).

Table 1. Company profile (2003).

NAICS 2002 sector	31: Manufacturing
Total Assets	€ 385 mio.
Annual revenue	€ 762 mio.
Net profit	€ 22 mio.
No. of employees	2,587
No. of customers	100s
No. of suppliers	10,000s
No. of recorded subsidiaries	2
Founded	1989
Publicly quoted	No
Legal form:	Incorporated
IS/IT division represented at board level	No
IS/IT strategy defined	Yes

3.1 Decision Making Approach

As already indicated, MAN has aligned their IT infrastructure to the needs not only of their business but also to the whole firm. The ERP project was initiated by the controlling company, although MAN was allowed to undergo its own evaluation and selection process. Besides the pressure from their controlling company, there were a number of reasons for revising their IS. Firstly, they experienced pressure from the value chain from business customers and suppliers and secondly, operational problems due to multiple systems, interfaces and databases. They needed a cross-functional IS to support the needs of all business functions with specific capabilities in the production planning section. MAN has paid a great amount of attention to the evaluation of the organizational fit of major ERP systems. MAN's decision making process was characterized by driving ERP as a strategic concept, thereby emphasizing that ERP was seen as an IT infrastructure investment designed to support the competency of the firm.

The decision making process can be described as follows. After the decision committee had received recommendations reflecting the current strategic directives, they decided to evaluate ERP. The next decision was to either choose from among a number of ERP systems and their modules, or to regard no ERP system or module as suitable for the firm specific needs. As alternatives MAN chose the solutions provided by SAP and BaaN. SAP was selected due to their market leadership in the ERP software sector and BaaN due to their relative strength in area of production planning. In making the ERP system selection decision, the committee needed to accomplish several objectives. First, they wanted the system to achieve a high ERP utility score through simple additive weighting based on a number of pre-selected attributes reflecting their specific range of targeted functionalities and benefits. Second, they wanted to assess the level of organizational fit for each ERP system, which the committees analysed without using any specific methodical aid. The third objective was to minimize costs assessed through standard financial accounting techniques. Table 2 denotes the assessed decision making characteristics.

The ERP project was staffed with 5 members (from key application owners) and interestingly help was only aquired from hardware vendors. No consultants and software vendors directly supported the evaluation process. This excludes meetings with vendors to gather information on both systems. The aquisition process was costly (approx. 1 mio. €) and lasted for 1 year.

The decisional outcome was to choose only certain modules from SAP and rely on a custom development in terms of the primary production process. Therefore, MAN's ERP project can be seen as support ERP purchase. It targets support processes, which provide inputs that should allow the primary activities to take place [11]. ERP projects can be seen as primary ERP purchases, when they are targeted at the primary activities of organizations covering the four functions: research and development, production, marketing and sales, and services [11]. Support processes involve human resources and/or financial/accounting modules. MAN has reached the conclusion that no ERP solution provided the necessary level of organization fit and functionality for the primary activities (production planning) of the company.

Table 2. ERP decision making characteristics.

Size of project team	5 key members
Structure of involved project team	Participative decision making including members of all or almost all parties (Matrix)
Help from hardware vendors	Yes
Help from software vendors	No
Help from external consultants	No
Main information search activity	Meetings with vendors
Applied evaluation method	Ranking and scoring based on simple additive weighting
Definition of scores and weights	Expert judgments
Acquisition costs	Approx. € 1 mio.
Length of acquisition period	12 months
Man power needed	10 man-months
External man power proportion	50%
Acquisition effort estimation	Yes
Considered ERP software	SAP, BaaN
Chosen ERP software	SAP
Acquired ERP modules	From SAP: Finance (FI/CO), Human Resources (HR) In-house development: (Production)

4 Organizational Impact

4.1 Implementation Stage

MAN relied on a slow phased-in implementation approach supported by organizational learning. They concurrently introduced Just in Time and Agile/Lean manufacturing strategies with their support ERP project. They also used the opportunity to reengineer their business processes. The business process reengineering (BPR) efforts were undertaken at the same time as the ERP implementation took place, but were independently organized.

MAN's decision making approach was intrinsically based on the evaluation of organizational fit of ERP, thereby ensuring a high feature function fit. As a consequence the needed level of ERP software adaptations was low. Here software adaptation was divided into two subcategories: configuration, and programming. Configuration is the customization part of the adaptation process where the adaptor has to set parameters and to choose among the available reference processes. Programming involves changing and extending source code. The only problems occurring during the implementation in MAN were challenges of integration with legacy systems. The other explicitly asked generally known implementation problems (user resistance, cost escalation, time escalation, availability and retention of skilled people, high degree of organizational change just to meet the needs of the software, capability of organizational infrastructure to contend with new technology, and lack of management support) were not applicable to MAN.

Table 3 gives an overview of implementation process characteristics with common practice (mean) evaluations from the empirical survey. The most obvious impact on the implementation stage is that MAN's implementation process was very cost-friendly in comparison with other LEs. It only took a little longer than their decision making process (14 months), while needing only 45 man months in comparison with 400 man months in the average (for the group of LEs). In addition, the external man power proportion was very low which can be seen as a major cost driver. The main reason for their cost-effective implementation was the mentioned low software adaptation levels needed, which again can be seen as a consequence of their chosen decision making approach.

Table 3. ERP implementation characteristics.

| Variable | Common Case Benchmarks | | | | Case |
| | All companies | | LEs | | |
	ME	SD	ME	SD	
% of the desired ERP system functionality that was implemented	80.50	14.20	85.00	13.65	**70**
Implementation time (months)	9.88	8.70	75.00	15.50	**14**
Man power expended (man months)	25.48	53.45	400.0	56.93	**45**
External man power proportion (%)	30.61	22.04	80.00	39.40	**10**
Proportion of total implementation expenses for customizing (%)	32.61	31.41	39.89	36.95	**5**
Proportion of total implementation expenses for programming (%)	26.65	24.51	21.89	23.36	**5**

4.2 Use and Maintenance Stage

In evaluating the performance in the usage stage traditionally two different perspectives, the financial and the technical view, can be defined. The balanced scorecard (BSC) is a well known approach used for controlling based on multiple attributes aligned along four different perspectives. It was first proposed in 1992 [14] and soon after applied [15]. The BSC is a well established measurement framework which links strategic objectives and performance measures. Its application promises strategy mapping between each of the perspectives. The idea of a BSC is to find a set of measures that maintain a balance between short- and long-term objectives, between lagging and leading indicators, between financial and non-financial criterions, and between internal and external performance perspectives [13]. To assess the performance in system usage, this study has drawn on suggestions provided in academic literature, mainly on [16] where the BSC was developed for ERP controlling. Table 4 denotes the four considered ERP controlling perspectives with attributed measures. Based on the gathered data, the overall conclusion is that ERP impact in terms of all measured dimensions was considerable more successful in the case study compared to the average values. Again, the subgroup consisting of LEs is better qualified for the comparison of values. MAN achieved in nearly every factor a better outcome.

In terms of the *financial perspective*, it can be seen that ERP has different impacts on cost drivers. Costs attributable to the IT/IS department have increased. In the other (functional) areas, costs were considerable decreased. It remains unclear to see from the data, if these trade-offs mean reduced costs at the bottom line.

In terms of the *customer perspective*, the situation has also improved on a higher level as compared to the general case. Only the coverage of business processes is relatively weak, which is a direct consequence of MAN's decision to rely on custom development in terms of their production processes.

In terms of the *internal process perspective*, the situation the outcome of ERP implementation is very successful, especially important for the efficiency and effectiveness of operations. Problems with reports on demand are unchanged to the situation prior to ERP and are accounted more often compared to the mean case. Utilized ERP functionality out of the implemented areas was given as very high in terms of the chosen modules. Again, this should be seen as very positive, since only minor resources assigned to ERP implementation were wasted for not used functionalities. Another benefit arising from the minor software adaptations undertaken during implementation is the observed ease with updates reflected by the average time to upgrade and the actuality of release levels.

In terms of the *innovation and learning perspective*, the assessed training hours needed for system usage are much lower in comparison with the common case. Again, this can be seen as an effect from choosing an ERP strategy based on high feature fit, i.e. only minor modifications were needed in terms of the reference model (and processes) available with sound documentation in any ERP software solution.

Table 4. Usage/maintenance impact in relation to the situation prior to ERP across BSC perspectives.

	All companies		LEs		MAN	
Financial perspective[1]	ME	SD	ME	SD	Val	Diff
Procurement costs	3.36	0.88	3.48	0.85	4	+
Inventory holding costs	3.21	0.99	3.46	0.91	5	++
Transportation/logistics costs	3.16	0.76	3.30	0.77	4	+
Hardware/Technology costs	2.93	0.80	2.87	0.70	3	+
IT/IS maintenance costs	2.83	1.14	2.39	1.23	2	-
Overall IT/IS costs	2.79	0.96	2.31	1.13	2	-
IT/IS consulting costs	2.67	0.91	2.41	1.11	5	++
Customer (supplier) perspective						
Coverage of business processes[2]	3.94	1.18	3.81	1.35	1	-
Transactions finished on schedule[1]	3.62	0.71	3.64	0.77	4	+
Problems order processing or mgmt.[1]	3.56	1.04	3.41	0.96	4	+
Communication with supplier[1]	3.17	0.85	3.61	0.84	4	+
Internal process perspective[2]						
Availability of ERP services	3.96	0.84	3.89	0.77	5	+
Average time to upgrade the system	3.31	1.05	3.11	1.04	5	++
Release levels lagging behind actual[3]	1.34	0.76	1.54	0.91	1	+
Effectiveness/Productivity	3.86	0.70	3.84	0.97	4	+
Efficiency/Profitability	3.82	0.79	3.74	1.05	4	+
Financial close cycle	3.55	0.96	3.84	1.01	4	+
Problems with reports on demand	3.53	0.95	3.47	1.01	3	-
Problems with warehouse processes	3.41	0.90	3.40	0.93	4	+
Problems with standard reports	3.37	1.05	3.66	1.05	4	+
Exploited ERP functionality[4]	66.16	20.71	73.39	23.49	90	++
Innovation and Learning perspective[5]						
Training hours per developer	3.24	0.88	3.02	1.03	4	+
Training hours per user	2.94	0.76	2.95	0.96	4	++

[1] Rated on a scale between 1 (poor rating/higher costs) and 5 (good rating/lower costs) in comparison to the situation prior to ERP
[2] Rated on a scale between 1 (poor rating/decreased) and 5 (good rating/increased) according to planned level of support
[3] Rated on a scale between 0 (no lag) and 3 (3 levels behind)
[4] % of the implemented ERP system functionality
[5] Rated on a scale between 1 (increased) and 5 (decreased) in comparison to the situation prior to ERP adoption

5 Conclusions

The ERP project initiated by MAN Austria can be seen as stereotype for how successful IS projects with strategic value can be designed. It followed general guidelines of ERP decision making, i.e., considered their strategic needs, analysed organizational fit of the ERP alternatives, assigned a participative decision approach, and applied a multi-dimensional evaluation methodology. As a consequence, MAN believes that their competitive priorities are well supported through the chosen solution, respectively ERP strategy. MAN chose a decisional alternative that comprised only the modules from one vendor that provided enough organizational fit to introduce the modules with minor adaptations to the company. The consequence was a short and relatively non-expensive ERP implementation with a successful ERP outcome in terms of all four measured BSC scorecard dimensions. The only more technical limitation is the problem of having many interfaces that need to be engaged with so-called glue software code, which is known as another IT related problem domain. The integration of IS, respectively decision making and evaluation therefore will be addressed by future research.

Besides giving more analytical insights on the decision making process, this research has also provided numerous indications for on-going benefits in ERP operation in a Balanced Scorecard based assessment. Measures used should be applicable to other settings, where costs and utility of ERP need to be observed, respectively controlled.

Table 5 summarizes the main conclusions and supports the originally postulated and observed preposition that achievable ERP value should be dependent on sound decision making based on strategic planning and alignment as well as top-level management responsibility. Another observation was that high efforts and a longer process time in decision making were more than compensated by the low efforts and short length of subsequent system implementation. Future research will consider in more detail the methods and methodologies needed to support governance of ERP in a more general IT Governance framework.

Table 5. Summary of key variables with their values for the case environment.

Decision making	Implementation	Usage & Maintenance
Costs/Efforts (high)	Costs/Efforts (low)	Financial impact (diverse)
Length (long)	Length (short)	Customer impact (very positive)
Strategic guidance (yes)	User resistance (no)	Internal process impact (very positive)
Organizational fit analysis (yes)	Adherence with schedule (yes)	Innovation & Learning impact (very positive)
Participative decision making (yes)	Cost or time escalation (no)	
Multi-dimensional evaluation of costs and benefits (yes)	Man power shortage (no)	
Utilization of internal competence (yes)	Organizational change (low)	
Autonomous decision making w/o guidelines from controlling company (yes)	Management support (high)	

References

1. Ansoff, I.: Corporate Strategy. Penguin Books, London (1988)
2. Bergeron, F., Raymond, L., and Rivard, S.: Ideal patterns of strategic alignment and business performance. Information & Management, In Press, Corrected Proof
3. Bernroider, E. and Leseure, M. L.: Enterprise resource planning (ERP) diffusion and characteristics according to the system's lifecycle: A comparative view of small-to-medium sized and large enterprises, Institute of Information Processing and Information Management, Vienna University of Economics and Business Administration, Vienna 01/2005, (2005)
4. Bernroider, E. and Mitlöhner, J.: Characteristics of the Multiple Attribute Decision Making Methodology in Enterprise Resource Planning Software Decisions. Communications of the International Information Management Association (CIIMA), 5 1 (2005) 49-58
5. Bernroider, E. W. N. and Hampel, A.: Enterprise Resource Planning and IT Governance in Perspective: Strategic Planning and Alignment, Value Delivery and Controlling. Proceedings of Fifth International Conference on Electronic Business (ICEB), Hong Kong, China, (2005)
6. Boubekri, N.: Technology enablers for supply chain management. Integrated Manufacturing Systems, 12 6 (2001) 394-399

7. Broadbent, M., Weill, P., and Neo, B. S.: Strategic context and patterns of IT infrastructure capability. The Journal of Strategic Information Systems, 8 2 (1999) 157-187
8.   Esteves, J. and Pastor, J.: Enterprise Resource Planning Systems Research: An Annotated Bibliography. Communications of the Association of Information Systems, 7 8 (2001) 1-52
9. Esteves, J. and Pastor, J.: An ERP Lifecycle-based Research Agenda. Proceedings of International Workshop on Enterprise Management Resource and Planning Systems (EMRPS), Venice, Italy, (1999)
10. Henderson, J. C. and Venkatraman, N.: Strategic alignment: leveraging information technology for transforming organizations. IBM Systems Journal, 32 1 (1993) 4-16
11. Hill, C. W. L. and Jones, G. R.: Strategic Management: An Integrated Approach. 5th edn. Houghton Mifflin, Boston (2000)
12. Jacobs, F. R. and Bendoly, E.: Enterprise resource planning: Developments and directions for operations management research. European Journal of Operational Research, 146 2 (2003) 233-240
13. Kaplan, R. S. and Norton, D. P.: The Balanced Scorecard - Translating Strategy into Action. Harvard Business School Press, Boston, Mass. (1996)
14. Kaplan, R. S. and Norton, D. P.: The Balanced Scorecard – measures that drive performance. Harvard Business Review (1992) 71-79
15. Kaplan, R. S. and Norton, D. P.: Putting the Balanced Scorecard to Work. Harvard Business Review (1993) 134-147
16. Rosemann, M. and Wiese, J.: Measuring the Performance of ERP Software – a Balanced Scorecard Approach. Proceedings of Australasian Conference on Information Systems, (1999)
17. Sauer, C. and Willcocks, L.: Establishing the Business of the Future: The Role of Organizational Architecture and Information Technologies. European Management Journal, 21 4 (2003) 497-508.

SCOLDSS: A Decision Support System for the Planning of Solid Waste Collection

Eugenio de Oliveira Simonetto[1], Denis Borenstein[2]

[1] Federal Center of Technological Education of Sao Vicente do Sul (CEFET-SVS) , CIET,
20 de Setembro, S/N , 97420-000, Sao Vicente do Sul-RS, Brazil
[2] Federal University of Rio Grande do Sul, EA-UFRGS, Washington Luis, 855 , 90010-460, Porto
Alegre-RS, Brazil

eosimonetto@gmail.com[1] , denisb@ea.ufrgs.br[2]

Abstract. This paper presents the conception, modeling, and implementation of a decision support system applied to the operational planning of solid waste collection systems, called SCOLDSS. The main functionality of the system is the generation of alternatives to the decision processes concerning: (a) the allocation of separate collection vehicles, as well as the determination of their routes, and (b) the determination of the daily amount of solid waste to be sent to each sorting unit, in order to avoid waste of labor force and to reduce the amount of waste sent to the landfills. To develop the computer system, a combination of quantitative techniques was used, such as: simulation of discrete events and algorithms/heuristics for vehicle allocation and routing. The system was validated using a field test in Porto Alegre, Rio Grande do Sul.

Keywords: Decision Support Systems, Waste Management, Operations Research

1 Introduction

Concern within the international community regarding the limits of development of the planet began during the 1970s, when the first debates took place on the risks involved in environmental degradation. Those discussions led researchers to reach the conclusion that if the rate of industrialization, pollution and exploitation of natural resources were to continue at the current rate, the limits of the developmental limits of the planet would be reached within a hundred at most [14].

Environmentally healthy management of solid waste is part of larger, more important issues for the maintenance of the environment of the Earth and, mainly to achieve a sustainable and environmentally healthy development in all countries [20]. As a consequence, the destination of solid waste is a central concern of municipalities around the world. As space for building landfills becomes increasingly difficult to find, solid waste management becomes an ever more important issue. Municipalities are increasing the use of recycling as the best strategy for dealing with the disposal of this kind of waste.

However, recycling is a very expensive task for municipalities, since involves collection, handling, and reuse of the solid waste.

Recycling is, according to [16], the process by which materials otherwise destined for disposal are collected, processed or remanufactured, and are reused. Recycle can be defined as being the separation of domestic waste, such as paper, plastic, glass, and materials, aiming at bringing them back to the industry to be benefited. These materials are once again transformed into tradable products. Solid waste management is receiving increasing attention due to its impact on the public concern for the environment. In general, the municipality is responsible for the collection and transportation of the solid waste. These are very expensive services, being responsible for 75-80% of the solid waste management budget [3].

The implementation of a solid waste management program is a continuous process, which is gradually developed. The first step is related to public awareness campaigns, convincing the population of the importance of recycling and giving instructions on how to separate the waste in containers for each type of material. Afterwards, a collection plan must be created, defining equipment, vehicles, areas, and the waste collection frequency. After the collection, recyclable materials must be transported to a unit equipped with places for sorting, so that a more judicious selection of the materials is made, aiming at their commercialization. It is important for the population to be adequately instructed, so that only tradable materials are separated as solid waste, thus avoiding additional expenses with transportation and handling of waste that cannot be recycled. After the implantation of the separate collection, the municipality must maintain the population permanently active through awareness and environmental education campaigns [6].

Recycling solid waste is an excellent alternative to provide the preservation of natural resources, energy savings, reduction in the landfill area, creation of jobs and income, and the awareness of the population for environmental issues. However, to have an effective functioning, it is extremely important to implant a properly designed solid waste collection system in a city, where recyclables are separated at home and collected by the municipalities. Despite being an excellent alternative for the reduction of waste destined to landfills, only 4.7%, on average, of wastes are reused or recycled in Brazilian cities, according to CEMPRE (Non-Governmental Organization Company Commitment for Recycling). One of the reasons for this small amount of recycling is due to the bad conditioning of wastes by the population, which is generated by the lack of information about solid waste. Other factors that contribute to the small recycling index of wastes are: (a) the high cost of the solid waste collection for municipalities [16]; and (b) the lack of a system correctly designed and operated in terms of storage capacity and waste processing at the sorting units. The main goal of this paper is to develop a tool for aiding managers to overcome those two barriers.

The main objectives of the developed decision support system (DSS) is to support the operational planning of the solid waste collection, aiming at the reduction of the involved costs, as in other studies presented in the literature [1, 15, 11, 10, 6, 3, 19] but also trying to reduce the amount of recyclable waste that is lost due to the lack of control in the storage capacity and work processing at sorting units. Thus, the main contribution of this research is to present an operational management tool that considers the solid waste processing capacity of sorting units. For the development of the computational system, quantitative techniques originate from the Operational Research field were used, such as discrete-event simulation and algorithms/heuristics for solving the well-known vehicle routing problem (VRP). The use of such techniques aims at adding quality to the decision process, since in many cases decisions on planning the solid waste management are taken based only on the experience of managers [6]. This fact, according to those authors, contributes to the high cost and low performance of waste collection systems in several cities. The use of quantitative analysis tools for solid waste management is a feasible alternative to the treatment of the complexity inherent to the solid waste collection process, since by using these tools it is possible to represent a situation of the real world, study its behavior (by executing formal models), and making decisions based on the analysis made.

The paper is organized as follows: Section 2 describes the developed decision support system – SCOLDSS, focusing on its architecture. Section 3 presents the validation process of the DSS in the operational planning of the solid waste collection system. Finally, section 4 presents the final considerations of the paper.

2 SCOLDSS – The Decision Support System

SCOLDSS aims at subsidizing the operational decision making process of solid waste managers related to the solid waste logistics, from the collection stage until the waste delivery at sorting units. The computational system specifically supports the following tasks: (i) reducing the amount of solid waste destined to the landfill; (ii) assuring a waste input percentage at each sorting unit; (iii) assigning vehicles to collection trips; (iv) defining their route; and (v) estimating the work capacity (productivity) of sorting units, in relation to the waste arrival and processing (separation). The system basically aids the solid waste collection operational management through the generation, analysis, and assessment of possible operational scenarios for this type of collection. It is considered that the design of the solid waste collection system (in terms of defining the equipment, human resources, areas, and separate collection frequency) has already been previously defined.

The research methodology adopted for the development of *SCOLDSS* is the one usually developed in Operational Research [13]. This methodology consists basically of the following stages: (1) exploratory studies, in which the problem was identified and structured; (2) solution development by building formal models capable of representing the problem. The problem complexity demanded the integration of several modeling techniques, including discrete-event simulation and algorithms/heuristics for vehicle routing and allocation problems; (3) computational implementation of the solution, using the decision support systems technology; (4) solution validation through laboratory and field tests, in order to verify if the results obtained are in accordance with the observed reality. The validation was carried out by using real data from the solid waste collection in the city of Porto Alegre, Brazil. Porto Alegre is the capital of the southernmost state in Brazil, with a population of 1.3 million inhabitants. The municipality of Porto Alegre was a pioneer in the establishment of the solid waste collection in Brazil and its program nowadays is a reference for other cities in Brazil and Latin America.

To develop *SCOLDSS*, the decision support systems architecture proposed by [18] was used, which is composed of the three following subsystems: database subsystem, model-based subsystem, and user interface subsystem. *SCOLDSS* architecture can be seen in Figure 1.

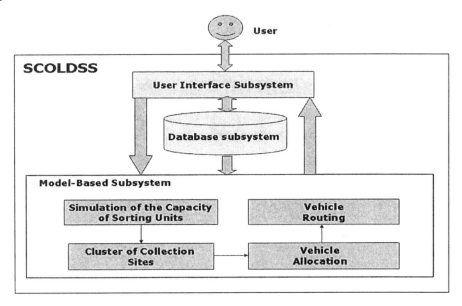

Figure 1. SCOLDSS architecture

2.1 Database Subsystem

The basic premise to build SCOLDSS database subsystem was to select data which were extremely important for providing information to managers, as well as to feed the mathematical and simulation models existing in the model-based subsystem. To develop the database, we have used: (i) studies performed prior to this paper [10, 19, 3, 8, 6]; (ii) technical manuals related to Solid Waste Management [15, 16] and (iii) interviews to investigate requirements from experts in solid waste management.

The relational database model developed in SCOLDSS, after the specification of the system requirements, is composed of data structures, attributes, and descriptions.

2.2 Decision Model Subsystem

The model-based subsystem was created using different techniques of quantitative modeling: the computational simulation of discrete events and the development of algorithms/heuristics for vehicle allocation and routing problems. Simulation is used to determine the sorting unit demands, since it presents a quite dynamic behavior profile, basically attributed to seasonalities and to the population consumption profile. The solid waste collection was modeled as a typical multi-depot VRP with a heterogeneous fleet, in which collection sites offer solid waste to be demanded by a sorting unit. Algorithms and heuristics were developed to solve this problem.

The use of these techniques is justified by the distinct nature of the problems being addressed. Firstly, the determination of the waste processing capacity is defined by the simulation model; secondly, the determination of solid waste flow (vehicles and routes), as a consequence of simulation results, is solved using heuristic methods for the multi-depot VRP. Based on the interaction of the waste processing simulation at sorting units and the execution of the multi-depot VRP with a heterogeneous fleet, the waste collection vehicle routing, as well as the final destination of the waste carried by them is determined, in order to calculate the waste processing capacity for one day.

2.2.1 Simulation Model

The simulation model mainly aims at estimating the solid waste processing capacity at sorting units. The determination of the processing capacity is a particularity of recyclable wastes and has its origin in the input and output flow of this type of waste at sorting units. This is not the case of solid waste destined to the landfill, once there is no solid waste output (only waste input) in this type of final disposal. The commercial software ARENA [12] was used for simulation.

To execute the simulation, which will depend on the processing capacity of each sorting unit, the following information is necessary:

- *Mean rate of waste generation* – mean amount of waste generated by the population in Kg per minute. In the mathematical formulation of the decision model, it is represented by variable λ;
- *Amount of waste waiting to be processed* – amount of waste waiting in Kg to be processed in each sorting unit;
- *Mean waste processing rate by sorters* – mean amount of waste that each sorter is able to process in Kg per minute. In the mathematical formulation of the decision model, it is represented by variable μ.

The identification of the previously described information will influence in determining the *total amount of processed waste* per day at each sorting units. The total amount of processed solid waste, including the recycled ones and the others that will be destined to the landfill have to be taken into account by the simulation, since both temporarily occupy physical space and also consume a given period of time to be processed by workers. The *Pickstation* module of the simulator Arena 5.0 was used to distribute solid waste among sorting units. This module selects the unit to send the raw material (waste) in precedence order, according to the number of resources (personnel) used in each sorting unit (in order to avoid idleness) and by the amount of post-consumption raw material waiting to be processed, since in each sorting unit there is a maximum capacity of waste storage. In this selection, occasional interruptions at work (lunch, change of work team) and the production variation from one shift to another were considered. The main information generated by the simulation model is the solid waste demand (in Kg) that each sorting unit is able to process at a certain day of work, obtained by the average of n simulation runs. The integration module of the Arena simulator, based on text files, was used to generate the file with the results.

2.2.2 Grouping of Collection Sites and Vehicle Allocation

The subsequent stage of using the model based subsystem is characterized by having n sorting units (which demand already have been defined by the simulation model) and m collection sites with recyclable solid waste to be collected by the vehicles. Such description clearly identifies the multi-depot VRP [4, 7]. The approach proposed by [9] was used for modeling and solving this problem, implemented in the form of "grouping for later routing" heuristic. In this approach, collection sites must first be associated to specific sorting units, through assignments such as "solid waste from collection site x will be sent to sorting unit y". As a result of this step, collection sites are clustered in accordance with the sorting unit in which the solid waste collected will be unloaded. Also, in this stage the minimum percentage of solid waste input is assured in each of the sorting units, according to the maximum processing capacity provided by the simulation model. The main objective is to avoid imbalanced trip assignments to sorting units, where some facilities may be allocated excessive collection trips, and other facilities may be idle. Such solutions should be rejected when the social benefit of the solid waste program is considered.

2.2.3 Determining the Solid Waste Collection Routes

The aim of this sub problem is to generate the collection routes to be covered, as well as to assign the vehicles that should cover each route. The output of this sub problem has the following structure: vehicle v will cover collection sites a, b, and c (in this order) and unload its cargo in sorting unit x. For the solution development, a heuristic developed by [17] was used. This heuristic was specifically developed to solve the VRP with a heterogeneous fleet, in case there are vehicles with distinct load capacities. The basic processing stages of the heuristic are: the determination of the distance order in relation to each sorting unit, route generation using the different types of vehicles available, and the selection of the lowest cost combination among the several generated routes. For executing this heuristic, the following additional information is required:
1. The sorting unit to which the planning will be made;
2. The selected collection sites to send waste to the unit (from the grouping stage);

3. The distance between collection sites, as well as their distance until the sorting unit (it is worth mentioning that the distance covered from the garage is being taken into account to calculate the distance related to the sorting units);
4. The mean waste offer at each collection site for each month;
5. The vehicles allocated to the sorting unit (from the vehicle allocation stage);
6. The load capacity of each allocated vehicle.

2.3 User-Interface Subsystem (Dialogue)

The user interface subsystem in *SCOLDSS* is responsible for the definition of the solid waste collection operational scenarios. This module has graphical and interactive facilities, and menu-data driven dialogues that offer a friendly environment for the user to define all needed data to run the models existing in the DSS. This module is also responsible for the overall control of the DSS, accessing and changing information with other subsystems within the DSS. The main SCOLDSS interface screen is presented in Figure 2. The vehicle routes are presented in the map of this figure.

The interface functioning, when using the decision support system, basically occurs in the following way: the user informs the weekday on which the separate collection planning will be made, the month (in order to consider the occasional seasonalities existing in the process), the operating waste sorting units. Next, the simulation can be performed in order to determine the amount of waste that each operating unit is able to process every day. Afterwards, the user will execute the functionalities of the system step by step: vehicle allocation, collection route generation, and reports with main results. The main results of the system include: the identification of the vehicle to be used in each collection trip, its route, an estimation of the quantity of solid waste collected, and the recycling facility in which this vehicle will unload its cargo. In the map of Figure 2, the route of each vehicle is presented interactively. The system provides text or graphical reports for all vehicle upon request, using button *Report.*

The interface validation of *SCOLDSS* was developed with the participation of potential system users (academics and professionals), who, after receiving instructions on its functioning, used it aiming at verifying if it was user-friendly and adequate. The main goal of the interface validation was to achieve consistency between the visions of the system analyst/modeler and the potential user of the model, in a way that is appropriate and cost effective.

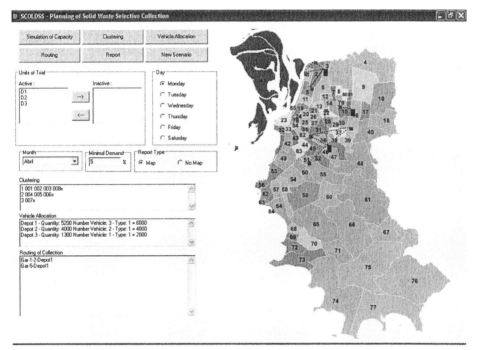

Figure 2. Main *SCOLDSS* interface screen

3 SCOLDSS Validation

The *SCOLDSS* system basically consists of the development of quantitative analytical methods and simulation for supporting the operational planning of the solid waste collection. A model can be defined as a representation of the real world, so it is desirable that the representation behavior is the same (or as closest as possible) as the reality being analyzed, under certain specific conditions. This process is called validation, and it is a fundamental step towards an effective computer based system. This section briefly describes the tests carried out to validate the DSS. The emphasis of the validation process is on determining the potential value of the computer based system [5].

The computational implementation of the heuristics were verified – referring to build the system "right" – by running test cases and comparing their output with the output provided for classical examples in the OR-Library [2] for the VRP problems. So far, only very minor discrepancies were identified (inferior to 1%), probably consequence of using different solvers and CPU processors. In addition, for each heuristic, sensitivity analysis were performed by systematically changing the input variable values and parameters over a large range of interest and observing the effect upon the heuristics output. Such analysis led to a better understanding of the model-based subsystem with respect to real systems.

The experiments of the validation were performed for fifteen distinct dates (5 in March, 5 in April, and 5 in May). Experiments were performed in a Pentium 4, Processor 2.0 GHz, 256Mb RAM. An example of the results obtained in the validation is presented in Table 1.

Table 1. Comparison concerning distances between the current system and *SCOLDSS*

	Current Distance	*SCOLDSS Distance*	*Mean Reduction in Distance*	*Reduction Percentage*
Monday	546.5 km	500.7 km	45.8 km	8.39%
Tuesday	522.8 km	478.4 km	44.4 km	8.49%
Wednesday	442.8 km	400.4 km	42.4 km	9.58%
Thursday	591.8 km	537.2 km	54.6 km	9.23%
Friday	374.9 km	343.1 km	31.8 km	8.57%
Mean	495.76 km	451.95 km	43.8 km	8.82%

4 Concluding Remarks

This paper presents the conception and development of a decision support system for the operational planning of solid waste collection. The DSS supports the main operational stages of the solid waste collection process, namely the collection by trucks, and the solid waste unloading at sorting units. The major contribution of this research is the DSS's capacity to incorporate the control of the storage and processing capacity of the material at sorting units, a fact which was neglected by previous studies in this area. The possible benefits to be obtained by using *SCOLDSS* include: (a) reduction of the distances to be covered by collection vehicles; (b) reduction in the number of trips; and (c) balance in the distribution of waste collected among sorting units.

Specifically for the case study performed with data from Porto Alegre, RS, Brazil, the following results were obtained:

- Routing solutions, in average, 8.82% better than the routing currently implemented by the DMLU;
- Reduction of 17.89% in the number of collection vehicle trips;
- Through the simulation of waste processing at sorting units and the definition of the minimum demand percentage of waste per unit, the distribution of waste per collection day among the units could be balanced.

With further studies, we intend to develop researches concerning the knowledge and generation of relevant information on solid wastes, through the development of data warehouses and the application of data mining techniques on databases about solid wastes. The development and application of these techniques will allow the identification of relevant behavior standards from waste generation until its final disposal.

References

1. Barlaz, M.A. (et al.) (1995). Life-Cycle Study of Municipal Solid Waste Management System Description. U.S. Environmental Protection Agency, Washington DC,USA.
2. Beasley, J.E. (1990). OR-Library: distributing test problems by electronic mail. Journal of the Operational Research Society 41, 1069-1072.
3. Bhat, V.N. (1996). A model for the optimal allocation of trucks for the solid waste management. Waste Management & Research 14, 87-96.
4. Bodin, L.D. and B. Golden (1981). Classification in vehicle routing and scheduling. Networks 11, 97-108.
5. Borenstein, D. (1998). Towards a practical method to validate decision support systems. Decision Support Systems 23, 227-239.
6. Chang, N. and Y. Wei (2000). Sitting recycling drop-off in urban area by genetic algorithm-based fuzzy multiobjective nonlinear integer programming modeling. Fuzzy Sets and Systems, 114, 133-149.
7. Cordeau, J.F., M. Gendreau, G. Laporte, JY Povtin and F. Semet (2002). A guide to vehicle routing heuristics. Journal of the Operational Research Society 53, 512-522.
8. Everett, J.W. and S. Shahi (1997). Vehicle and labor requirements for yard waste collection. Waste Management & Research 15, 627-640.
9. Gillet, B. and L. R. Miller (1974). A heuristic algorithm for the vehicle dispatch problem. Operations Research 22, 340-349.
10. Huang, G.H., B.W. Baetz and C.G. Patry (1998). Trash-flow allocation: Planning under uncertainty. Interfaces 28, 36-55.
11. Kulcar, T.(1996). Optimizing solid waste collection in Brussels. European Journal of Operations Research 90, 71-77.
12. Kelton, W.D., R.P. Sadowski and D.T. Sturrock (2004). Simulation with Arena. 3rd. Ed., McGraw-Hill, New York, USA.
13. Law, A.M. and W. D. Kelton (1991). Simulation Modeling and Analysis. 2* Ed., McGraw-Hill, New York, USA.
14. Meadows, D.H. (1972). The Limits to Growth. Universe Books, New York, 1972.
15. Monteiro, J.H.P.(et al) (2001) Manual de Gerenciamento Integrado de Resíduos Sólidos. Rio de Janeiro: Instituto Brasileiro de Administração Municipal. 2001. (In Portuguese).
16. O'Leary, P.R. (et al.) (1999). Decision Maker's Guide to Solid Waste Management.Vol. 2. Environmental Protection Agency, Washington DC, USA.

17. Renaud, J. and Boctor, F.F.(2002). A sweep-based algorithm for the fleet size and mix vehicle routing problem. European Journal of Operational Research 140, 618-628.

18. Sprague, R. and Watson, H. (1993). Decision Support Systems: Putting Theory into Practice. 3rd. Ed., Prentice-Hall, USA.

19. Tung, D.V. and Pinnoi, A. (2000). Vehicle routing-scheduling for waste collection in Hanoi. European Journal of Operational Research 125, 449-468.

20. Zutshi, A. and Sohal, A. (2002) Environmental management systems auditing: auditors´experiences in Australia. International Journal Environment and Sustainable Development, 1, No. 1, 73-87.

IV. EVOLVING TECHNOLOGIES:
Next Generation Systems

Semantic Web Technologies for Enhancing Intelligent DSS Environments

Ranjit Bose[1], Vijayan Sugumaran[2]

[1]Anderson School of Management, University of New Mexico, Albuquerque, NM 87131, USA
[2] Department of Decision and Information Sciences, School of Business Administration, Oakland University, Rochester, MI 48309, USA

bose@mgt.unm.edu[1], sugumara@oakland.edu[2]

Abstract. The next generation Web, called the Semantic Web (SW), is receiving much attention lately from the research and development communities globally. Many software designers, developers, and vendors have recently begun exploring the use of SW technologies within the context of developing intelligent Web-based Decision Support Systems (DSS) since they provide an attractive, application-neutral, platform-neutral, Web environment that operates on top of the existing Web without having to modify it. They are envisioned to provide machine interpretation and processing capability of the existing Web information. With these powerful potential advantages, there is a need for the DSS designers and developers to not only understand the SW technologies in terms of what they are and do, but also how and where they could be effectively used in Web-based DSS to enhance its environment. This study addresses that and characterizes a semantic DSS environment to assist the researchers and developers to investigate in more detail the SW technology applications and challenges within the context of DSS.

Keywords: Decision Support Systems, Web-based DSS, Semantic Web, Intelligent DSS, Semantic Web Technologies.

1 Introduction

Decision Support Systems (DSS) are a class of computerized information systems that interactively support the decision-making activities of a decision maker in solving un-programmed, and unstructured (or "semi-structured") problems. Almost over three decades, DSS have witnessed continued growth and maturity in several areas such as their component design, emerging technology applications, functionality, intelligence, and the technological proficiency of their user among others [33]. Due to this evolving nature, the compromises that were made with system designs in the past years in order to facilitate the use of DSS by non-savvy users are no more necessary now. Simultaneously, the current technologically advanced users are increasingly expecting more intelligence and functionality in the DSS environments they use [4].

In recent years, WWW or the Web has become the platform of choice for building DSS. Consequently, Web-based technologies are having a major impact on design, development, and implementation processes for all types of DSS [5, 22]. Distributed DSS over the Internet and intranets enable the dissemination of DSS applications at a reasonable cost. Power [31] defines a Web-based decision support system as a computerized system that delivers decision support information or decision support tools to a manager or business analyst using a "thin-client" Web browser such as Netscape Navigator or Internet Explorer. Besides having a focus on DSS design that incorporates distributed resources such as databases and that makes use of intelligent and/or soft computing systems such as intelligent agents, considerable attention is now being given to channel these trends to the design and development of e-commerce decision support [8, 9]. Furthermore, several DSS vendors now are offering ASP (application service provider) services in which companies can lease both DSS development tools and ready-made DSS applications thus providing them with more flexibility for selecting their DSS development approach and for analyzing the cost effectiveness of the available alternatives [6].

In spite of these developments, most of today's Web content is only suitable for human consumption. Typical uses of the Web today involve users searching for and making use of information, reviewing catalogs on online stores and ordering products by filling out forms. These activities are not particularly well supported by software tools. Apart from the existence of links that establish connections between documents, the most valuable and indispensable tools today are the search engines. At present, the main obstacle to providing better decision support to Web users is that the meaning of Web content is not machine-interpretable. That is, currently there are tools available that can retrieve texts, split them into parts, check spelling, count the number of words and so on, but when it comes to interpreting sentences and extracting useful information for users, the capabilities of current software are still very limited.

The next generation Web, called the Semantic Web (SW), is envisioned to represent Web content in a form that is equally meaningful to the humans as well as to the computers [3]. The SW, which is a Web technology that provides machine interpretation and processing capability of the existing Web information, lives on top of the existing Web without modifying it. This extension of the current Web, to one where information is given well-defined meaning (semantics), better enables computers and people to work in cooperation and to use intelligent techniques to take advantage of these representations. Thus SW intends to create a universal medium for information exchange by giving semantics, in a manner understandable by machines to the content of resources [40]. The World Wide Web Consortium (W3C) spearheaded the SW development project, which is the international standardization body for the Web.

The idea behind the SW is to add defining tags to information within Web pages and to provide links to this information so that an application can discover data and make associations between different data elements [20]. Essentially, the SW is a way of creating a globally distributed database where data can more easily be found, accessed, and incorporated into applications. The SW relies on three basic technologies filling key roles: XML for syntax and structure, Ontology systems that define terms and their relationships, and the resource definition framework (RDF), which provides a model for encoding ontology defined meaning.

As the dynamics of the global markets increase, the need for accurate, more diverse and immediate information by the decision makers will continue to grow. Since the volume of data and human-centered information available to decision-makers today continues to increase at an ever-accelerating rate, the need to represent this information in software-process able formats becomes more apparent. At the same time, the availability of information from diverse sources through the WWW also provides the opportunity to widen the scope of input to DSS, if this information can be made accessible through automated means. SW technologies are primarily designed to be a powerful means for supporting information-centric interoperability and reducing the costs of data reuse, and to provide intelligent content for use by automated systems, enabling software services to perform distributed reasoning using Web resources [14]. Within this environment, intelligent agents will be able to solve complex problems by gathering information from diverse sources and synthesizing results tailored to the decision makers' requirements [2, 25].

With these powerful potential advantages, there is a need for the DSS designers and developers to not only understand the SW technologies in terms of what they are and do, but also how and where they could be effectively used in Web-based DSS to enhance its environment. This study addresses that and characterizes a semantic DSS environment to assist the researchers and developers to investigate in more detail the SW technology applications and challenges within the context of DSS.

2 Overview – Semantic Web Technologies & Web-based DSS

Today's technologies such as the Internet, the Web, and telecommunications technology have made it possible to create an organizational environment that is increasingly more global, complex, and connected. The Web environment is emerging as a very important DSS development and delivery platform, particularly the rapid dissemination of information to the decision makers. The Web's impact on decision-making has been to make the process more efficient and to make the DSS technology easy to understand and use.

Most Web sites today produce some amount of dynamically generated content. The SW builds on this idea with the aim of providing machine-process able information, which is made possible by the addition of "semantic markup" to Web-based resources. In contrast to HTML markup, semantic markup includes definitions of concepts and relationships involved in the information being transmitted. This richer definition allows client programs to process the contents instead of merely the markup.

Today's Web sites can be designed to provide one or more of the following kinds of communication: (1) human-to-human communication (humans place Web pages on a site, other humans read it); (2) machine-to-human communication (server-side software assembles information, formats it for the Web, passes the result to humans to read); and,

(3) machine-to-machine communication (software assembles information, formats it to make it machine-process able, passes the result to other software).

The following two subsections provide a brief description of the basic SW technologies and Web-based DSS including Web services.

2.1 Semantic Web Technologies

The word *semantics* implies the study of meaning. The SW provides a common framework to: (a) represent data on the Web or as a database that is globally linked, in a manner understandable by machines, to the content of documents on the Web; and (b) allow data to be shared and reused across application, enterprise, and enterprise boundaries. If a computer understands the semantics of a document, it doesn't just interpret the series of characters that make up that document: it understands the document's meaning. SW technologies therefore help separate meanings from data, document content, or application code, using technologies based on open standards. SW technologies represent meaning using ontologies and provide reasoning through the relationships, rules, logic, and conditions represented in those ontologies [13].

The metadata, data about data, is one of the core organizing concepts behind the W3C's vision of the SW. To represent the SW knowledge, one uses the following technologies: (a) RDF (a standard syntax for describing data); (b) RDF Schema (a standard means of describing the properties of that data); and (c) Ontologies – defined using OWL, the Web Ontology Language (a standard means of describing relationships between data items).

RDF – Resource Description Framework. The RDF is the underlying unified data model for representing semantics. The data model and XML serialization syntax is used for describing resources both on and off the Web. RDF makes use of unique identifiers (URI, Uniform Resource Identifier) for describing metadata. URIs are used to describe things, also called resources, which could be people, places, documents, images, databases, etc. All RDF applications adopt a common convention for identifying these things. A subset of URI, the Uniform Resource Locator or URL, is concerned with the location and retrieval of resources, while URI is a unique identifier for things or resources that we describe but that may not necessarily be retrievable. However, RDF provides a consistent, standardized way to describe and query Internet resources, from text pages and graphics to audio files and video clips.

RDF Schema. RDF Schema is a standard means to describe the properties of resources defined using RDF. For example, if we say that a resource is of a particular type, or has a certain relationship to another resource, or has some specified attribute, we need to uniquely identify these descriptive concepts. RDF uses URIs for these too. Different development communities can invent new descriptive properties (such as person, employee, price, and classification) and assign URIs to these properties. Since the assignment of URIs is decentralized, one can be sure that uniquely named descriptive properties don't get mixed up when we integrate metadata from multiple sources.

In other words, RDF Schema is a semantic extension of RDF. It provides mechanisms to describe groups of related resources and the relationships between those resources [7]. The RDF Schema class and property system is similar to the type systems of object-oriented programming languages such as the Java language. RDF differs from many such systems. Rather than define a class in terms of the properties of its instances, the RDF vocabulary description language describes properties in terms of which classes of resource that the properties apply to.

Both RDF and RDF Schema are based on XML and XML Schema. The existence of standards for describing data or other resource (RDF) and data or other resource attributes (RDF Schema) enables the development of a set of readily available tools to read and exploit data or other resource from multiple sources. The degree to which different applications can share and exploit data or other resource is called syntactic interoperability. The more standardized and widespread these data manipulation tools are, the higher the degree of syntactic interoperability, and the easier and more attractive it becomes to use the SW approach as opposed to a point-to-point integrated solution.

Ontology. The term ontology, also known as a domain model, refers to a hierarchical data structure containing the relevant entities and their relationships and rules within a specific domain. Ontologies define data models in terms of classes, subclasses, and properties. Before multiple applications can truly understand data – and treat it as information – semantic interoperability is required. Syntactic interoperability is about parsing data correctly, which requires mapping between terms. Semantic interoperability is about content analysis, which requires formal and explicit specifications of domain models, which define the terms used and their relationships.

Ontologies provide shared semantics to metadata, enabling a degree of semantic interoperability [27]. The challenge for the designer is to identify how to represent, create, manage and use both ontologies as shared knowledge representations, but also large volumes of metadata records used to annotate Web resources of a diverse kind. That is, to achieve knowledge integration through ontologies, semantic metadata and databases of annotations. The aim of building ontologies is to share and reuse knowledge. Since the SW is a distributed network, there are different ontologies that describe semantically equivalent things. Therefore, it is necessary to map elements of these ontologies if one wants to process information across applications or domains.

W3C's OWL (Ontology Working Language) Web Ontology Language is a popular language used to represent ontologies on the Web. OWL facilitates greater machine interpretability of Web content than that supported by XML, RDF, and RDF Schema by providing additional vocabulary along with formal semantics. The basic components of OWL include classes, properties, and individuals. Classes are the basic building blocks of OWL ontology. A class is a concept in a domain. Classes usually constitute a taxonomic hierarchy (for example, a subclass-superclass hierarchy). Properties have two main categories: (a) Object properties, which relate individuals to other individuals; and (b) Datatype properties, which relate individuals to datatype values, such as integers, float, and strings. OWL makes use of XML Schema for defining datatypes. Individuals are instances of classes, and properties can relate one individual to another.

Examples of ontologies include catalogs for online shopping sites like Amazon.com, domain-specific standard terminology like UNSPSC (a terminology used for products and services), or various taxonomies on the Web, like the "My Yahoo" categories.

2.2 Web-based DSS & Web Services

Since the beginning of the last decade, DSS technology and applications have enabled significantly powerful DSS functionality. The Web, in particular, has enabled both intra- and inter-organizational DSS [11] for individuals, workgroups, and teams and has given rise to numerous new applications of existing technology as well as many new decision support technologies themselves [33]. The Web has also helped to extend the capabilities of DSS to a very large number of users. The standard Web browser has been used as the user interface/dialog means that companies could introduce new DSS technologies at their sites at relatively low cost when compared to client-based DSS. A Web browser user interface allowed the implementation of DSS technology with very little user training.

Web-based DSS are computerized systems that deliver decision support information or decision support tools to managers or business analysts using "thin-client" Web browser such as Netscape Navigator or Internet Explorer that are used for accessing the Global Internet or a corporate intranet. The server computer that hosts the DSS application is linked to the user's computer by a network with the TCP/IP protocol. Web-based DSS are classified into several categories such as communications-driven, data-driven, document-driven, knowledge-driven, model-driven, and hybrid. Web technologies are used to implement any of these categories of DSS. The term Web-based means the entire application is implemented using Web technologies.

The potential exists for Web-based DSS to increase productivity and profitability, and speed the decision making process without regard to geographic limitations [21]. Through increased decision making ability, reduced costs, and reduced support needs, Web-based DSS can significantly improve companies' use of their existing infrastructures. More executives and managers can have access to technology that increases overall organizational efficiency and effectiveness [23].

Web Services. An advanced technology that is relevant to the field of SW and DSS is Web services. Web services are "services" offered by one application to other applications via the Web [44]. Developers can aggregate the services to form an end-user application, enable business transactions, or create new Web services. They are software components and applications that use Internet technologies and standards, and they can be accessed through the Internet, intranet, or extranet. Their applications are growing and it has been projected that most of the next generation Internet- intranet-based e-business systems will be based on Web services [26]. The popularity of Web services is due to the fact that it is designed to allow enterprises to move to a more "plug-and-play" business IT infrastructures, which would provide tremendous flexibility in managing IT resources and budgets.

Web services provide DSS designers and builders the ability to design, create, and deliver applications more quickly and cost-effectively. The three fundamental methods in a Web services system are: register; discover; and bind. When an organization exposes services on its Web site, the services are ready to use, but only by clients that know in advance where the service is and how to access it. To increase the number of potential customers, Web service providers will *register* their services in a public registry. Registries provide the equivalent of a phone book for Web services. Once services have been registered, would-be service consumers can locate systems that provide relevant operations and information. Registry specifications include interfaces for various kinds of query, including industry type, name of service, key word descriptions, etc. The registry provides enough information for service consumers to *discover* Web services dynamically and to learn how to access them. Once a service consumer has located a relevant service in the registry, the consumer has the information it needs to use that service. Connecting to the service provider, passing correctly formed input, and receiving the results, is called *binding* to the service.

Web services can bind together autonomous heterogeneous applications, data services, and components residing in distributed environments. Thus, they facilitate universal interoperability and integration [10], and hence the common intersection with the semantic Web technologies.

3   Semantic DSS Environment

In this section we attempt to identify how and where SW technologies could be used effectively in conjunction with Web-based DSS to bring out the best of each to create a more friendly, capable and intelligent DSS environment for the users. We use the term *Semantic DSS Environment* to denote such an environment resulting from such a combination. We envision *Semantic DSS* (the combination of SW and Web-based DSS) to provide programmatic assistance in managing Web-based DSS resources, components, applications, and knowledge for coordination of required DSS processes for carrying out decision-making sessions by the users through the systematic application of SW technologies. For example, consider the scenario where a decision maker has to access data and other knowledge resources that are scattered across a global enterprise in order to solve a particular problem at hand. Typically, these resources are heterogeneous and are not readily usable within a Web-based DSS environment. However, if the same resources are made available using Semantic Web technologies, then the DSS can make use of these resources seamlessly.

As discussed earlier, the SW currently offers the means to integrate heterogeneous systems across organizations or organizational units in a meaningful way by incorporating various technologies such as *ontology*, a common, standard and shareable vocabulary used to represent the meaning of system entities; *knowledge representation*, with structured collections of information and sets of inference rules that can be used to conduct automated reasoning; and *intelligent agents* [37] that collect content from diverse sources and exchange semantically enriched information. These three are envisioned to form the foundation technology for Semantic DSS.

One of the challenges for DSS researchers therefore is to provide insight into how and where to effectively apply the SW technologies to support the transparent flow of semantically enriched information and knowledge, including content and know-how, to enable, enhance and coordinate collaborative DSS processes within and across organizational boundaries. Accordingly, the semantic DSS processes will be characterized by the seamless and transparent flow of semantically enriched information and knowledge for their effective operations.

3.1 Ontology Development and Application for Semantic DSS Environment

The realization of the Semantic DSS will require the construction of ontologies for the various representation languages, query languages, and inference technology that are needed to support the Semantic DSS environment [16]. A key endeavor in this regard would be the design and modeling of Semantic DSS repositories and distributed knowledge-based systems for their use. Criteria and rules must be established that would allow Semantic DSS ontologies to do true information integration and automatic reasoning across data and information derived from different sources.

The Semantic DSS ontologies would form a network of concepts, relationships, and constraints that would provide context for data and information as well as processes within the DSS environment. They would enhance service discovery in Web services, modeling, assembly, mediation, and semantic interoperability. Additionally, they would provide formal specification of DSS components and their relationships that facilitate machine reasoning and inference. They would tie DSS subsystems together using metadata, much as a database ties together discrete pieces of data.

Some of the key areas the DSS researchers need to study and investigate would include, but not limited to: (a) developing ontologies with OWL for DSS information retrieval and incorporating Web services facilities within DSS environment, (b) designing effective tools for development and management of DSS ontologies, (c) developing ontologies for semantic DSS data modeling, (d) developing applications that focus on using semantics to manage interoperation in DSS databases, and (e) designing applications using ontologies for DSS data/knowledge integration.

3.2 Semantic Search – Ontology Mapping and Matching

As SW technologies see widespread use in the near future, effective semantic search capabilities will become a must for DSS environments. A semantic search engine would seek to find documents that have similar 'concepts' not just similar 'words'. However, in order for the semantic-based search engines to not suffer from performance problems from the scale of a very large semantic network, they have to be intelligent to be effective in finding responsive results and reducing the amount of irrelevant results. These search engines would therefore need the ability to do ontology mapping and ontology matching.

Since the SW is distributive, numerous resource descriptions are introduced where two concepts are equivalent, but are described using different terms. The resolution of such terminology conflicts requires ontology mapping and matching. Ontology mapping enables interoperability among different sources in the semantic Web. It is required for combining distributed and heterogeneous ontologies based on semantic relations that have been defined between them.

The problem of finding the semantic mappings between two given ontologies is called ontology matching, which lies at the heart of numerous information processing applications. Virtually any application that involves multiple ontologies must establish semantic mappings to ensure interoperability.

Ontology matching is a key solution to the semantic heterogeneity problem. It finds correspondences between semantically related entities of the ontologies. These correspondences can be used for various tasks, such as ontology merging, query answering, data translation, or for navigation on the semantic Web. Thus, matching ontologies enables the knowledge and data expressed in the matched ontologies to interoperate.

It is therefore important for the DSS researchers to find effective methods for ontology construction, matching, and mapping, which support semantic search engines.

3.3 Semantic Knowledge Management

The systematic management of the semantic knowledge to enhance the capability and value of the DSS environment is another need to address by and a challenge for the DSS researchers. Semantic knowledge management would incorporate: semantic knowledge access, semantic search engines, and use of intelligent DAML-S agents [15]. The DAML (DARPA Agent Markup Language) program's focus is to develop an agent language and tools to facilitate the concept of SW [12]. DAML-S [1], an extension of DAML, provides a standard way to define Web services based on ontology, which allows for context-based service discovery.

Semantic knowledge management can help enhance the DSS users' experience within the environment. For example: Web portals using OWL can gather relevant links more rapidly, and syndicate their content to other like-minded sites with ease; within the semantic knowledge repositories, semantic annotations for multimedia collections such as images, audio, and other non-textual objects will make them searchable and easy to locate; DAML-S agents can provide the capability to understand and integrate diverse information resources; and OWL-S, the ontology Web language for semantic Web services can help integrate Web services within knowledge management.

3.4 Semantic User Interface

The end-user interaction with or touch point to the SW can be conceptualized as the semantic user interface. The semantic user interface should be designed in a way that would separate the functions of the user interface from its visual appearance. That is, the designers must adopt a view of the user interface that goes beyond look and feel. It must be intelligent, distributed, and knowledge-intensive. It will exist as a continuum of the rest of the Web and will include knowledge agents, which know how to assemble information for user interaction. These agents will specialize in forms of knowledge useful in interacting with human users as well as with application processes.

The direct manipulation user interfaces common today have proven popular in desktop applications for many years. Graphic controls, such as list boxes, pull-down menus, pop-up menus, tree menus, scrollbars, and tool tips have all been used to considerable advantage. The current user interface provided by the Web browsers is necessary but insufficient, for delivering the SW to the desk or palm top. The semantic user interface must not only provide the delivery mechanism for system functionality, but for it to be effective, it must draw upon the underlying capabilities of the applications to enable the user to do what needs to be done.

The semantic user interface design is quite challenging to the designers since the underlying applications in SW are implemented on a confederation of loosely affiliated elements. The user in a SW environment would typically encounter collections of distributed entities, conscripted on call to the user's goals and aspirations. To make this encounter interesting and beneficial to the user, a deeper understanding of the user interface is critical.

The semantic user interface would guide the distributed entities to interoperate by exchanging ontology-based information instead of data expressed in standardized formats. The use of ontologies would provide a context that will enhance the ability of application to reason about information received from outside sources.

3.5 Semantic Web Services for the DSS environment

Although SW concepts and Web services specifications were developed by different groups of researchers and organizations, there is now a growing understanding of the benefits of combining the two to form "semantic Web (SW) services" [28, 34]. Web services provide a uniform infrastructure for the provision of services leveraging Web technologies, but they offer only syntactical descriptions that are hardly amenable to automation. SW services will combine the meaningful representation of information, relationships and context from the SW community with the dynamic discovery and binding of the Web service specifications to create a DSS environment that will allow contextual discovery and use of Web services [19, 36]. For example, Web services within DSS environment could provide different modeling applications to a problem-solving session such as data mining or simulation.

In a Web services model there are three key roles. First, the service requestor, namely, customer, in this case the DSS user; second, service providers, namely, specific online businesses who provide services; and third, service brokers, who maintain registries (catalogs) of services and their capabilities. Service providers publish the capabilities of their services and rules to access them, using WSDL (Web Services Description Language) descriptions to the service registries which follow the Universal Description, Discovery and Integration (UDDI) standards. Interaction amongst these three roles is supported by the Web service model, which also provides facilities for service composition and service execution for fulfilling service requests.

In a SW service environment service registration would include a semantically rich description of the service model [30]. Service consumers will be able to discover service providers based on reasoning about the context within which the service is defined. This semantics-based discovery process will help loosen the coupling between service consumers and service providers, allowing for greater flexibility across the DSS environment. SW services will also improve on current methods of binding a consumer to a service. When service operations are registered using current Web service specifications, the parameter and return types must be exactly defined. If, however, the service is defined using ontologies, it is possible for would-be consumers to learn the context in which the parameter and return classes are defined [17]. This will allow the consumer i.e. the user to relate those classes to classes in its own information model. DAML-S specifications provide a standard way to define services based on ontologies, which will allow context-based service discovery [29].

4 Semantic DSS Environment Architecture

Organizations are beginning to explore the use of semantic web technologies within their decision support application development [22]. The integration of web services into the decision support environment provides several business benefits that include lowering costs, improving application sharing, increasing flexibility, and innovative model execution and problem solving. However, there are a few obstacles that need to be overcome before widespread adoption of semantic web technologies into decision support systems can happen [39]. They include searching for appropriate decision support services, availability of relevant services, their reliability, composition of these services, and performance of web services based decision support systems. The semantic web technologies discussed in the previous section help to design a flexible, intelligent, and sophisticated decision support environment. These technologies also help minimize the cognitive burden on the user in solving complex problems by providing the user with additional knowledge and interface resources.

The architecture of the proposed Semantic DSS Environment is shown in Figure 1. The two major subsystems that comprise the architecture are (a) Internal Components, and (b) External Components. The internal components subsystem contains modules or resources that are available and under the control of the organization as well as the components that typically constitute a decision support system. The internal components subsystem is composed of: (a) intelligent user interface, (b) database and model base, (c) knowledge base, (d) ontologies, (e) DSS manager, (f) semantic search mechanisms, and (g) semantic web service discovery and composition mechanism. The external components consist of: (a) semantic web service providers, (b) semantic web service registry, and (c) ontological and knowledge resources. These components are briefly described below.

4.1 Internal Components

Intelligent User Interface. The user interface contains intelligent agents that can act on behalf of humans and assist them in executing complex tasks. They can be integrated into knowledge-driven semantic web DSS environments to shield the complexities and help novice users tackle unstructured problems. Development of multi-agent systems is also increasing [24, 41] and these systems contain agents that are capable of acting autonomously, cooperatively, and collaboratively to achieve a collective goal. An agent by itself may not have sufficient information or expertise to solve an entire problem; hence mutual sharing of information and expertise is necessary to allow a group of agents to produce a solution to a problem. Agent collaboration involves joint work by a group of agents on a common task. The interface agent provides mechanisms for the user to interact with the system. It enables the user to carryout various modeling and analysis tasks and renders the forms and reports created by the system as well as other outputs generated during data analysis and model execution. It also maintains user profiles and facilitates customization and parameterization of the tasks.

Database and Model Base. The database component provides data support for the operation of the semantic DSS environment. Data management component provides access to attribute and spatial data. It may encompass traditional databases as well as GIS databases. Thus, the data management component provides easy access to large volumes as well as different types of data. It also provides mechanisms to derive new data sets from existing data based on various criteria and the problem at hand.

The model base component provides access to a large number of models necessary for analyzing and solving unstructured problems. The model base supports both aspatial and spatial models. It also facilitates development and testing of new algorithms and models. For example, in the domain of facilities planning, Multi-Criteria Evaluation (MCE) technique is frequently used, which allows evaluating several criteria in the decision process. This requires a diverse source of information as well as generating multiple versions of the model with varying weighted linear combinations of attributes.

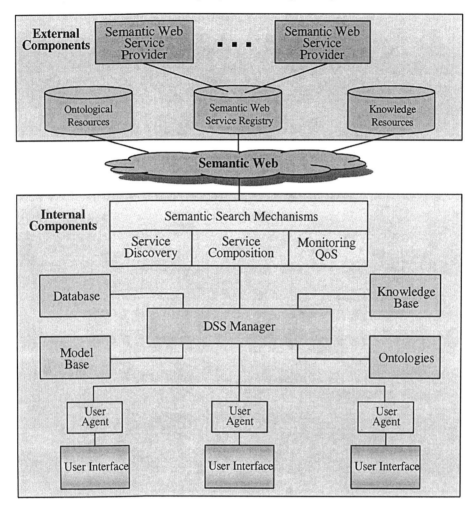

Figure 1. Semantic DSS Environment Architecture

Knowledge Base. The knowledge base contains domain specific knowledge relevant to a particular problem. It also contains rules that enable the user to select the appropriate type of model to use for a particular task and perform sensitivity analysis. It may also contain organizational policies, procedures, business rules and constraints that may be relevant for the problem at hand. This helps in ensuring that developers adhere to the organization wide standards that need to be followed during application development.

Ontologies. Ontologies have been proposed as a way to capture common sense knowledge about the real world and can be used to increase our semantic understanding for decision support. An ontology describes one's world, although there are many different definitions, descriptions, types and approaches to ontology development. An ontology generally consists of terms, their definitions, and axioms relating them. For this research, the most relevant ontologies are domain ontologies that specify conceptualizations specific to a domain [42]. Ontological resources may incorporate a combination of different lexical and ontological sources of knowledge. For example, different kinds of information can be gathered from WordNet [18] and the DAML ontology library (http://www.daml.org/) that are useful for disambiguating terms and providing additional semantic information.

DSS Manager. The DSS manager serves as the controlling unit that takes care of the communication between the collaborating modules and coordinates the various tasks that need to be executed in order to solve the problem that the user is working on. This module essentially drives the "what-if" scenario analyses. It maintains meta-data about the various models that are part of the semantic DSS environment and provides interface to the model base and helps the user in model selection as well as execution. It coordinates the results generated by other modules which carry out specific sub-tasks related to problem solving.

Search Mechanism. While solving unstructured problems, decision makers may need to search and retrieve relevant information from a number of external sources, particularly, the information sources on the Web. However, typical search mechanisms are inadequate to support the semantic searches required. This component enhances the search process by incorporating semantics into query formulation and execution. It relies on term co-occurrence to improve query relevance and word-sense disambiguation [35]. For example, a user is more likely to find a result relevant if it contains not only the original query term, but also includes additional terms that are related to the desired sense of the query term and excludes terms that are related to unwanted senses of the query term.

Service Discovery and Composition. Organizations are acquiring the necessary semantic web tools in order to facilitate efficient DSS application development. These tools are in three major areas: a) service discovery, b) service composition, and c) monitoring. Service discovery tools help search for appropriate services available on the semantic web. This involves gaining access to various service registries and identifying those services that match the requirements of the problem currently being solved. If perfect matches are not found, then, these tools can suggest partial matches and suggest how to customize those services. The service composition tools help determine whether the selected services can be composed together and successfully solve the problem at hand. These tools also help in optimizing the services in terms of setting the appropriate values for various parameters. Once a semantic DSS application is constructed using one or more semantic web services, they have to be monitored continuously. The monitoring tools can be configured to make sure that those services meet the quality of service thresholds set forth in the service agreement. Many of these tools can be implemented as agents and made available to developers throughout the entire organization.

4.2 External Components

Semantic Web Service Providers. The semantic web service providers primarily consist of vendors that provide one or more web services that might be integrated into a decision support application. These services may support specific functionalities with well defined interfaces and extensive documentation as to how to use them in a particular application. The success of web service providers greatly depends on describing and advertising their services correctly and efficiently. Web service providers face the problem of how to publicize their services so that service seekers can easily find these services and evaluate their suitability. After all, if the service seekers can't find or get appropriate information about a particular web service, then the likelihood of some one using that service is grim and hence the service provider stands to lose lot of market share [43]. Semantic web service providers typically model the requirements and functionalities that their web service can satisfy, and then transform this model into appropriate ontologies.

Semantic Web Service Registry. The semantic web service registry is a central repository that publishes the availability of web services. Web services are modeled using DAML-S or other ontology languages, which contains ServiceProfile, ServiceModel, and ServiceGrounding [38]. The ServiceProfile describes what a service can do and contains contact information about the service provider and an extensible set of service characteristics. This helps in advertising the service as well as spotting by service seekers.

Ontological and Knowledge Resources. The ontological and knowledge resources contain information about various web services, computational and model execution, which can be used by applications for reasoning and exhibiting intelligent behavior. Domain specific knowledge resources may contain knowledge that is relevant to a particular application domain that the organization specializes in. This knowledge would be of great help to semantic DSS developers.

   The semantic DSS architecture described above is modular in nature and additional domain specific components can be easily added to the system as long as the interfaces are clearly defined. Using this environment, decision makers can tackle complex problems and the system provides a number of facilities for tapping into the data, model, and knowledge bases available both within and outside the organization. The system supports interoperability between internal and external components through ontologies and existing standards. It also improves communication with other existing applications.

5 Future Research

While several research areas and topics were identified in the previous sections, this section tries to summarize a few of them and also provide some new ones.

   First and foremost, there is a need for the design and development of several types of tools to proliferate the use of SW in DSS environments. A few of them are: tools for development and management of DSS ontologies; automated tools for dynamic service discovery in SW services and annotation of results of services with semantic information; new tools and algorithms for semantic search must be developed and tested for efficiency and effectiveness; and tools for ontology mapping and matching. Despite SW's pervasiveness, today ontology matching is still largely conducted manually, in a labor-intensive and error-prone process. The manual matching has become a key bottleneck in building large-scale SW-based systems.

Second, there is a need for developing various SW applications for the DSS environment. These applications could represent pilot projects and research prototypes to show the way in which the SW technologies can strengthen the current Web potentials within DSS environments. Applications such as semantic Web mining, semantic knowledge portals and semantic knowledge management within each DSS components – data, model and interface would be a good starting point.

Finally, the DSS technology of the future will lead to ubiquitous access to information and decision support tools through the use of mobile tools, mobile e-services, and wireless protocols such as wireless applications protocol (WAP), wireless markup language (WML), and iMode. Adaptations of existing SW and Web services to the wireless environment will pose some unique and new challenges to DSS researchers.

6   Concluding Remarks

The WWW is the biggest repository of information ever created, but it is difficult to make sense of this content by computer systems because they do not understand the meaning of the content or information about the content. A semantic Web in its envisioned form, it can provide the ability to tag all content on the Web, describe what each piece of information is about and give semantic meaning to the content item. This chapter has attempted to study the semantic Web technologies in terms of what they are, as well as how and where they could be effectively used in Web-based DSS to enhance its environment.

In this chapter, we have discussed the core technologies that contribute to the semantic Web and discussed why organizations might want to adopt those technologies. With the semantic Web technologies, organizations can provide a single, unified view of data across their applications, which allow for precise retrieval of information, simplifies interoperability, reduces data redundancy, and provides uniform semantic meaning across applications. They are essential for building future DSS environments.

References

1.   Ankolekar, A., Burstein, M., Son, T.C., Hobbs, J., Lassila, O., Martin, D., McDermott, D, McIlraith, S., Narayanan, S., Poalucci, M., Payne, T., Sycara, K., and Zeng, H. (2001) "DAML-S: semantic markup for Web services," *The First Semantic Web Working Symposium*, Stanford University, California, pp. 411-430.

2. Benjamins, R. (2002) "Agents and the semantic Web: a business perspective," *Agent Technology Conference (ATC).*

3. Berners-Lee, T., Hendler, J., and Lassila, O. (2001) "The semantic Web," *Scientific American,* 284, May, pp. 34-43.

4. Bharati, P. and Chaudhury, A. (2004) "Am empirical investigation of decision-making satisfaction in Web-based decision support systems," *Decision Support Systems,* 37, pp. 187-197.

5. Bhargava, H.K. and Power, D.J. (2001) "Decision Support Systems and Web technologies: a status report," *Seventh Americas Conference on Information Systems.*

6. Bhargava, H.K.; Krishnan, R.; and Muller, R. (1997) "Decision support on demand: emerging electronic markets for decision technologies," *Decision Support Systems,* 19, pp. 193-214.

7. Brickley, D., and Guha, R. (Eds.) (2002) *Resource description framework (RDF) schema specification. W3C Working Draft 30 April 2002* Cambridge, MA: W3C. Available at: http://www.w3.org/TR/rdf-schema.

8. Burstein, F., Bui, T., and Arnott, D. (2001) "Decision support in the new millennium," *Decision Support Systems,* 31, pp. 163-164.

9. Carlsson, C. and Turban, E. (2002) "Decision support systems: directions for the next decade," *Decision Support Systems,* 33, pp. 105-110.

10. Chung, J., Lin, K., & Mathieu, R.G. (2003). "Web services computing: Advancing software interoperability," *IEEE Computer,* 36(10), pp. 35-37.

11. Cohen, M., Kelly, C.B., and Medaglia, A.L. (2001) "Decision support with Web-enabled software," *Interfaces,* 31(2), March-April, pp. 109-128.

12. DAML Coalition (2001) *Darpa Agent Markup Language,* http://www.daml.org.

13. Davies, J., Fensel, D., and van Harmelen, F. (Eds.) (2002) *"Towards the Semantic Web: Ontology-Driven Knowledge Management,"* Wiley, NY: New York.

14. Dell'Erba, M. (2004) "Exploiting semantic Web technologies for data interoperability," *AIS SIGSEMIS,* 1(3), pp. 48-52.

15. Denker, G., Hobbs, J., Martin, D., Narayanan, S., and Waldinger, R. (2001) "Accessing information and services on the DAML-enabled Web," *Proceedings of the 2nd International Workshop on the Semantic Web – SemWeb'2001,* May.

16. Ding, Y., and Fensel, D. (2001) "Ontology library systems: the key for successful ontology reuse," *The First Semantic Web Working Symposium,* Stanford University, pp. 93-112.

17. Dogaac, A., Laleci, G., Kabak, Y., and Cingil, I. (2002) "Exploiting Web service semantics: taxonomies vs. ontologies," *IEEE Data Engineering Bulletin,* pp. 10-16.

18. Fellbaum, C. (1998) *WordNet: An Electronic Lexical Database.* MIT Press, Cambridge, MA, 1998.

19. Fensel, D., Bussler, C., and Maedche, A. (2002) "Semantic Web enabled Web services," *Proceedings of the International Semantic Web Conference,* LNCS, Springer, pp. 1-2.

20. Fensel, D., Hendler, J., Lieberman, H., and Wahlster, W. (Eds.) (2003) *"Spinning the Semantic Web,"* Cambridge, MA: MIT Press.

21. Gregg, D.G.; Goul, M.; and Philippakis, A. (2002) "Distributing decision support systems on the WWW: the verification of a decision support systems metadata model," *Decision Support Systems,* 32, pp. 233-245.

22. Hagel , J. (2002). Out of box: Strategies for achieving profits today and growth through web services. Harvard Business School Press, Boston: MA.

23. Hallett, P. (2001) "Web-based analytics improve decision making," *DM Review,* www.dmreview.com.

24. He, M., and Jennings, N. R. (2003) "SouthamptonTAC: An Adaptive Autonomous Trading Agent," ACM Transactions on Internet Technology (TOIT), Vol. 3 No. 3, 2003, pp. 219 – 235.
25. Hendler, J. (2001) "Agents on the semantic Web," *IEEE Intelligent Systems*, 16(2), pp.30-37.
26. Kreger, H. (2003) "Fulfilling the Web services promise," *Communications of the ACM*, 46(6), pp. 29-34.
27. Maedche, A., and Staab, S. (2001) "Ontology learning for the semantic Web," *IEEE Intelligent Systems*, 16(2), pp. 72-79.
28. McIlraith, S.A., and Martin, D.L. (2003) "Bringing semantics to Web services," *IEEE Intelligent Systems*, 18(1), pp. 90-93.
29. Pahl, C. and Casey, M. (2003) "Ontology support for Web service processes," *Proceedings of the 9th European Software Engineering Conference*, September.
30. Paolucci, M., Kawmura, T., Payne, T., and Sycara, K. (2002) "Semantic matching of Web services capabilities," *Proceedings of First International Semantic Web Conference*.
31. Power, D.J. (1999) Decision Support Systems Glossary. *DSS Resources, World Wide Web*, http://www.DSSResources.com/glossary.
32. Power, D.J. (2000) "Web-based and model-driven decision support systems: concepts and issues," *Proceedings of the Americas Conference on Information Systems*, pp. 352-355.
33. Shim, J.P., Warkentin, M., Courtney, J.F., Power, D.J., Sharda, R., and Carlsson, C. (2002) "Past, present, and future of decision support technology," *Decision Support Systems*, 33, pp. 111-126.
34. Sivashanmugam, K., Verma, K., Sheth, A., and Miller, J. (2003) "Adding semantics to Web services standards," *1st International Conference of Web-Services*, 395-401.
35. Snasel, V., Moravec, P., Pokorny, J. (2005) "WordNet Ontology Based Model for Web Retrieval," *Proceedings of the International Workshop on Challenges in Web Information Retrieval and Integration, WIRI '05*, April 2005, pp. 220 – 225.
36. Sollazzo, T., Handschuh, S., Staab, S., and Frank, M. (2002) "Semantic Web service architecture – evolving Web service standards toward the semantic Web," *Proceedings of the 15th International FLAIRS Conference*, AAAI Press.
37. Stroulia, E., and Hatch, M.P. (2003) "An intelligent-agent architecture for flexible service integration on the Web," *IEEE Transactions on Systems, Man and Cybernetics*, Part C 33 (4), pp. 468-479.
38. Sycara, K., Paolucci, M., Ankolekar, A., and Srinivasan, N. (2003). "Automated Discovery, Interaction and Composition of Semantic Web Services," Journal of Web Semantics, Vol. 1, No. 1, pp. 27 – 46.
39. Tilley, S., Gerdes, J., Hamilton, T., Huang, S., Miller, H., Smith, D., & Wong, K. (2004). "On business value and technical challenges of adopting web services," Journal of Software Maintenance and Evolution: Research and Practice, 16, 31-50.
40. Trastour, D., et al. (2002) "Semantic Web support for the business-to-business e-commerce lifecycle," *WWW2002*, Honolulu, Hawaii, pp. 89-98.
41. Wang, H., Mylopoulos, J., and Liao, S. (2002) "Intelligent Agents and Financial Risk Monitoring Systems," Communications of the ACM, Vol. 45, No. 3, pp. 83 – 88.
42. Weber, R. (2002) "Ontological Issues in Accounting Information Systems," Sutton, S. and Arnold, V., (Eds.), *Researching Accounting as an Information Systems Discipline* Sarasota, FL: American Accounting Association, 2002b.
43. Zeng, L., Benatallah, B., Lei, H., Ngu, A., Flaxer, D., and Chang, H., (2003). "Flexible Composition of Enterprise Web Services," *Electronic Markets*, 13 (2), pp. 141 – 152.
44. Zhao, J.L. and Cheng, H.K. (2005) "Web services and process management: a union of convenience or a new area of research?" *Decision Support Systems*, 40, pp. 1-8.

Towards a Unified Representation Framework for Modelbases and Databases

Thadthong Bhrammanee[1], Vilas Wuwongse[1]

Computer Science & Information Management Program, School of Engineering and Technology, Asian Institute of Technology, Thailand.

{ttb,vw}@cs.ait.ac.th

Abstract. Modelbases and databases are complementary to each other in Decision Support Systems. Hence, there exists a need for a framework to uniformly represent modelbases and databases in order to facilitate information exchange and integration between them. Because of the advancement in Web technologies and business globalization, such a framework must be Web-based, promote reuse and share modelbase and database information among branch locations, and be able to express user-defined rules, which are culturally diverse. This paper proposes a unified framework for modelbases and databases. It comprises two major components: Ontology and Schema. The former provides the meanings of specific terminology widely agreed upon by concerned communities; the latter, contains purely generic schematic descriptions of specific information. The framework is represented by means of OWL Declarative Description (ODD)—a language with well-defined semantics and expressive means for direct and uniform representation of database and modelbase components, as well as inferences and rules.

Keywords: Web-based DSS, unified representation, modelbase, database, ontology, OWL, ODD.

1 Introduction

A modelbase and a database are integral parts of a Web-based Decision Support System (DSS) [14]. A modelbase stores a collection of decision models, referred to here as quantitative models used in Management Science and Operations Research (MS/OR), such as optimization and financial models. In contrast, a database performs data organization and retrieval using database queries; it focuses on representing large amounts of simple datasets.

Modelbases and databases need data models. Data models are a framework that modelbases and databases use to represent and describe their information items, relationships, and constraints in an abstract way. Modelbase representations seem to heavily borrow data models from databases, in order to employ those data models as their underlying conceptual foundations. Uses of database data models to represent modelbases/databases are classified as: (1) Use of the *relational model*, by which decision models and data are organized based on relations or tables (e.g., [11, 12]), (2) Use of the *data abstraction/frames* to represent decision models and data by using frame structures (e.g., [4]), (3) Employment of the *data abstraction/Object-Oriented model* to represent decision models and data using the Object-Oriented (OO) model in order to exploit the OO benefits, such as an inheritance hierarchy and a polymorphism, and adopting query languages of the OO Database Management System (ODBMS) to retrieve a dataset (e.g. [7, 10, 13]), (4) Use of a *semi-structured model* to make decision models and data self-described so as to associate the information that is normally coupled with a schema within themselves (e.g. [5, 8]).

Business organizations, particularly global companies (companies having world-wide local locations), need modelbases and databases as part of their DSS applications. Current concerns that affect the design of modelbase and database frameworks are:

Regulations. The advancement of business globalization urges many companies to have geographically diverse locations, where local rules/regulations vary from place to place. Modelbase and database frameworks should be able to let the stored information abide by the appropriate regulations of each location (e.g., tax rate and wage rate) while taking into account the business policies of the company.

User Efforts. First, decision models and data are complementary to each other, but the lack of a uniform framework for modelbases and databases creates excessive effort for users of DSS applications. For example, they have to independently construct a query to retrieve and maintain decision models and data. Second, users may be unaware of available data that are essential to supplement the decision models in order to compute the solution result.

Web Technologies. First, the eXtensible Markup Language (XML)-based technologies are being promoted as a viable Web technology. As a result, modelbases inevitably require access to existing data sources that provide XML interfaces, and vise versa. Second, the Web has been considered as a widely accepted information infrastructure for global companies; modern Web-based applications, inclusive of Web-based DSS, require information that provides a formal semantic in order to communicate across the Web, to be reused across branch locations and application domains, and to infer new information automatically. Such application demands a description of business information in a way that is formal and independent of concrete system platforms.

Unfortunately, existing frameworks have been unsatisfactory in amending those realizations in one way or another:

Firstly, they lack the ability to express complex rules or handle cultural differences. For example, decision models and data using the relational model employ a table format of the Relational Database Management System (e.g., [11]). Such a format has limitations, such as limited capability to provide the specification of rules in a relatively precise context and limited set of data type; users cannot define a customized data type as part of business rules, e.g., the data type of numbers that are larger than 20. Moreover, this traditional data model does not support the creation of reusable modelbase/database components very well. This reuse of modelbase/database components is an opportunity to reuse core similarities across different businesses while adjusting details to fit distinct organization location/culture.

Secondly, there exists an incapability to intelligently retrieve data into decision models [4, 5, 8, 11, 12]. Some existing frameworks do not provide a modelbase/database data model that can effectively carry out unwritten semantics, "freight cost stored in a database is equivalent to a transportation cost in a modelbase; and if the value of the freight cost in the database does not violate federal law, then bring it to the decision model as a value of the transportation cost" is an example of unwritten semantics.

Lastly, many existing frameworks do not sufficiently address the issue of compatibility with Web technologies, partly due to the fact that they were not intended to directly support a Web-based environment [4, 11, 12]. The most recent trend in modelbase representation has been to use XML as the preferred mechanism to define model representations [5, 8]. However, XML cannot achieve the level of interoperability required by the application of Semantic Web ear. XML just defines the basic grammar for the document structure but does not recognize the semantics of the information contained in the document necessary to enable flexible dynamic mapping among decision models developed by different groups of people. In addition, XML does not take into account the ability to make inferences.

Overcoming these limitations while accommodating the advantages of the XML-based Web technologies, a new representation framework called "OWL Declarative Description for Modelbases and Databases" (OFMD) is proposed. It can uniformly represent modelbases and databases, as well as support seamless integration and reuse of decision models and data. In addition, it can represent rules which are different among local locations while abiding by the core policies of a company. OFMD is extensible and suitable for being incorporated into the Web-based infrastructure. It is comprised of two major components: Ontology and Schema. The former provides the meanings of specific terminology widely agreed upon by concerned business communities; the latter, contains purely generic schematic descriptions of specific information. Those basic components are ready to represent the modelbase and database by adopting the components as Model Ontology and Model Schema, and Data Ontology and Data Schema, respectively. OFMD employs "OWL Declarative Description" (ODD) as the underlying unified language that represents and describes the framework components, as well as the rules in a formal and declarative manner. ODD extends OWL (Web Ontology Language—the language for processing information on the web) [3]. ODD incorporates variables into OWL and enhances OWL's expressiveness and computational power by means of clauses (rules). Major components of OFMD, i.e. Ontology and Schema, are seamlessly interoperated because of their unified representation using ODD. Thus, the framework aims to flexibly represent both modelbases and databases under the same unified language and conceptual model and to facilitate information exchange and integration between them.

Section 2 introduces ODD; Section 3 proposes basic components of the framework; Section 4 shows the representation of modelbases and databases; and Section 5 is discussion. Finally, Section 6 draws conclusions.

2   Introduction to OWL Declarative Description (ODD)

Because of the trend to use OWL to describe business information, this paper employs OWL as a primitive language for describing modelbase and database information. OWL is a W3C's recommended ontology markup language for the Web. OWL is built on top of RDF—a framework for describing resources on the web; both RDF and OWL are usually written in XML. OWL can employ all RDF features, such as declaring properties and allowing creation of a subproperty hierarchy. More specially, OWL can define the information beyond the capability of RDF and XML, such as specifying classes as a logical combination of other classes. For example, local employees are the intersection of employees and persons who live in an area.

Although OWL is widely recognized as a formal language for specifying concepts and relationships, it still has limited expressive power to describe complex constraints and rules. Therefore, this paper proposes an underlying unified language, namely "OWL Declarative Description" (ODD), to represent and describe the framework components. ODD extends OWL's expressiveness. Generally, ODD is an extension of RDF Declarative Description (RDD) [1]—a modeling language that can directly represent all RDF-based languages. ODD extends RDD by 1) incorporating elements that contain an OWL namespace and 2) introducing ontological axioms for the support of OWL semantics.

ODD can directly represent OWL and it extends ordinary well-formed OWL elements by incorporation of variables for the enhancement of expressive power and representation of implicit information of a decision model into so-called OWL expressions. Every component of an OWL expression can contain variables, e.g., tag names or attribute names (N-variables), string or literal contents (S-variables), expressions (E-variables), pairs of attributes and values (P-variables), and some partial structure (I-variables). Every variable is prefixed by "$T:", where T denotes its type. Ordinary OWL elements—ground OWL expressions—are OWL expressions without variables. OWL elements with variables are called non-ground OWL expressions.

More complex and implicit information can be modeled by an ODD description. An ODD description is a set of OWL clauses, each of which has the form:

$$H \leftarrow B_1,..., B_m, \beta_1,..., \beta_n$$

where m, $n \geq 0$, H and B_i are OWL expressions, and each of the β_i is a predefined *OWL constraint*—useful for defining a restriction on OWL expressions or their components. The OWL expression H is called the *head*, the set $\{B_1,...,B_m, \beta_1,...,\beta_n\}$ the *body* of the clause. When the body is empty, such a clause is referred to as an *OWL unit clause* and the symbol '$\leftarrow$' will often be omitted; hence, an OWL element or document can be mapped directly onto *a ground OWL unit clause*. Given an ODD description P, its meaning is the set of all OWL elements that are directly described by and are derivable from the unit and the non-unit clauses in P, respectively. Paper [1] provides the theoretical details of the theory.

Support of OWL semantics can be carried out by means of OWL non-unit clauses, e.g., the meaning of owl: SymmetricProperty is modeled by an OWL non-unit clause as:

(the body of the clause) if a PropertyX is symmetric and an IndividualA (a member of class A) uses the PropertyX to refer to an IndividualB (a member of class A), (the head of the clause) then the IndividualB can use that property to refer back to the IndividualA. A concert example is: if "worksWith" is a symmetric property and Joe "worksWith" Tom, one can infer that Tom "worksWith" Joe.

3 Basic Components of the Framework

Ontology and Schema are core components of the proposed framework. They provide a high-level conceptual model which can be adopted by modelbases and databases. Table 1 outlines an ODD approach to a uniform representation of basic information of the framework.

Table 1. Modeling of basic information of the framework

Component	Formalized as
1. Ontology	OWL unit clauses: representing general terminologies.
2. Schema	OWL unit clauses: representing structures of information in a smaller scope.
4. Rules	OWL non-unit clauses: modeling principles of things.
3. OWL axiomatic semantic	OWL non-unit clauses: modeling ontological axioms for support of OWL semantics.

3.1 Ontology

"Ontology" provides formal, concise, uniform, and consistent terminology, in accordance with known and accepted classifications. The agreements of terminology are explicitly defined in a user and machine understandable fashion; Ontology allows reasoning of the stored information in many aspects, such as sameness. A set of rules are defined by means of OWL clauses to restrict the relationship of information items within Ontology. In short, ontology primitives comprise: *Concepts (Classes)*—that present domain concepts (things) in the domain of interest. *Relationships*—that relate those things. *Properties*—that is a binary relation between things. There can be property characteristics (e.g., symmetry) to enhance reasoning about a property. *Rules*—that define principles of things.

3.2 Schema

Information in Ontology may be too massive to be able to describe a small range of substances. Thus "Schema"—an accompanying part of Ontology—formally describes a structure of specific information in a smaller and more specific scope than Ontology. For example, a schema may describe assets of a company, employee profiles, and production lines, while Ontology may contain a broad collection of terms and definitions relevant to general existences. Terminologies used in Schema are drawn from Ontology.

Schema contains general primitives similar to those of Ontology, i.e. concepts, relationship, properties, and rules. ODD is a language representing both Schema and Ontology, and therefore, the framework is able to represent uniformly the Schema and the Ontology so as to yield less translation effort between both components when it borrows terms and performs meaning interpretation.

In the next section, the use of Ontology and Schema on modelbases and databases will be discussed.

4   Representing Modelbases and Databases

A modelbase and a database adopt the aforementioned basic components to describe their information items. On the modelbase side, the Ontology and Schema are adopted as "Model Ontology" and "Model Schema", respectively. On the database side, the Ontology and Schema are taken on as "Data Ontology" and "Data Schema", respectively. Figure 1 illustrates the use of Ontology and Schema for modelbases and databases. The rest of this section presents Model Ontology, Model Schema, Data Ontology, and Data Schema, and then presents an engine to process the ODD.

4.1   Model Ontology

In a modelbase, *Model Ontology* provides an indispensable and consistent terminology that can be used to describe different decision models, regardless of the specific type of decision models. Though a variety of existing ontologies or taxonomies related to MS/OR have some of the necessary concepts and relations which can serve as a shared conceptualization of decision models, unfortunately, none of them has all which are necessary. For example, the Guide to Available Mathematical software [6] lists the mathematical problems and covers most of the top concepts of the mathematical problem; however, it does not include many basic concepts of the real world domain, such as "quantity" and "activity". Therefore, this paper proposes an organization of Model Ontology which can accommodate existing related ontologies. It consists of four main areas: problem taxonomy, mathematical model entities, world concepts, and arithmetic-related properties.

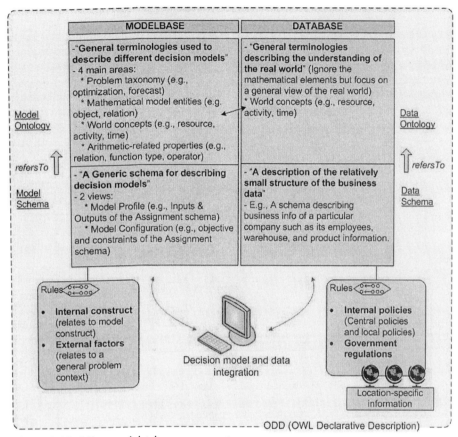

Figure 1. Modelbase and database components

Problem Taxonomy consists of concepts and classifications of mathematical problems e.g., optimization, simulation, and forecast.

Mathematical Model Entities encompass indispensable elements of a quantitative model e.g., *Object* and *Relation*, each of which may have its properties attached.

World Concepts bring together the views of the real world which necessarily relate to concerned decision problems. They also correspond to "mathematical model entities" in some sense. Their broad conceptual elements may cover *Resource, Activity, Time, Event, State,* and *Quantity*. They also have properties showing the relationships among them.

Arithmetic-Related Properties include a *Relation* denoting comparability between model elements, e.g., *Equal* and *Less Than*, a *Function Type* indicating a predefined procedure, e.g., *Sum* and *Mean*, and an *Operator* signifying an operator symbol, e.g., *Minus* and *Time*.

Restrictions (rules) on elements and relationships of Model Ontology, in the sense of general phenomena, can be formulated, e.g., Resource-Activity rule—if an activity X has special characteristics and resource Y (e.g. workforce and money) has capabilities that match those characteristics, then resource Y can perform activity X. If resource Y is a consumable resource (e.g. money), then it will be diminished during the activity process. OWL non-unit clauses model rules. The head is the rule's constructor describing the information to be yielded; the body is a pattern and condition.

4.2 Model Schema

Modelbase users have realized the need to specialize a generic pattern of a certain decision model to solve similar business problems in order to reduce excessive effort and time in formulating a decision model from scratch. Accordingly, the *Model Schema* presents a generic schema for describing a decision model, such as an Assignment problem and an Economic Order Quantity (EOQ) problem. The model schema can be generalized into the so-called model instance. For example, an assignment problem for project X of local location Y is a model instance of an assignment model schema. The terms used in Model Schema are borrowed from Model Ontology, eliminating vagueness for modelbase users and Web-based DSS applications. This Web-processible schema is composed of the "external view" and "internal view" of a decision model description; they are referred to as *Model Profile* and *Model Configuration*, respectively. Both views provide different insights into the decision models. The modelbase stores a collection of different decision models, each of which has an external view and internal view.

Model Profile. Model Schema is "presented" by Model Profile—a black box view. It provides the input and output information (e.g. data type and unit of measurement) of the model schema and it refers the classification of the schema to a problem name in the taxonomy of problem type in the Model Ontology.

Model Configuration. Model Schema is "described" by Model Configuration—a glass box view, which is comprised of major elements of model constructs. A model construct serves as skeletons, major model constructs (e.g., objective function, constraint, decision variable, and independent variable for an optimization model type) of a particular decision model. A model configuration also contains MathExpression elements to express each model construct in Mathematical Markup Language (MathML).

Figure 1 shows the partial schema describing a configuration of an assignment problem that is used as a running example in this paper; the problem is concerned with assigning exactly one agent to each task in such a way that the total cost of the assignment is minimized. The main constructs are objective function, constraints, decision variables, and parameters. Terms in the schema are selectively taken from Model Ontology. Due to space limitations, the schema is graphically shown by means of an RDF graph [9]; this is borrowed as an alternative to a text format of ODD. The (a) in Figure 2 shows example OWL elements that correspond to the bolded oval in the main illustration. It states that an

"AssignmentCost" has the property "costForAssignmentOf" which refers to an "AgentTask_Allocation". Sample instances of this schema are given in (b) of Figure 2. The statements convey that a "John01_MachineA" is of "AgentTask_Allocation" type. The cost for assigning the employee "John01" to the "MachineA" is S-Variable $S:CostX. Note that the cost is currently unknown; yet it can be fulfilled by taking data value from the database. The means of integrating the data from the database will be discussed in section 4.6.

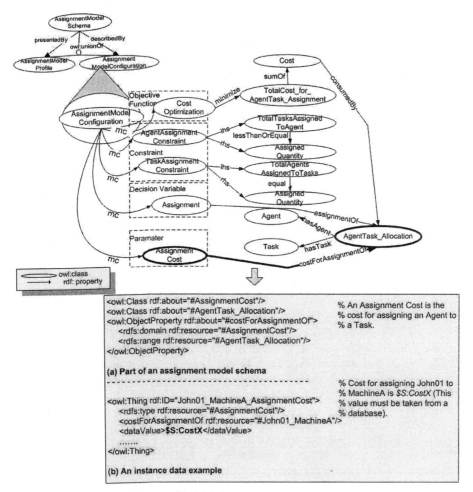

Figure 2. Part of the Assignment Model Schema

The rules which concern two main areas—"internal construct" and "external factors"—are attached to the Model Schema. The rules related to internal construct regard the internal structure of a model schema, e.g. the left-hand-side of the constraints in an assignment problem must uniformly be 1. Rules related to external factors concern factors that relate to the general problem context and are not directly related to the model constructs. For example, use of an EOQ model schema requires that the vendor characteristics stored in the database appears as "no stock out guarantee".

4.3 Data Ontology

Data Ontology contains high-level common terminologies. Data Ontology is comparable to Model Ontology yet it is different in the sense that the Data Ontology ignores the mathematical model entities but focuses on a general view of the real world. As a result, Data Ontology is analogous to the area of the World Concept defined in Model Ontology.

There exist various ontologies relevant to views of the real world, e.g., time ontology [16] and enterprise resources ontology [15, 17]. However, each of them may be too detailed or too limited to be readily adopted as Data Ontology. Thus, this research temporally accepts the ontology described in the World Concept (one area of Model Ontology) for the purpose of providing an example. In actual system development, a database developer can adopt or map other existing ontologies and justify details of information to fit the nature of the company.

4.4 Data Schema

While Data Ontology provides a high-level context agreement, *Data Schema* uses Data Ontology as a general reference to describe the relatively small structure of business data. Terminologies in the schema conform to the Model Ontology.

Consider XYZ Company, a global company, as an example. The company may define the schema to describe its project profiles, financial records, employee-task matching, etc. Such schemas can be shared and reused among local locations/branches. Figure 3 shows part of a data schema as well as schema instances adopted by the Minnesota USA location of the XYZ Company in order to describe its business information. The schema describes address and employee information. The schema instance contains information: for example, the cost for employee John01 to perform a task on MachineA and MachineB is US$25 and US$31, respectively.

Rules attached to Data Schema concern two main areas: "internal policies" and "government regulations". Internal policies regard the general business policies of the company. For example, an employee cannot operate a machine for more than 10 hours consecutively, and an employee of location B must have US$ 9 as a minimum wage rate. Government regulations express the regulations of diverse locations. Consider minimum wage rates; they are different in each country. For instance, the national minimum wage rate in the United Kingdom varies depending on the employee's age, and the rates in the United States of America (USA) are different from state to state. Figure 4 shows the minimum wage rate applicable to an office at a Minnesota location. The rate depends on the annual receipts of the company: the company with an annual receipt greater than or equal to US$625,000 and less than US$625,000 must pay the minimum wage of US$6.15 and US$5.25, respectively. Such government regulations also certainly affect "internal policy" rules. Consider the internal policy rules in Figure 5 as an example. They define the eligible pay rate for each agent-task allocation (e.g., the pay rate for assigning an employee X to task Y). One part of the rule forces the pay rate to be legitimated (i.e., conforms to the government regulation rules of Figure 3) by stating that the pay rate must be greater than or equal to the one specified in the minimum wage law.

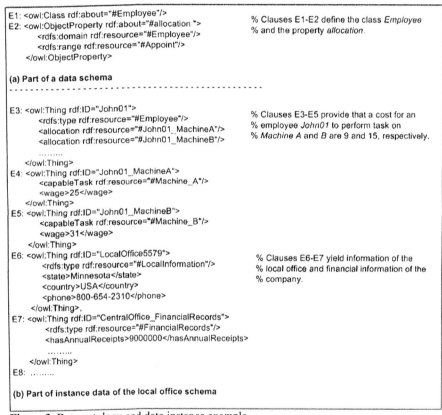

Figure 3. Data ontology and data instance example

```
R1: <MinimumWage per="$S:HourOrDay">$S:MinumumWage</MinimumWage>
    ←
        <owl:Thing rdf:ID="$S:ThingA">                        % If the local office is located in Minnesota,
            <rdfs:type rdf:resource="#LocalInformation"/>     % USA, and the company has annual
            <state>Minnesota</state>                          % receipts greater than or equal 625,000
            <country>USA</country>                            % then the minimum rate is 6.15 per hour.
            $E:Element1
        </owl:Thing>,
        <owl:Thing rdf:ID="$S:ThingB">
            <rdfs:type rdf:resource="#FinancialRecords"/>
            <hasAnnualReceipts>$S:AnnualReceipts</hasAnnualReceipts>
            $E:Element2
        </owl:Thing>,
        GreaterThanOrEqual($S:AnnualReceipts, 625000),
        AssignString($S:HourOrDay, hour),
        AssignString($S:MinimumWage, 6.15).

R2: <MinimumWage per="$S:HourOrDay">$S:MinumumWage</MinimumWage>
    ←
        <owl:Thing rdf:ID="$S:ThingA">                        % If the local office is located in Minnesota,
            <rdfs:type rdf:resource="#LocalInformation"/>     % USA, and the company has annual
            <state>Minnesota</state>                          % receipts less than or equal 625,000
            <country>USA</country>                            % then the minimum rate is 5.25 per hour.
            $E:Element1
        </owl:Thing>,
        <owl:Thing rdf:ID="$S:ThingB">
            <rdfs:type rdf:resource="#FinancialRecords"/>
            <hasAnnualReceipts>$S:AnnualReceipts</hasAnnualReceipts>
            $E:Element2
            </owl:Thing>,
        LessThan($S:AnnualReceipts, 625000),
        AssignString($S:HourOrDay, hour),
        AssignString($S:MinimumWage, 5.25).
```

Figure 4. Modeling of a minimum wage rate rule

```
R3: <owl:Thing rdf:ID="$S:AssignmentCost_ID">              % If the pay rate for an agent-task allocation
        <rdfs:type rdf:resource="#AssignmentCost"/>        % $S:Agent_Task is $S:CostX of which is
        <costForAssignmentOf rdf:resource="$S:Agent_Task"/> % greater than or equal a minimum wage
        <dataValue>$S:CostX</dataValue>                    % rate defined in the minimum wage law,
    </owl:Thing>                                           % then the cost $S:CostX is an eligible and
    ←                                                      % legitimate cost for the agent-task
        <owl:Thing rdf:ID="$S:AssignmentCost_ID">          % allocation.
            <rdfs:type rdf:resource="#AssignmentCost"/>
            <costForAssignmentOf rdf:resource="$S:Agent_Task"/>
            $E:Element1
        </owl:Thing>,
        <owl:Thing rdf:ID="$S:Agent_Task"">
            <capableTask rdf:resource="$S:Task"/>
            <wage>$S:CostX</wage>
        </owl:Thing>, _ _ _ _ _ _ _ _ _ Reference to other rule's constructor
        <MinimumWage per="$S:HourOrDay">$S:MinumumWage</MinimumWage>,
        GreaterThanOrEqual($S:Cost, $S:MinumumWage).
```

Figure 5. Modeling of the pay rate for an agent-task allocation

An example application has been built using the proposed framework as a conceptual foundation. Users can use the menu-driven interface to go through simple steps: selecting a decision model, running queries against the database, and receiving the decision model and associated input data retrieved from the database. This Web-based application employs XET as a computation and reasoning engine in the Windows environment. Note that not only are the exchange formats of decision model and data in XML (recall that OWL is written in RDF/XML) but also the output of XET computation is in XML. This allows the Web application developer to create an interface to the decision model and data using a variety of XML Web programming languages. Here, ASP.net is used as a Web programming language, and Protégé 3.1 is used as an ontology and schema editor tool. Visual Studio is used to build a Web interface design to execute the queries and view the result in a user-friendly design interface on the Web browser. Components of modelbases, as well as databases, are seamlessly interoperated because of the unified representation using ODD.

4.6 A Sample Scenario

Consider an example scenario of a Minnesota office which is one of the office locations of the global company, XYZ Company (Figure 6). The company has decentralized its DSS applications; each has its own processing facility yet all applications adopt this framework. The applications leverage Internet protocols in transmitting information. The technical details on communication among decentralized applications are beyond the scope of this paper. The Minnesota office needs to run an Assignment model for the Film Repair project, and for this reason the modelbase needs to integrate data from the database (as required input parameters) onto the Film Repair Assignment Schema. Three employees are suitable for this project, and there are three machines for repairing the film. Each employee will be working on only one machine, and each machine will be given to only one employee. The decision model schema requires the cost for assigning employees to machines, as input parameters. Those parameter values must be taken from the database. With respect to the data stored in the database together with rules, the wage (which does not violate the minimum wage law of Minnesota State) for hiring each employee (e.g., John01) to operate machines (e.g., machineA and machineB) will be automatically retrieved to fulfill the inputs of the Film Repair Assignment Schema.

One may use the pay rate rule of Figure 4 to return from the database the pay for each employee-machine. For simplicity, the paper assumes that Figure 3 contains the data of the three employees. Since the example data in Figure 3, the assignment model schema in Figure 2, and information inferred from Figure 5 match the body of the pay rate rule given in Figure 4, and also satisfy the rules filtering conditions, an example XML result described by the head of the rule is obtained as:

```
<owl:Thing rdf:ID="John01_MachineA_AssignmentCost">
        <rdfs:type rdf:resource="#AssignmentCost"/>
        <costForAssignmentOf rdf:resource="#John01_MachineA"/>
        <dataValue>25</dataValue>
</owl:Thing>.
```

Based on the results, Figure 7 illustrates an example HTML output.

Finally, the Film Repair Assignment Schema is ready for a mathematical computation engine (i.e., a solver) to generate a solution result. At this stage, application developers may use pre-defined rules written in ODD or other transformation languages, such as Extensible Stylesheet Language Transformations (XSLT), as a way to transform the schema to a solver's native format and send it to the solver. This allows users to focus on the decision problem context without bothering about how to interface with the solver.

Other locations of XYZ Company can exploit the modelbase and database integration in the similar manner. Data values of input parameters will be appropriately supplied from the database by taking into account the location of the project and the government regulations of that particular location. Note that when one location demands information from another location, an exchange of information between diverse locations must take into account cultural differences, such as currency units and aspect ratios. Those concerns will also be handled by means of OWL non-unit clauses (rules).

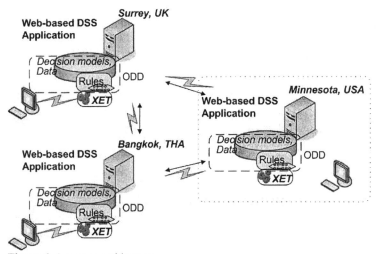

Figure 6. A system architecture

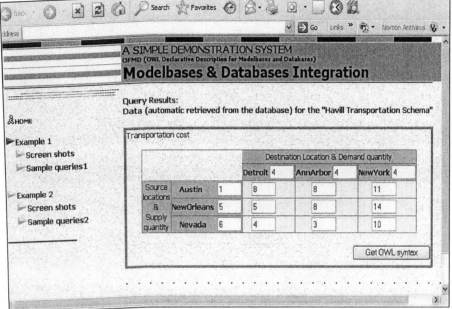

Figure 7. A client browser showing data values that serve as inputs to the decision model

5 Discussion

The proposed framework can overcome the common limitations appearing in existing frameworks while accommodating their merits.

First, ODD has facilities for the creation of rules to define central and local company regulations in an expressive manner. Existing frameworks that employ XML as a representation language [5, 8] do not address means to express rules. In addition, this capability goes beyond that of traditional data model, such as the relational model, where the table format does not fit the complex rules well.

Second, both decision models and data are able to carry the information and unwritten semantics that each of them can understand and access using the same underlying language—OOD. This information can be accessed and processed by the XET engine without having to convert to another format.

Third, the data on the Web and decision making information are semistructured in nature; the proposed ODD approach employs an XML-based concept which is well-known as a data model for representing such information. Yet, using ODD as an underlying language of the framework yields advantages over existing frameworks that merely use basic XML language because ODD also supports features of other kinds of data models, such as the class/property inheritance of the OO paradigm.

Last, the proposed conceptual framework is compatible with XML-based Web technologies. It can be implemented in a Web-based environment using the XET engine for inference making and query computation. Application developers can use available Web programming languages for user creating interaction and presentation on a Web browser.

A sample application based on the proposed conceptual framework has been built using an ODD and XET engine. The following limitations were found during the implementation. First, ontology and schema were written in XML-based syntax, which is lengthy and difficult to hand-code and maintain. Code writing and maintenance therefore have to be carried out via an interface of ontology building/editor tools. Each tool tends to modify the original code/syntax to fit its own format, thus, creating a difficulty when the information is exported to other tools from different vendors. Users may need to limit their freedom of choice to only one tool. Second, the interface between decision models and solver must be predefined for every generic model schema (e.g., assignment and transportation) and the solver pair. A newly customized model schema, such as an assignment problem with an added time dimension, requires generating a new rule for transforming the schema to solver's required format. Last, ontology in the sample application contains limited terminologies; it may not be robust enough to be borrowed by the schema. In actual practice, ontology and schema should contain information of a suitable size for an organization. Yet, the organization can incrementally increase the information size because OWL is extensible.

Further work may involve investigating a solution to supplement these limitations.

6 Conclusions

An approach towards a unified framework for modelbases and databases of Web-based DSS has been developed. This unified framework provides the means to describe both decision models and data in a formal and declarative manner, under the same representation approach, and in the context of the Semantic Web. By employment of the ODD language, modelbases and databases can be seamlessly integrated and processed. Moreover, the proposed framework readily enables reuse and sharing of decision models and data among diverse locations of a global company through the use of a scheme as well as a common understanding stored in ontology. The expressiveness of non-unit clauses of ODD enables the creation of rules to handle flexibly specific local restrictions as well as differences among geographic locations, and to maintain integrity. Reasoning and query processing are computed by the XET engine, without it being necessary for data conversions to other formats, because XET is friendly with languages defined in the XML-based syntax. The framework provides interoperability by using an XML-based standard as a foundation (ODD, OWL, and XET follow XML standard). By providing interoperability, different local locations can implement the application regardless of platforms. Ongoing research includes an extension of the development technique to store decision models and data in other kinds of native XML database systems, development of additional user interfaces for other operations on modelbases and databases, and to enlarge the scope of terms in model ontology and data ontology.

References

1. Anutariya C., Wuwongse V., Akama K., and Nantajeewarawat E., "RDF Declarative Description (RDD): A Language for Metadata". Journal of Digital Information Vol. 2(2), (2001)
2. Anutariya C., Wuwongse V., Akama K., Wattanapailin V., "Semantic Web modeling and programming with XDD", Proceedings of 1st Semantic Web Working Symposium (SWWS'01), CA (2001)
3. Bechhofer S., Harmelen F., Hendler J., Horrocks I., McGuinness D., Patel-Schneider P., and Stein L., OWL Web Ontology Language reference, W3C Recommendation 10 February 2004, http://www.w3.org/TR/owl-ref/
4. Dolk D., "A Generalized Model Management system for Mathematical Programming", AMC Transactions on Mathematical Software, Vol.12(2), (1986)
5. Ezechukwu O. and Maros I., "OOF: Open Optimization Framework", Departmental Technical Report 2003/7, Imperial College London, (2003)
6. Guide to Available Mathematical software (GAMS), NIST, Available online: http://gams.nist.gov
7. Huh S. and Chung Q., "A model management framework for heterogeneous algebraic models: Object-oriented data base management systems approach", Omega, International Journal of Management Science Vol.23(3), (1995)
8. Kim H., "An XML-based modeling language for the open interchange of decision models", Decision Support Systems Vol.31, (2001)
9. Klyne G. and Carroll J., "Resource Description Framework (RDF): Concepts and Abstract Syntax", W3C Recommendation, http://www.w3.org/TR/2003/WD-rdf-concepts-20030123/
10. Kwon O. and Park S., "RMT: A modeling support system for model reuse", Decision Support Systems Vol.16, (1996)
11. Liang, T., "Integrating Model Management with Data Management in Decision Support Systems", Decision Support Systems Vol.1, (1985)
12. Lin S., Schuff D., and Louis R., "Subscript-Free Languages: A tool for facilitating the formulation and use of models", European Journal of Operational Research Vol.123(3), (2000)
13. Potter W., Byrd T., Miller J., and Kochut K., "Extending Decision Support Systems: The integration of data, knowledge, and model management", Annals of Operations Research Vol.38, (1992)
14. Power D. and Kaparthi S., "Building Web-based Decision Support Systems", Studies in Informatics and Control Vol.11(4), (2002)
15. Smith S., and Becker M., "An Ontology for Constructing Scheduling Systems", Working notes for 1997 AAAI Spring Symposium on Ontological Engineering, Stanford (AAAI Press), CA, March (1997)
16. Time ontology, SRI International's Artificial Intelligence Center (AIC), Available online: http://www.ai.sri.com/daml/ontologies/time/Time.daml
17. Uschold M., King M., Moralee S., and Zorgios Y., "The Enterprise Ontology", The Knowledge Engineering Review (13), Special Issue on Putting Ontologies to Use, (1998)

A Multi-Attribute Auction Format for Procurement witn Limited Disclosure of Buyer's Preference Structure

Atul Saroop[1], Satish K. Sehgal[1], K. Ravikumar[1]

[1] India Science Lab, General Motors R&D
3rd Floor, Creator Building, ITPB, Whitefield Road, Bangalore 560066, India

{atul.saroop, satish.sehgal, ravikumar.karumanchi}@gm.com

Abstract. In this paper, we present a hybrid, two-round procurement auction that can be used when a buyer wants to procure a single unit of a multi-attribute item. In such cases, bids are measured on many attributes like price, quality, reliability, past history of the bidder, geographical distance between the locations of the bidder and the buyer. The problem is even more acute for Global Enterprises where additional attributes like tax and tariff structures of the country of the supplier become important as well. While such multi-attribute bids are commonplace in sealed bid tenders where the analysis of the bids can be carried out after all of them have been placed to determine the winner; it is difficult to handle such multi-attribute bids in other auction formats like English and Dutch auctions. The difficulty arises because in holding multi-attribute forms of English and Dutch auctions, the buyer needs to communicate information about his true preference amongst attributes to the participating suppliers. But by passing the information on preference between various attributes (termed as the preference structure), the buyer risks revealing sensitive strategic information to the suppliers. In this paper, we present a two-phase auction mechanism that guides the multi-attribute bidding of the participating suppliers, but ensures that only limited information about the buyer's preference structure can be reverse interpreted by the buyers. We also provide results relating to proper choice of the amount of information that should be disclosed in such manner.

Keywords: Multi-attribute auctions, Limited information disclosure.

1 Introduction

Procurement is an important function in any enterprise, and is often one of the most influential ones due to the amount of money involved. Contracts and purchases often run into hundreds of millions, if not billions, of dollars. Effective low-cost and long-term viable procurement is a difficult ballgame, and is becoming the focus of a lot of business activity due to the emergence of third-world countries as effective low-cost suppliers of materials and services. It is difficult to design effective decision support systems around a primarily human-based negotiation process that is often used for procurement of items. Characteristics of items to procure – the technical expertise required in manufacturing the item, the competition in the sub-market of the item, the uncertainty of prices of raw materials are some of the factors that drive the mechanism through which the item is deemed proper to be procured. Such mechanisms could vary from strategic contracts and inviting tenders through sealed bids to purchasing directly from the open market. There are two decision making scenarios in the procurement process that should be of interest to the decision-support community. One is that of a proper choice of mechanism for procurement, based on the characteristics of the item involved. The other pertains to the study of "optimally" designing these individual mechanisms to suit the short- and the long-term needs of the procuring company. In this paper, we concentrate on the second scenario of optimizing the procurement mechanism of a technologically developed item[6] that requires evaluation of the suppliers on multiple attributes, has a competitive sub-market so that a large enough number of suppliers is able to participate in the procurement mechanism when the pre-verification of all participating suppliers has been carried out.

Auctions have been used to procure items for centuries [2], and many formats have evolved over time into mature purchasing mechanisms. Their recent popularity in business procurement stems from the very much publicized air-spectrum sale of rights carried out in various countries, some of which have been more successful than the others. Much of the reason for the varied success of the air-spectrum auctions has been attributed to the differences in their mechanism design [3], leading to a lot of interest in the research community. Auctions have traditionally been used in selling commodities, but have not been used very frequently for procurement in the manufacturing industry. Traditionally, auctioning mechanisms have performed exceptionally well in terms of stimulating competition between suppliers of a product to drive down its price. However, in a manufacturing industry like the automotive industry, the procuring manufacturers or OEMs themselves are under severe price pressures from the final consumers. Under such cases, it is necessary not only to stimulate competition amongst various suppliers of an item, but also to have effective margin-sharing mechanisms between suppliers and manufacturer OEMs to adjust for such downward price pressures.

While there exists a developed literature for analysis of auctions [4], most of it concentrates on models that do not take price pressures on buyer into account. To further complicate matters, the value or contribution of each of the components in an assembly process to the final sale becomes obtuse. In sale of items like fish, the contribution of a fish catcher can be easily calculated as the fish catcher deals with the same product as the one that is sold to the final consumer. However, in the automotive industry, where the OEM assembles sub-assemblies from a number of suppliers, the contribution of each of the parts to the final selling price becomes a difficult quantity to estimate even for the OEM. In such a scenario, propagating the price pressures on the OEM to the individual component suppliers is not straightforward. While this paper does not answer the question of how much price pressure on the final product should be propagated to an individual component supplier, it does propose an auction mechanism that facilitates sharing of such price-pressures across the buyer and its suppliers. Note that this feature is in contrast with a

---

[6] By "technologically developed", we mean an item whose production does not require substantial research & development effort. Design competitions like the ones discussed in [1] are deemed better suited for procurement of products that require substantial research & development efforts.

simple auction mechanism like an English auction, where the supplier with the lowest cost wins the auction at a price approximately[7] equal to the second lowest cost amongst the participating suppliers. The usual practice of today to address the issue of profit-sharing amongst the buyer and the supplier is to procure items through a two-phase mechanism: a sealed bid auction where the price gets determined by the competition between various suppliers, followed by a negotiation phase where the manufacturer negotiates with the top suppliers based on the market-pressures that he faces. Such two-phase auction mechanisms have earlier been analyzed to some detail in [1]. The reader is referred to [1, 5, 6, 7, 8, 9] for some other works in the area of multi-dimensional auctions.

This paper is organized as follows: This section discusses the background of multi-attribute auctions in a manufacturing industry. Section 2 proposes the single-item multi-attribute auction mechanism as a sequence of steps. For stimulating competition between suppliers in a multi-attribute procurement scenario, the buying OEM needs to guide the bidding to a portion of the attribute space that it prefers. However, such guidance of the bidding process also discloses confidential information about the buyer's structural cost and its preference structure amongst various attributes. Section 3 discusses these forms of information disclosures that take place between the buyer and the sellers during the auctioning mechanism, while noting the downsides of such information sharing. Section 3 also discusses an information disclosure algorithm that limits the amount of manufacturer related information that can be reversely interpreted from the bids in the auctioning mechanism. However, as noted in Section 2, while information disclosure prompts suppliers to submit more meaningful bids and guides the competition in a direction beneficial to the buyer; the associated revelation has negative effects on the final deal that the buyer gets. Hence, in a mechanism like this, it is an important decision for the buyer to decide the degree of information that should be disclosed to the suppliers during the bidding process. Section 4 deals with this decision and points to the process of finding the appropriate amount of information disclosure. Section 5 concludes our discussion and lays down various areas of future research.

2 Proposed Single-Item Multi-Attribute Auction Mechanism

The proposed auctioning mechanism can be detailed in terms of the following steps and in terms of the activity chart of Figure 1:

1. Collect the list of attributes that are to be considered for evaluating suppliers' bids.
2. Segregate the attributes into "Generic attributes" and "OEM-specific attributes'". OEM-specific attributes denote the attributes that contain sensitive competitive information in them.
3. For the generic attributes, carry out axis corrections. Axis correction for an attribute ensures that the possible values of that attribute are arranged in

---

[7] The approximation of the final winning price to the second lowest cost arises due to the finiteness of the minimum bid increment that is usually operational in practical English auctions.

decreasing order of preference of the buyer. The corrected axes (and hence the order of preference on the possible values) are declared to all participating suppliers.

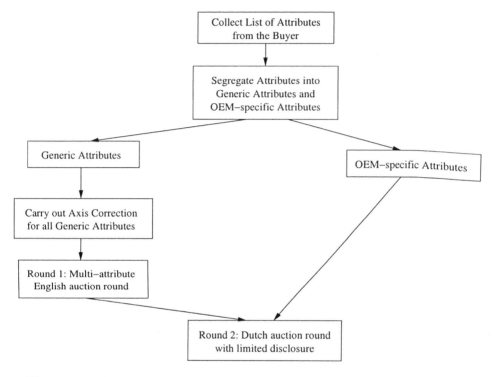

Figure 1: Activity Chart for the proposed Multi-dimensional Auction Format

4. Auction Round 1 (Multi-Attribute English auction round)
   a. Suppliers specify bids on all attributes, but compete only on Generic attributes.
   b. At any stage of bidding, a bid-envelop of all bids is calculated in terms of Generic attributes. The bid-envelop represents the set of best bid-combinations present in the bids specified by the suppliers. The "bid score" of a bid is calculated in terms of the distance from the bid-envelop. A Data Envelopment Analysis [10] based formulation would be helpful for calculating the bid-scores of individual bids. Under such a scheme, bids on the bid-envelop have a score of 1.0, while those further away have scores tending towards zero.
   c. Suppliers place more and more competitive bids during the bidding process, thereby pushing the bid-envelop further towards the origin (since the axes

have been transformed so as to have more preferred values near the origin). This process has been shown in Figure 2.

d. Bidding continues till the bid-envelop keeps improving at least at a threshold rate.

e. Participation rules: To ensure a healthy competition during this round, the buyer should announce that suppliers would not be allowed to improve their specifications on Generic attributes by more than say 10% in Round 2 with their bids in Round 1 as the basis.

f. The suppliers compete in terms of their bid-scores, which can be improved by improving specifications on one or many attributes, thereby giving the round a multi-attribute nature. Also, while in this auction round the suppliers compete only on generic attributes; the bids that they place also specify the corresponding OEM-specific attribute values without any guidance from the buyer. These values however, would be utilized by the buyer in organizing the Round 2 of auctioning.

5. Auction Round 2 (Multi-Attribute Dutch auction round):

a. Ask the buyer to specify the amount of disclosure required on OEM-specific attributes, and input these values to the Limited Information Disclosure algorithm of Section 3. This issue is discussed in detail in Section 4.

b. Find the final bid-envelop in terms of Generic attributes as an output of Step 4 (Auction Round 1). Also, find out the set of best combinations that can be obtained on OEM-specific attributes. Note that the set of best combinations can be found by looking at the quotes on OEM-specific attributes in Round 1 or can be taken as an input from the buyer. Input both these sets of values to the Limited Information Disclosure algorithm.

c. Take the M bid-points that form the output of the Limited Information Disclosure algorithm and declare these bid-points one-by-one in order of decreasing preference to all the participating suppliers. This ensures that suppliers are not able to infer the buyer's preference structure by reverse-engineering the bids.

d. The bid-points are declared to the suppliers till the point any supplier accepts to supply the declared bid-point combination.

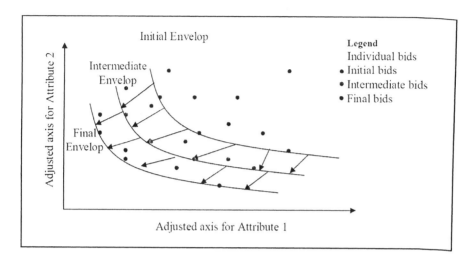

Figure 2: Bidding Process during Auction Round 1 (Multi-attribute English auction round)

3 Limited Information Disclosure Algorithm

In the supplier-OEM interactions, there are two types of information that are susceptible to disclosure: disclosure of OEM's "cost structure" and disclosure of OEM's "preference structure". Cost structure of an OEM refers to the information about the contribution of each component to the selling price of the final product. Knowledge of the cost structure of an OEM gives negotiating suppliers an upper hand their negotiations as they would know the OEM's valuation completely in that case. Also, since suppliers would also be able to interpret the margin available between the OEM's cost structure and the competitive price of the item, they would try to extract this margin completely to their advantage. Usually, suppliers tend to form bidding collusions to reduce competition and keep the margin with themselves rather than the OEM. For more discussions on bidding rings, the reader is referred to [4].

The preference structure of an OEM denotes the relative preferences that he has for attributes of an item. In simplest of the multi-attribute auction designs, the preference structure of the OEM is used as a scoring function to convert the multi-dimensional bids into a scalar score value. However, knowledge of preference structure of an OEM can help a supplier reverse engineer the OEM's cost structure. Also, uncertainties in suppliers' minds about OEM's preference structure can be utilized to maintain symmetries between participating suppliers. This issue is discussed in detail in Section 4.

The main feature of an information disclosure algorithm is to "limit the information that can be reverse interpreted from the auctioning mechanism about the buyer's preference structure on any bid attribute combination". The algorithm presented here calculates bid attribute combinations to achieve the desired level of Information Disclosure. Here, we refer to "Preference Space" as the space constructed from preferences on all attributes. This is in contrast with the "Attribute Space" that represents the space constructed from all attribute-values. $X_1=(x_1, y_1, z_1...), X_2=(x_2, y_2, z_2...),..., X_M=(x_M, y_M, z_M...)$ denote bids in terms of their attributes in the Attribute Space. The goal is to limit the disclosure on Preference Space while ensuring enough bid-points are specified on the Attribute Space.

1. Take as input the sets of bids near (say within 10% distance) the bid-envelop of all the bids placed in terms of:
   - Generic attributes alone
   - OEM-specific attributes

   and calculate the union U of the two sets of bids so obtained.

2. Ask the buyer to input her preferences on attributes as a point in the Preference Space. Also, ask for the degree to which she wants her preferences to be interpretable by the suppliers (in case they reverse engineer the rankings on bids).

3. In the Preference Space, ascertain the region representing the preference structure specified by the buyer along-with the associated amounts of acceptable disclosure. Find a set of *(M-1)* planes that do not pass through this region. This may be achieved by inscribing the region in an ellipsoid and by choosing *(M-1)* of its tangent planes randomly.

4. The coefficients of these *(M-1)* tangent planes in the Preference Space represent the difference in Attribute Space between two subsequent bids announced during the Dutch auction Round. So, to generate the M bid combinations to be announced during the Dutch auction Round, choose the first bid combination to be declared as the best bid-combination from the set U (or a point close-by).

5. Choose any one of the randomly generated tangent planes. The coefficients in the equations of the tangent should be used as the differences on individual attribute axes for Limited disclosure. Calculate the next bid combination by finding the difference between attribute values of previous bid and the coefficients of the equation of the chosen tangent.

6. Repeat step 5 above for generating the rest of the bid-combinations to be declared.

7. In case the buyer specifies more than one point in the Preference Space corresponding to different sets of values of attributes, repeat steps 3 to 6 above for the new region.

4 Choice of Amount of Information to be Disclosed

A supplier that has a cost-structure well aligned with the manufacturer's preference structure would have distinct advantages over other suppliers. In particular, such a supplier can be expected to have cost advantages over other suppliers. However, as shown in [4, p. 46], bidders with a priori advantage in an auction mechanism tend to be less aggressive in terms of their bidding behavior. Also, as discussed in Section 3, the suppliers would try to reverse interpret the manufacturer's cost structure also using knowledge of the preference structure. Hence, it is necessary to ensure that the suppliers are not able to interpret their positions relative to other suppliers and the manufacturer before the start of the bidding process itself. For achieving this, the buyer would like to specify a large safe-area around her preferences on attributes in Step 2 of the information disclosure algorithm. But, for the auctioning mechanism to succeed, and for the suppliers to be able to make competitive bids, they need to have a fair idea of the manufacturer's preferences on attributes. In the following discussion, we illustrate calculation of the appropriate amount of information disclosure (radius r of the information disclosure algorithm of Section 3) so that an advantaged supplier (S_1) is not able to a priori judge (statistically) his advantage to another supplier (S_2).

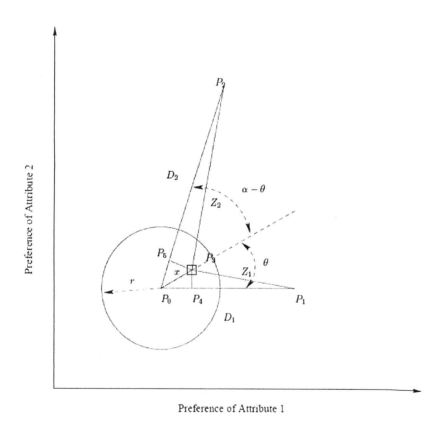

Figure 3. Information Disclosure - choosing the correct value of disclosure

Theorem 1: As the radius r of the safe-area circle of the information disclosure algorithm increases, it becomes difficult for an advantaged supplier to interpret his cost-advantages over other bidding suppliers. The buyer can decide the appropriate value of r based on the statistical confidence with which he wants the advantaged supplier to reject the hypothesis that he has an apriori advantage over other bidders.

Proof: Refer to Figure 3, let P_1 and P_2 denote the cost-structures of two suppliers S_1 and S_2 on the preference space. Let the circle centered at P_0 with a radius r denote the safe-area inputted by the buyer in step 2 of the information disclosure algorithm. Let D_1 and D_2 denote the distances P_0-P_1 and P_0-P_2, the distances of the supplier cost-structures from the center of the safe-area circle, and let Z_1 and Z_2 denote the distance of the supplier cost-structures from the hidden but true preference structure of the buyer, shown as point P_3. Also, let x be the distance P_0-P_3. Then

$$Z_1 = \sqrt{(D_1 - x\cos\theta)^2 + (x\sin\theta)^2} \tag{1}$$

$$Z_2 = \sqrt{(D_2 - x\cos(\alpha - \theta))^2 + (x\sin(\alpha - \theta))^2} \tag{2}$$

$$\text{Prob}(Z_1 > Z_2) = \text{Prob}\left[(D_1 - x\cos\theta)^2 + x^2\sin^2\theta > \{D_2 - x\cos(\alpha - \theta)\}^2 + x^2\sin^2(\alpha - \theta)\right] \tag{3}$$

$$= \text{Prob}\left[\sin^2\theta - \sin^2(\alpha - \theta) > \left\{\frac{D_2}{x} - \cos(\alpha - \theta)\right\}^2 - \left\{\frac{D_1}{x} - \cos\theta\right\}^2\right] \tag{4}$$

$$= \text{Prob}\left\{\left(\frac{D_2}{x}\right)^2 - \frac{2D_2}{x}\cos(\alpha - \theta) - \left(\frac{D_1}{x}\right)^2 + \frac{2D_1}{x}\cos\theta < 0\right\} \tag{5}$$

For $D_2 = \rho D_1$, where $\rho > 1$

$$= \text{Prob}\left\{\left(\frac{D_1}{x}\right)^2 (\rho^2 - 1) - \frac{2D_1}{x}(\rho\cos(\alpha - \theta) + \cos\theta) < 0\right\} \tag{6}$$

Minimum value of L.H.S. corresponds to the case when $\cos\theta = \cos(\alpha - \theta) = 1$, at which point for L.H.S. to be negative

$$\left(\frac{D_1}{x}\right)^2 (\rho^2 - 1) - \frac{2D_1}{x}(\rho + 1) < 0 \tag{7}$$

$$\left(\frac{D_1}{x}\right)(\rho + 1)\left[\frac{D_1}{x}(\rho - 1) - 2\right] < 0 \tag{8}$$

As $\dfrac{D_1}{x} > 0$ and $(\rho + 1) > 0$, the condition is satisfied only when

$$x > \frac{2}{(D_2 - D_1)} \qquad (9)$$

Since P_3 can be located anywhere in the safe-area circle, a value of x can be chosen appropriately for desired confidence levels of statistically rejecting the hypothesis that $Z_1 > Z_2$. ∎

5 Conclusions

In this paper, we have presented an auctioning mechanism for holding single-unit multi-attribute procurement auctions in a manufacturing industry setting. In industrial procurement, it is of utmost importance that sensitive cost information be preserved from outside agencies. On the other hand, in an auctioning mechanism, suppliers need to have a fair bit of an idea about the buyer's preferences to be able to bid meaningfully. To achieve this fine balance, we have presented an information disclosure algorithm that limits the amount of preference information disclosed to the suppliers during the bidding process, but still allows the auctioning mechanism to suitably guide the suppliers' bids to a desirable bid-attribute combination. We also address the issue of finding the appropriate amount of information that should be disclosed by the buyer.

This work can be extended further in the following ways:

1. Equilibrium bidding strategies of suppliers: theoretical analysis of the bidding strategies of participating suppliers in multi-round auctions seems to become intractable in this case. However, a simulation based analysis of their bidding strategies can still be carried out.

2. Extensions to multi-unit auction formats: the auctioning mechanism presented in this paper can be extended to accommodate procurement of multiple units of an item. One way of achieving this would be to add an Multi-unit auction Round 3 that allows the suppliers to place multi-unit bids in an English auction format. In particular, some characteristics of this auction round would be:

   a. The set of winning suppliers are calculated in real-time by calculating their scores according to the preference structure of the buyer. Note that while deciding the set of winners, the number of units being supplied and various Vendor-related constraints are decided as per a combinatorial multi-unit auction formulation. The set of winning suppliers and their bids are announced to all participants, who then revise their bids in a competition to win the contract. Note that due to Round 1, suppliers would know how to improve their bids on Generic Attributes; and due to Round 2, they would know how to improve their bids on OEM-specific attributes.

b. The bidding closes either at a pre-announced closing time or continues till a point when bidding-activity reduces below threshold levels. At this stage, the set of winning suppliers are announced as winners and are allotted the contract.

3. Designing appropriate participation rules to spur competition during the multi-attribute English auction Round 1: For the success of the proposed auctioning mechanism, it is important that suppliers compete with each other in the first round of multi-attribute English auction as well. The buyer decides upon the bids of the Dutch auction Round based on these bids only. To restrict suppliers from remaining dormant during the English auction phase, it is important for the buyer to design appropriate participation rules. While we have mentioned a participation rule in this work, a careful choice can reap higher benefits to the buyer.

References

1. Che, Y. K.: Design competition through multidimensional auctions. Rand Journal of Economics, 24:668–680, 1993
2. Cassady, R. Auctions and Auctioneering. University of California Press, 1967
3. Klemperer, P. D.: What really matters in auction design. Journal of Economic Perspectives, 16(1):169–189, 2002
4. Krishna, V.: Auction Theory. Academic Press, San Diego, California, USA, 2002
5. Bichler, M.: An experimental analysis of multi-attribute auction. Decision Support Systems, 29:249–268, 2000
6. Branco, F.: The design of multidimensional auctions. Rand Journal of Economics, 28(1):63 –81, 1997
7. Vulkan, N., Jennings, N. R.: Efficient mechanisms for the supply of services in multi-agent environments. Decision Support Systems, 28:5–19, 2000
8. Parkes, D. C.: Iterative multi-attribute vickrey auctions. Technical report, Harvard University, 2005
9. Strecker, S., Seifert S.: Electronic sourcing with multi-attribute auctions. In: Proceedings of the 37th Hawaii International Conference on System Sciences, 2004
10. Charnes, A., Cooper, W.W., Rhodes, E.: Measuring efficiency of decision making units. European Journal of Operations Research, 2:429–444, 1978

A Generic Model of Self-Incrementing Knowledge-Based Decision Support System Using the Bolzmann Machine

Tapati Bandopadhyay[1], Pradeep Kumar[2]

[1] ICFAI Business School,Bangalore,Karnataka, India,
[2] ICFAI Business School,Gurgaon,Haryana, India

chatterjee_tee@yahoo.com[1], pkgarg@ibsdel.org[2]

Abstract. Knowledge-driven decision support systems (DSS) rely significantly on the currency of it's back-end knowledge-base for improved quality of support that it can provide to the decision making process. In this paper, a model has been developed and presented to support this purpose i.e. making the knowledge base of a knowledge-driven DSS as self-incrementing. First, the necessity of such a model for maintaining knowledge currency and the importance of knowledge currency in the context of DSS supporting operational decision processes, are discussed. Then, a generic model is presented using customer-email as input knowledge sources, frames as a knowledge representation scheme, and Bolzmann machine as the self-incrementing mechanism. The model can be further extended or fine-tuned both in terms of the input options and process options. The input options can include other types of knowledge inputs with varying degrees of structuredness. The process options may include other algorithms and machine learning processes.

Keywords: Decision Support System, Bolzmann Machine, Knowledge Currency.

1 Introduction

Decision support systems have been defined by researchers using different viewpoints including the 'negating-definitions' view as expressed by Keen [5] -"there can be no definition of decision support systems, only of decision support". Turban [12], on the other hand, gave a comprehensive definition as "an interactive, flexible, and adaptable computer-based information system, especially developed for supporting the solution of a non-structured management problem for improved decision making. It utilizes data, provides an easy-to-use interface, and allows for the decision maker's own insights." From this inclusive definition it can be broadly seen that decision support systems have been considered and analyzed from the viewpoints of 1) computer-based application, 2) supporting mechanism implementing some decision models, 3) input-handling and processing mechanisms applicable primarily in the context of structured and semi-structured inputs, 4) human-computer interaction in terms of the ease-of-use and technology acceptance (or rather acceptability to support the human decision making process to whatever possible extent).

Accordingly, the classification or taxonomies of Decision Support Systems (DSS) also have been done from these viewpoints. In the context of this paper, Power's classification is used, as this classification would give an idea about the basic building blocks for each of the types of DSS. According to Power [8] there are five basic types of DSS, primarily based on the inputs they can handle and the decision models that they support. These are: communication-driven DSS, data-driven DSS, document-driven DSS, knowledge-driven DSS, and model-driven DSS. A communication-driven DSS is meant for supporting decision making in a group environment where data and decision processes are shared [11]. A data-driven DSS primarily aims at generating analytical reports or visualizations from structured data e.g., internal company financials data or external database data. A document-driven DSS manages, retrieves, and manipulates unstructured information in a variety of electronic formats. A knowledge-driven DSS uses knowledge engines and different formats like facts, rules, procedures, logical structures, etc. to store a knowledge-base in a re-usable form. A model-driven DSS emphasizes access to and manipulation of a statistical, financial, optimization, or simulation model.

Consequently, any generic DSS architecture includes basic components such as a backend database, a model-base and the model-base management system and the interface. If these generic components are related to the viewpoints covered under the DSS gamut as discussed in the first section, it is apparent that the database component supports viewpoints 1 & 3, the model-base component supports viewpoints 1 & 2, and the interface component supports viewpoint 4. So, these components can be fairly representative of all the aspects that any generic DSS should minimally cover.

Now, depending on what type of inputs and models a DSS employs, the back-end database structure would vary. Here it is important to follow the distinctive features of data, information, and knowledge where data is a collection of raw, unprocessed facts and figures, information is processed data in some useful format for decision making support and application support, and knowledge is, simply put, actually applied information for making decisions or taking specific actions. In the case of a knowledge-driven DSS, the source of knowledge might be a highly structured database to highly unstructured sources like free-flowing text messages from email servers' file systems. For example, in the context of a DSS supporting a routine Management Information System (MIS), data input based decision making would have a highly structured input data format and standardized decision models like time-series analysis, demand forecasting techniques etc. So, the back-end for this kind of DSS would also be fairly structured, in the form of a standard database as with OLTP (On-Line Transaction Processing) kind of systems. But, when a DSS is meant to support a complex decision making environment with semi-structured or flexibly structured data inputs, the database tends to take a flexible form like a knowledge-base with different knowledge representation forms such as frames, facts, association rules, production rules, semantic nets, logic constructs and so on. Each of these representation schemes has a different degree of structuredness. For example, frames are well structured, association rules and production rules - if expressed using predicate logic notations - can also be fairly structured. But any source with free-flowing data inputs e.g. emails or chat messages or SMSs are highly unstructured. For example, a DSS to support decision making on a Customer Relationship Management (CRM) strategy about how to reach a customer in the best possible way, might derive its input from some archived communication history of all the customers, e.g., call records, e-mails, on-line self-help, access log files etc. Information from these semi/ unstructured sources can not be mapped onto an OLTP backend-type highly structured database. So, these would be represented by other flexible knowledge representation forms like frames, rules or semantic nets. Accordingly, the processing engine implementing the decision-making models would also have to accommodate these flexible knowledge formats. This is where a knowledge-based DSS can perform whereas the data-driven or other models are inadequate to accommodate the system flexibility, both in terms of handling inputs as well as supporting decision support process models.

2 Knowledge-Driven DSS: Components and Quality

Knowledge driven DSSs generally have knowledge storage - often referred to as a *knowledge base*, a processing engine to retrieve and process that stored knowledge and an interface mechanism to display or generate reports based on the knowledge processed. A knowledge base can be thought like a special database which can store knowledge in various forms and supports easy storage, search and retrieval of knowledge. Simple knowledge bases can be used to capture explicit knowledge of an organization, including troubleshooting, articles, white papers, user manuals and others. Capturing knowledge from various sources to create the knowledge base is a typical research problem as knowledge can be explicit or implicit or tacit [7]. It can exist in various forms e.g. structured (as in a database, spreadsheets or structured files) or semi-structured (as in databases which store indexed Binary Large Objects (BLOB) or Common Large Objects (CLOB)) to unstructured free-flowing text (e.g. word documents, emails, chat messages) and so on. It can be seen that the enterprise tacit knowledge sources contain knowledge in various forms like textual content [2, 6] as in e-mail messages, [1] or voice recording as in a telephonic feedback session and so on. [13, 14]. With the complexity of knowledge capture being dependent on the type of knowledge source, minimally the knowledge base of a knowledge-driven DSS should provide the means for computerized collection, organization, and retrieval of knowledge. More advanced knowledge bases are equipped with logical processing elements and mechanisms through which they can extract knowledge from these various sources and put them in reusable forms of varying structured ness again e.g. frames with slots(highly structured), predicate logic forms, semantic nets(highly abstract) etc. These knowledge bases can be processed using advanced algorithms and tools like automated deductive reasoning etc. Determining what type of information is captured, and where that information resides in a knowledge base is determined by the processes that support the system. A robust process structure is the backbone of any successful knowledge base. For the advanced type of knowledge bases as used in knowledge-driven decision support systems or expert systems, there are various application possibilities of Artificial Intelligence (AI)-based algorithms to support these knowledge-handling processes, as follows:

In knowledge extraction and capture: pattern recognition, pattern discovery algorithms can be used and then for storing them in a reusable and easily retrievable form, clustering algorithms can be used, to sort, classify, cluster and put the reusable knowledge items in groups. Machine learning and Neural Networks (NN) algorithms also find numerous applications here.

For knowledge retrieval, various advanced search techniques ranging from heuristic-based search algorithms to genetic algorithm based searching can be used.
Knowledge representation in itself is a section of AI, frames, semantic nets, predicate logic etc. being part of it.

Finally, to achieve a generic structure applicable for any knowledge-base architecture, ontology may be used to specify its structure (entity types and relationships) and its classification scheme, with a set of instances of its classes constituting the knowledge base.

2.1 Quality of a Knowledge-Driven DSS and Knowledge Currency

Quality of a DSS can be directly or indirectly reflected across various facilities or parameters e.g. the level of support it provides to a decision making process, analytical flexibility and options, presentation flexibility and options, drill-down facilities etc. It also gets reflected by the availability, accessibility, user-friendliness, data integrity, consistency, redundancy, and data currency. In the context of currency, it is all the more important for a DSS environment than an expert system type of environment because, as DSS generally supports operational decision making more than strategic ones, currency of the data/knowledge base and quality of support provided by the DSS are often seen to be linearly related.

Generally speaking, irrespective of the structure, the support provided by a knowledge base for decision making can only be as good as the quality of knowledge that it contains. The best knowledge bases are kept up to date supported by an excellent information retrieval system (search engine), and a carefully designed content format and classification structure. Whatever be the type of the knowledge base, in the context of the DSS, one of the prime quality issues for the support that it would provide to the decision-making processes, is the issue of currency of the knowledge that is available in the knowledge base. As DSS aims at supporting operational level decision making, a knowledge-driven DSS should ideally reflect a real-time currency of the knowledge base. At least, it should have a minimal delay in extracting and capturing knowledge from the operational sources. OLTP systems maintain a very high level of data currency. So, in context of a data-driven DSS which has a fairly structured database support in the backend as the source of data, the currency of the backend database can be made almost as good as the actual OLYP database either by using the same database through one or more application interfaces or by mirroring the database onto the DSS data source backend. But the same level of currency may be not adequately captured or reflected in the knowledge base of a knowledge-driven

DSS for the same organization, simply because the knowledge sources being varied from highly structured (like an OLTP database) to highly unstructured (like a chat server's file system / log files) – it is computationally very costly to have a real-time update continuously running on the knowledge-base of the knowledge-driven DSS. Nevertheless, if not real-time, but a high-frequency automatic update mechanism can be installed to improve the knowledge For example, if the marketing team wants to use a knowledge-driven DSS for supporting its decision making process on *"to which customers the promotional offers should be sent this week?"*, they can make better judgment if the knowledge-base that the DSS they are using is refreshed with the latest customer communication inputs. This is precisely the issue which the authors have addressed in the following sections by introducing a generic model for knowledge-driven DSS support for improved knowledge currency and handling heterogonous(structured/ unstructured) data sources at the same time.

2.2 Self-incrementing Property of the Knowledge Base of DSS and Knowledge Currency

The necessity of having the knowledge base of a knowledge-driven DSS to be auto-refreshing or self-incrementing gets justified when there is a need to maintain knowledge currency. In context of operational decision making, knowledge currency, as discussed earlier, becomes one of the prevalent properties required as the input quality for supporting the decision making processes. Logically, a knowledge base with any of the pre-defined structure types e.g. frames or semantic nets can be made auto-refreshable or auto-updatable or self-incremental using a number of algorithms e.g. neural network algorithms like back-prop, genetic algorithms for classifying the new entries into the knowledge base and then putting them into an appropriate cluster, or general machine learning algorithms based on induction, deduction or abduction – especially if the knowledge base is made of production rules. In this paper, Bolzmann machine concept has been used for designing the self-incremental model of the knowledge base of a knowledge-driven DSS. The reasons for this choice will be explained in the following section.

3 Bolzmann Machines

Bolzmann machines are variations on the basic concepts of Hopfield Networks, [9] which was initially proposed as a theory of memory with the following features:
1. Distributed representations: memory as a pattern of activations across a set of processing elements.
2. Distributed and asynchronous control: the process elements (can be represented as Knowledge maps in the context of this paper) evolves itself based on its local situation i.e. in a context-free domain.
3. Content-addressable memory.

4. Fault-tolerance: if a few elements fail, the network still functions.

Pairs of units in a Hopfield network are connected by symmetric weights and the units update their states asynchronously by looking at their local connections to the other units. The Hopfield network works well as content-addressable memories. They can also be used for constraint-satisfaction problems where each unit can be thought as a 'hypothesis' [9]. Then the network can try to reach a state of equilibrium by adjusting weights as follows:

1. Place positive weights on connections between pair of units representing compatible or mutually supporting hypotheses.
2. Place negative weights on connections between pairs of units representing incompatible or in-conflict hypotheses.

By definition, Hopfield networks settle on a number of local minimum, which is workable in case of content-addressable memory, but for hypotheses-based situations, a global equilibrium is to be reached. Towards this end, the concepts of Hopfield networks were combined with that of simulated annealing - another AI algorithm for searching and constraint satisfaction, and this effort produced the idea of Bolzmann machines.

This concept can be exploited very effectively in case of capturing knowledge elements from any knowledge sources. When this process is continuously executed by the Bolzmann machine, it increments or adds the captured/ extracted inputs from the knowledge sources, on the fly. Thereby a knowledge base supported by a Bolzmann machine which is running continuously or at least at an acceptable pre-defined frequency of intervals, can maintain knowledge currency to a much greater degree than any other options e.g. the developer/ administrator responsible for maintaining the back-end knowledge base adding data/ knowledge periodically. In the following section, a model for this process is presented.

Other methods like ANNs (Artificial Neural Networks) or various other machine learning algorithms can also serve the same purpose. But Bolzmann machine has been chosen in this paper over the other techniques because:

1. It is simple, easy to understand, explain and thereby justify, in contrast with ANN for example where the learning happened in the hidden layers and the weight adjustments are not visible to the users or programmers, therefore making it difficult to explain and justify the incremental changes to business application communities.
2. Bolzmann machine concepts can be quickly merged with unstructured data management issues using simple scores like similarity/ dissimilarity matrices. This is not the case with other machine learning algorithms where pre-processing knowledge for incremental loading can take a significant portion of computational resources.

4   The Basic Model of Self-incrementing Knowledge Base for a Knowledge-Driven DSS

The knowledge base forming the backend of a knowledge-driven DSS will certainly have a specified structure for knowledge representation, say frames, production rules, semantic nets etc. For this paper, these units of knowledge representation are considered as nodes in the Hopfield network.

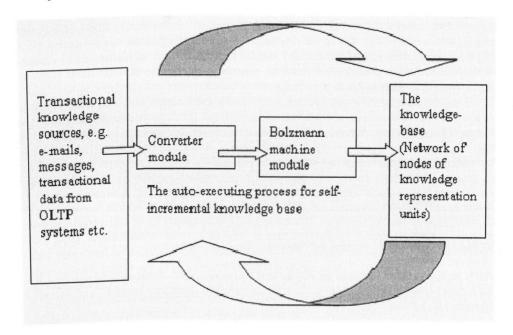

Figure 1: The basic model of self-incrementing knowledge base for a knowledge-driven DSS

The converter module: Converts the knowledge sources with various structures (e.g. database dump files, Comma Separated Values (CSVs), Tab Separated Values (TSVs), spreadsheet documents (structured) or word files, email messages (unstructured, free-flowing text) to the specified knowledge representation scheme e.g. frames/ rules. This involves pattern extraction process for extracting knowledge elements and fitting them into the specified knowledge form i.e. slots in case of a frame-type knowledge form. This process in itself is already a significant research area and still has a lot of research potential both in academic and commercial application domains, e.g. IBM's project on UIMA (Unstructured Information Management Architecture). For this paper, an elaborate discussion on these issues is beyond the scope. Therefore, only the function of this module i.e. 'what it does' has been explained.

and existing nodes as defined, each new node will either be absorbed into an existing node or will add a new node in the graph.

7. All the nodes of the existing network are also treated as hypotheses but they are already tested hypotheses which have been included and used for building up the initial network.

8. Each new hypothesis is tested with all the existing hypotheses or nodes.

9. The network places positive weights on connections between pair of hypotheses which are compatible or mutually supporting.
   a. So, where the similarity value > threshold value, the module will place a positive weight on the connections.
   b. Where the dissimilarity value > threshold value, the module will place a negative weight on the connections.

10. So, the module places negative weights on connections between pair of hypotheses which are incompatible or in conflict.

11. Steps 1 to 10 are repeated for n number of messages, or can go on as a continuous process when the entire model becomes truly self-incremental and the knowledge captured gets converted and stored almost in real-time with a small amount of delay/ latency (may be due to computational power limitations.) The weights can be dynamically adjusted as all the n messages are input and tested.

12. Ultimately at the end of one incremental phase with n email messages, the network will have the new hypotheses included along with their weights to different existing hypotheses.

13. For a new node say Ni, i= 1 to n, it's connections (edges) to all the existing nodes will have positive or negative weights on them.

14. If for Ni, the maximum positive value (similarity score) over it's edges with the existing nodes m, say, with existing node j is W_{ij} , then
    a. If W_{ij} is more than a given threshold value, Ni will be included in node j.
    b. If W_{ij} is less than the given threshold value, Ni will be represented as a new node creating another cluster in the network.

15. Same process will be done with the edges with negative nodes, in the reverse way.

For example, let us take a network as follows in Figure 2:

Say the existing network has m nodes. So S_{ij} will be measures such that i = 1 to n (new nodes), j= 1 to m (existing nodes)

For a new frame F_i, if the S_{ij}, j= 1 to m, is calculated as follows (similarity values in the + domain, dissimilarity values in the – domain):

If threshold = +/- 2, then two possibilities are there:

1. On the connections where the similarity >2, the frame F_i gets absorbed into the frame with the maximum similarity score e.g. +6 in this case.

2. If the dissimilarity score for any node to the new entry F_i > threshold as is the case with both nodes with -3 and -10 values, the new node should add itself to the network with connections to the other existing nodes given the similarity/dissimilarity values as shown on the connections in Figure 2.

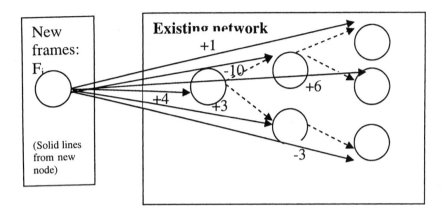

Figure 2: Similarity and Dissimilarity Value assignment in An Existing graph w.r.t. a New Frame Fi

Out of these two possibilities, as the aim is get a new node with maximum difference with the existing nodes e.g. max(max(dissimilarity), min(similarity)), the maximum dissimilarity of -10 will be considered here as $|10| > |2$:threshold$|$. Therefore, the node will be added as a new node to the network and the edges/ connections linking this new node to all other existing nodes will be the values that are already shown on the connections in Figure 2.

The whole example process can therefore be summarized as follows:

Steps summary:

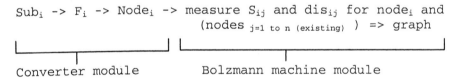

```
Sub_i -> F_i -> Node_i -> measure S_ij and dis_ij for node_i and
                          (nodes j=1 to n (existing) ) => graph
```

Converter module   Bolzmann machine module

Process logic:

'*For similarity values only*
If S_{ij} > threshold for any existing node say node$_k$, then node$_i$ gets absorbed in node$_k$

Else,

Node$_i$ creates a new node, the connection weights get adjusted to the values between S_{ij} (j=1 to n-existing) accordingly.

'For dissimilarity values only (for conflicting nodes)

If Dis$_{ij}$ > threshold for any existing node say node$_m$, then node$_i$ becomes a new node with weights adjusted on the existing connections and the new connections,

Else,

Node$_i$ gets absorbed in node$_m$.

In the example, however, a combination of both similarity and dissimilarity scores have been used to explain the most comprehensive possibilities scenario and for the ease of explaining it in case of the simple example.

6 Conclusion

In this paper, the model of a self-incrementing knowledge base to support a knowledge driven DSS has been developed, presented, and explained with a simple example using customer email subjects as inputs, frames as the knowledge representation scheme and Bolzmann machines as the self-incrementing mechanisms. The concept can be further extended in terms of handling more types and volumes of inputs, systems performance, algorithm performance analysis and measurement, knowledge representation models and self-incrementing mechanisms like genetic algorithms, neural networks and so on. However, the application of NNs and other machine learning algorithms may require different handling approached towards treating unstructured input data sources, the reasons of which are explained in the section on introduction to Bolzamann machines. This concept can also be further extended in the frequency of update domain, ideally to the extent of a real-time knowledge base supporting the decision processes. This being a generic framework can also be tried and tested in specific knowledge-driven DSS environments (for example- CRM decision support) as a route to further expansion of the generic theme of this work.

References

1. Bharat, K., Henzinger. M.R.,(1998) *Improved algorithms for topic distillation in hyperiinked environments.* Proceedings of the Twenty-First International ACM SIGIR Conference on Research and Development in Information Retrieval. New York: ACM Press. pp. 104-111.
2. Fuld, L.M.: Singh. A.: Rothwell. K.; and Kim, J.(2003) *Intelligence Software Report™ 2003: Leveraging the Web.* Cambridge. MA

3. He. X.; Ding. C; Zha. H.; and Simon, H. (2001) Automatic topic identification using Webpage clustering. In X. Wu. N. Cercone, TY. Lin, J- Gehrke. C. Clifton. R. Kotagiri. N. Zhong. and X. Hu (eds,). *Proceedings of the 2001 IEEE International Conference on Data Mining.* Los Alamitos. CA: IEEE Computer Society Press. 2(X)I. pp. 195-202.

4. He, Y, Hui. S.C. (2002) Mining a Web citation database for author co-citation analysis. *Information Processing and Management. 38.* 4. pp. 491-508.

5. Keen, P. G. W. (1980). *Decision Support Systems: A Research Perspective.* New York, Pergamon Press.

6. Mowshowitz. A., Kawaguchi. A.(2002) *Bias on the Web. Communications of the ACM, 45.* 9, pp. 56-60.

7. Nonaka, I; Takeuchi H.,(1995), *The Knowledge-Creating Company: How Japanese Companies Create the Dynamics of Innovation,* Oxford University Press.

8. Power, D. J. (2002). *Decision Support Systems : Concepts And Resources For Managers.* Westport, Conn., Quorum Books.

9. Rich E., Knight K.(2001), *Artificial Intelligence,* Tata McGrawHill Publishing Company Ltd, N. Delhi.

10. Shneiderman, B.(1996) The eyes have it: A task by data type taxonomy for information visualizations. In *Proceedings of IEEE Symposium on Visual languages.* Los Alamitos, CA: IEEE Computer Society Press, pp. 336-343.

11. Stanhope, P. (2002). *Get In The Groove : Building Tools And Peer-To-Peer Solutions With The Groove Platform.* New York, Hungry Minds.

12. Turban, E. (1995). *Decision Support And Expert Systems : Management Support Systems.* Englewood Cliffs, N.J., Prentice Hall.

13. Young, F.W.(1987), *Multidimensional Scaling: History, Theory, and Applications,* ed. R.M. Hamer. Hillsdale, NJ.

14. Zanasi A.(2000), "Web Mining through the Online Analyst," in *Data Mining II,* WIT press.com electronic library, pp. 3–14.

15. Z. Su, L. Zhang, and Y. Pan (2003), "Document Clustering Based on Vector Quantization and Growing-Cell Structure," *Proceedings of the IEA/AIE 2003, Developments in Applied Artificial Intelligence, 16th International Conference on Industrial and Engineering Applications of Artificial Intelligence and Expert Systems,* Laughborough, UK; Lecture Notes in Computer Science 2718 Springer, pp. 326–336.

Printed in the United States of America.